Guest Parking: Zita Johann

RICK ATKINS

Front cover: Zita Johann, photographed in London, 1930.
Back cover: Zita Johann photographed in New York, 1940s.

Guest Parking: Zita Johann
© 2011 Rick Atkins. All Rights Reserved.

No part of this book may be reproduced in any form or by any means, electronic, mechanical, digital, photocopying or recording, except for the inclusion in a review, without permission in writing from the publisher.

Published in the USA by:
BearManor Media
PO Box 1129
Duncan, Oklahoma 73534-1129
www.bearmanormedia.com

ISBN 978-1-59393-618-1

Printed in the United States of America.
Book design by Brian Pearce | Red Jacket Press.

Table of Contents

Acknowledgments 3

Epiphany/An Introduction 9

The Meeting 17

The Intermission 23

Broadway and Hollywood 31

Transitions 107

An Awakening 123

Crescendo 129

The Reawakening 135

And Then It Was Morning *by Zita Johann* 143

Afterword *by Liesl Ehardt* 297

Selected Bibliography 301

Appendix 303

Notes 323

Index 333

Zita Johann in New York, 1936.

This is for the children, for whom Zita Johann truly left her legacy… always.

ACKNOWLEDGMENTS

This book would not have been possible without the following guests. First and foremost, I want to thank Liesl Ehardt. Without her, my incentive to author this book would not have happened. Additional thanks go to David Simeur, JoAnn Surber, Kathleen Simeur Searl, Jane E. Moore, Anji Holtzman, Zachary Zito, David Marowitz, Rosemary Franck, Richard Finegan, John Ehardt, and Terry Salomonson. Extended thanks to my brother Dean, and to my sisters, Martha and Kathy, for their love and support. To the following organizations, The Chicago Public Library, The Newberry Library of Chicago, The New York Library, and The St. Lucie County Library Systems, I am grateful.

I must thank my dear parents, the late Dewey and Faye Atkins for their love and support of my interests and me. Also to the following posthumous, David Manners, Stanley Bergerman and Alan Napier. And to the loving memory of Rose MacGregor, better known to our family as Grandma Delaney. They have all enhanced this experience.

And last but not least, to my dear friend Zita Johann… You have touched my life in such a way that I feel as though I am one of those children you taught, building that *bridge of love* together. I understand that some have survived to advanced ages. They remember, as I do, unequivocally, the *lady* who made a difference in their lives. You have taught me how to adapt, but how to sometimes make changes in my life on my own terms objectively.

Thanksgiving Sunday, nine years after the epiphany of August 2000, was a delight. My way of giving back was to join the church choir. One of the highlights of the morning was singing alongside the children's choir with *"Look At The World"* by John Rutter. Zita, I give thanks for the times that we've shared and I'll cherish the fond memories with love, always.

CHAPTER 1

Epiphany/ An Introduction

Her portrait hangs on my living room wall. It captures the look of a familiar spirit, who I am proud to call my *friend*. My friend and I had once agreed that life is so precious yet temporary. It was something that we referred to as *Guest Parking*. When one stops to think about it, we really are only guests, alluding of course to our very temporal mortal existence here on earth.

One afternoon, while looking into her intriguing eyes in the portrait, I noticed something peculiar. Her face took on a rather pensive look to me. Remembering that my friend told me of her superstitions, it was as if I could hear her unique voice:

> Thank you for not memorializing me any earlier since my death. Nothing has gone awry, dear Rick. You are exactly where you are supposed to be in your life. And, as for *me*, <u>for later</u> has arrived and *you* have work to do. Your journey back will bring you good merit. However, <u>do</u> wait for that dreaded thirteenth year to pass. I am with you, always.

The thirteenth year has passed. My friend in the portrait is Zita Johann. She was a former star of stage, motion pictures and radio, and a treasure who inspired others. It is hard to believe that 1993 was the year she passed. I feel, as others do, that she is still here. My memories of her are many.

Undoubtedly, movie audiences will identify Zita Johann by her most memorable role as Helen Grosvenor, the daughter of an Egyptian mother and an Arab-English father in the film *The Mummy* that starred Boris

Karloff, in which Zita also appeared as an Egyptian Princess named Anck-es-en-Amon. *The Mummy* was released 75-plus years ago and is considered a "classic."

There is one fateful Sunday morning after Zita's passing that remains paramount in my memory. It was the morning of August 13, 2000.

Being awakened at five a.m. by the sound of wind whistling through my bedroom window was a start. This was immediately followed by the sound of breaking glass! Soon, I discovered that a picture frame that hung on the opposite side of my room had fallen off the wall and shattered. The picture in the frame was that of Zita Johann. Fortunately, the photo remained intact.

After the cleanup and a light breakfast, I walked out to my back porch. Clear skies and lovely breezes were welcome. The weather was identical to another Sunday long ago remembered, the day that Zita Johann and I met. An *inner prompting* led me to church that August morning.

The church service warranted the tone by which Zita would have deemed a suitable opening. The church program was entitled, <u>Discern Between Good and Evil</u>. The opening hymn was "*I Sing the Mighty Power of God.*" The hymn of preparation was "*I Will Lift the Cloud of Night.*" And the sermon came under the skillful title, <u>The Impatience of Job</u>.

Listening to the Pastor's steadfast sermon, memories were conjured of people no longer alive who meant a lot to me. Zita Johann was especially on my mind. As the Pastor continued with his sermon, I silently prayed, asking God, 'had I forsaken Zita Johann since her death?' Suddenly, it was as if Zita was speaking to me. "I trust you." The congregation was presented with the musical offering. A Saxophonist played Johann Sebastian Bach's "*My Heart Ever Faithful.*" Warm feelings continued through the closing hymn, "*Take My Gifts*" and through the parting song, "*Go, My Children, With My Blessing.*"

After returning home from church, rest became less important than locating a neglected storage box full of Zita memories. The contents hadn't seen light since they were packed away when our family relocated in October of 1993. The first item that was retrieved from the box was a book.[1]

Reading that book is how I first learned of Zita's whereabouts. Placed in the book, I found a phone bill marking the day when I first phoned Zita Johann. Some days before that, for the first time, I saw Zita in a television broadcast of *The Mummy*. Her performance intrigued me. According to the phone bill, I phoned her at exactly *9:15 a.m. Monday, February 25,*

1974. That day remained vivid in my mind. First, I had phoned New York directory assistance hoping that she would be listed. And she was! Zita was living in West Nyack, New York, located in Rockland County, New York.[2]

The telephone rang at least ten times before she answered with a reluctant, "Hel-lo." This nervous adolescent introduced himself to Zita. She replied quickly but cordially:

> Excuse me, Mr. Atkins. I don't want to sound rude and I would love to speak with you, but, would you be so kind as to phone me again next Tuesday after 2:00 p.m. I would appreciate it. This time is too early for me. I have insomnia, you see. I sleep better in the mornings. Forgive me, and thank you for your interest. Do call again.

We established more rapport with the second conversation. Zita seemed happy to talk with me. My age did not surprise her. In fact, Zita said:

> One knows what one wants to do from an early age. It is getting there and getting around those who stand as obstacles, if you will. My mother was against my being anactress, you see. She gave me no encouragement. I was sixteen and going to school. She wanted me to work. She didn't think that acting was equivalent to work. So, I started sitting for children. And that wasn't so bad. I love children. I always have. So people started sending their children to me. I'll tell you about Joe. He was a relative of mine. Joe was a young man, who one might refer to as a slow learner. So they had me sit for him. What I saw was a delightful personality starving for attention. When I was done with him, he had learned his multiplication tables.

As the conversation continued, I told her that she must feel something special toward children. She replied:

> I have learned that the charm of it all is the other person. It involves generosity, love, and charity. But the essence of charm is being genuinely interested in the other person.

At another point, I praised Zita's performance in *The Mummy*.

> Thank you. I'm surprised that they are still showing it. I never considered it a horror picture, but that's the category the producers put it in. It's now what they call *a classic*. I began working in the theater and I felt that was where I belonged… then along came Hollywood and I never cared for it, you see.

Before our conversation was over, Zita agreed to a live interview. Zita asked:

> Me? An interview? [She giggled] Don't you think that you already *have* one?

We laughed as Zita continued to talk:

> Tell me something about your parents? Do they know what you are doing, in terms of coming out here from Chicago? This is admirable of you. I'd be happy to give you an interview for your book. Perhaps your parents can come with you? You'd have to find a place to stay. Listen! Continue to keep in touch with me and you'll see that this will all work to your advantage. What I hear of you, I like. I'll be happy to know more about you. Call me anytime, when you feel the urge, but not at 9 a.m. [laughing]. It has been a pleasure talking with you.

Among the other items in the storage box was one of many scrapbooks that I had created. Keeping scrapbooks was something that Zita encouraged. One of the scrapbooks contained written correspondence between Zita and myself. One particular Christmas card read,

> Thank you for your letter and your card, which I am returning signed, together with this card. There is a seemingly attractive motel near here about 4 miles or so but little else that I know of. I'd invite you to stay here but I have no servants. Who has these days? All my best to you, Zita Johann.

A poignant moment between us came before we met. When she received news of my maternal grandmother's passing, she responded with the following:

> The moment my telephone rang, I had just finished re-reading your latest letter! Dear, you haven't lost your grandmother. If you look beyond the physical, you will see that she is always there. You'll see. I am sure of it. Your healing starts now.

Zita also wrote the following letter:

> Dear Rick,
>
> It was good to hear from you, especially at that particular moment. Regarding your participation in the EST experience — EST in my opinion is another cult movement enriching its leader by robbing its followers of what they have and are. It's having a rotten effect on this pupil of mine, counteracting all I put into him. Satan is having a ball these days. Keep tuned into God. And when I see you we'll go into more of the good in Life.
>
> Do pray for me and write when you feel the urge. My prayers be with you. Thank you for the drawing. Keep it up — it's another way of staying tuned in. But we must be careful of the dark forces (Satan) and the tools employed to disconnect the unaware. Here's a protective prayer from 'Astara:' 'I am surrounded by the Pure White Light of Christ. Nothing but good can come from me now. Nothing but good shall go from me. I give thanks. I give thanks. I give thanks with Love.' Always, Zita.[3]

The enchanting spirit known as Zita Johann has unequivocally touched many lives. Over the course of our nineteen-year relationship, Zita and I shared many conversations by telephone, written correspondence, and later in person regarding our individual lives. My spirited memories of Zita are of her lucidity, candor, and humor. Her faculties were in full swing! She said that specific dates were "of no importance," unless she volunteered them. Sometimes after she'd talk about happenings, and without thinking, I'd ask her 'when?' She'd answer such things as, "last week" or "Yesterday, for God's sake." Her remarks were sometimes followed by a laugh!

Zita talked to me about her tumultuous family. It was a subject that she shared with few people. She referred to her three marriages, to John Houseman, John McCormick and Bernard E. Shedd as her "three biggest mistakes." Zita shared "important" newspaper articles that she sent to various publications, some of which were later read to me. And it greatly pleased me that Zita trusted me with a small assortment of her stage and movie photographs. From her personal collection, she autographed several to me.

What makes Zita Johann transcend above other women of the Twentieth Century were her outstanding listening skills. She alluded to being psychic and was aware of her spiritual strengths and weaknesses. She was intrigued by the writings of the American psychic Edgar Cayce and French existentialist philosopher, Jean Paul Sartre. She said of another, Michel Nostradamus:

> I have studied, *the eternal seer* but never delve too deep into *his* prophecies. I've been writing some of my own.

As a teenager, Zita absorbed herself in classic drama literature. Her reading interests over the years included poetry, master painters of history and their artworks, and American and European history.[4]

According to Zita, her greatest reward began working with children soon before the end of World War II. Later, through her church, her challenge was to work with mentally challenged children and those with developmental disabilities. She was passionate about this. Zita saw her expressions of love for these children a gift. Some of the children also came to her home and lived there temporarily.

The essence of success with these children were "with the help of the power of the Holy Spirit." Zita also trained young aspiring theater actors, some being groomed as late as the 1980s. Her special something was explained by her this way:

> Well, I treat children as equals. I work hard to gain their trust and in a sense, offer to build a bridge of love between us. I would expect that they would meet me halfway across. I listen to them…and I love them. And I think, inside, they know I will never betray them — that I will always love them for being so fresh and alive and full of hope.

Throughout life, Zita modeled the spirit of hope. She tried her hand at writing, but was not in favor of writing her own memoirs. However, she left me with a story, and her unpublished mystical play, entitled, *And Then It Was Morning* published here in its entirety. And I believed that the play's author deserved a fair introduction.

I consider that Sunday in church an epiphany. There were feelings of elation and a strong sense of remembrance regarding my friend. It was then that I knew something was more to come. And yet, Zita's words, "for later" had not yet found their proper perspective. In my pondering of those two short words, a familiar bittersweet emotion returned. As a result, I was prompted to re-seal the storage box with everything intact, except for the cherished picture of Zita that was later replaced with a new wall frame.

Zita's words mesmerized me for years. They still do. However, it wasn't until 2005 that I became acquainted with Liesl Ehardt, a Johann family descendant. Since that day, the storage box was reopened and a translation of "for later" has come to fruition.

Zita Johann's allotted guest parking on earth was eighty-nine years, two months, and three days. She and I once prayed together that her memory might be ushered into the Twenty-first Century. Perhaps now, her words may see the light of day.

CHAPTER 2

The Meeting

The day had finally arrived! It was a Saturday, May 1st, 1982. I found myself at LaGuardia airport in New York City. Was I dreaming?

The next day drive to West Nyack was very pleasant. Clear skies and gentle breezes filled the air. Zita had previously given me precise road directions to her home. I stopped along the way to purchase yellow mums for friendship. However, the florist was out of yellow mums, so I chose white mums instead. Zita's road directions were impeccable, as the home seemed to appear from nowhere.

The house had a personality of its own. It stood in a wooded area far off in the distance, inconspicuously in the haze of the mid-morning sunshine on Sickletown road. For a few short moments, I had a vision of Zita's house in its original splendor. I began imaging a woman wearing a long gray skirt and blazer with a ruffled white blouse, pacing along the downstairs porch of the two-story structure. As I came to my senses, I could smell the fresh country spring air and the sound of a barking dog.

As the car was parked, I walked towards the house carrying the potted white mums. There was a slight sound of music playing from Zita's house. I heard Zita's voice before she could be seen, clearly shouting, "PEANUTS! PEANUTS, DEAR!…Quiet!" Zita appeared through the front door and walked out to the porch smiling. Different to my vision, she was wearing brown slacks and a bright red corduroy garment with a colorful silk scarf around her neck. She looked at me with her large ageless eyes. I walked up on the porch to a warm embrace as Zita said:

> You're finally here, Rick! You've finally made it! How wonderful to see you here. Welcome! The weather is just perfect today, isn't it? You had no trouble finding the place?

My head nodded the answer as I handed Zita the potted mums with a courteous smile. She accepted them by saying:

> Mums are my favorite, most special dear. Thank you! How sweet of you. What a nice gesture of warmth.

I followed Zita down the porch steps as she laid the mums on a tree stump nearby. She went to leash her dog to a post some fifty feet away. The dog had first greeted me. Zita said, "Peanuts meet Rick! Rick, Peanuts!" The dog was black and cross-eyed. I told Zita about a cat from my childhood that was named Peanuts and *he too* was black and cross-eyed. Zita said, "How about that!" Peanuts was a mix of Labrador retriever and Saint Bernard.

Without hesitating, Zita walked from the dog post toward a pair of gardening gloves nearby. She slipped them on and took the pot of white mums, saying: "Since it is such a beautiful day, I'll plant your mums right now. This is wonderful!" As she pointed to the ground with the planting spade in her hand, she said, "This very spot is where I plan to have my ashes scattered someday. I feel that this house and I have been around for centuries."

As soon as Zita finished planting the flowers, we walked the short porch steps and into the front door of her home. A painting hung between the storm door and the front door of Zita's home. At the end of the short inner hallway was an oak wood staircase that led to the second floor where other paintings were placed. Zita asked, "Do you like primitive landscapes?" I answered, 'Yes. Absolutely!'

> The artist was a good friend of mine, Henry Varnum Poor. He lived here in Rockland County. He painted mostly primitive landscapes. He liked to work in my house. He said that my home brought him some peace.[1]

Zita learned prior to the visit that my late maternal grandmother Mamie, who loved painting landscapes. She also painted scenes on canvas as she imagined stories from the Bible. I reminded Zita of a prior conversation: My grandmother took an opportunity to visit a local gallery in her town, where she had taken one of her paintings. The proprietor admired her work against the multitudes of the newer abstract painting craze. My grandmother and the proprietor agreed that there was no comparison to landscapes over abstract art. Zita agreed with this by saying:

I prefer landscapes to abstract art. However, beauty *is* in the eye of the beholder. Artists and I seem to gravitate to each other. There is a relation, you see. But to *see*, first hand, the torment that an artist goes through, and then to see something beautiful come from it is quite a phenomenon. I see it as a gift from God. Writing is similar. I've done both painting and writing. I respect writers with patience. Now you *are* here after all of these years! Welcome.

Zita told me the music that I heard was coming from her portable cassette tape player. She referred to the player as the "magical tape recorder" used with her students and the children with whom she worked. This conversation was taking place in the foyer of Zita's house. When I asked her the title of the musical piece, she said,

It's Samuel Barber's "Adagio for Strings." Some people say that it's the saddest composition that they'd ever heard. I disagree. I think it is quite a beautiful piece and soothing to the soul. I see in your eyes that you agree.[2]

We entered the living room. Zita told me to make myself comfortable and instructed where to place my belongings. I complemented Zita on her home. She thanked me and said:

Welcome to Winter Quarters. It's a Dutch Redstone farmhouse. It goes back before the American Revolution. I have eight acres of land with it. I bought it many years ago. It took many years to repair. Would you care for some sort of refreshment? Apple juice? Lemonade? Root Beer? Milk? Apple pie?

My reply to Zita was, 'Did I hear milk and apple pie?' Zita answered with a smile:

Yes you did. I made one when I knew you were coming. Would you like it now? I nodded. Zita said, Let me shut the music off and after you eat your pie we can get on with our interview. You may have a cup of coffee later, if you wish, with some more pie.

As Zita walked to her kitchen, I asked her, 'May I come in?' She said:

Glory! Your Mother taught you well. May I. <u>I love that!</u>

While she cut the homemade apple pie, Zita teased me that it came from a box. Moments later she smiled by saying:

> No. I really made it. I think that's what the men in my life liked about me, that I baked. If nothing else [laughing]! Come on, we'll go back into the living room where you can enjoy your pie. And I'll look for something to read.

There we were. I was sitting on the sofa, eating a piece of Zita's delicious homemade apple pie as she sat in her cozy chair, reading the newspaper with her large, dark framed reading glasses down on her nose! She was adorable!

We started a casual conversation. My first question to Zita was about the pronunciation of her last name. She answered:

> You found me out [laughing]! Many people say Yo-Hon, or Yo-Han, but it really is Joe-Han. That's very good. You know that I'm Hungarian. I am not German. But I can also speak German. I'm mostly Hungarian and Romanian. It is hard to find people around here who speak Hungarian. I did speak the Hungarian language with [first husband, John] Houseman. He was from Bucharest, you know.

When I asked Zita about the village near Temesvar, Hungary, where she was born, she said:

> That village is somewhere between Banat and Temesvar. I don't know exactly. I was very young when I came here. My mother kept no records. Perhaps someday you may find out?

Elisabeth Johann, was born in Deutschbentschek, Hungary/Romania, July 14, 1904, the first of three girls born to Magdalena (Zimmermann) and Stefan Johann.[3]

Zita was six when she arrived in America with her father, Stefan, mother, Magdalena, and her four-year-old sister Magda. The ship ported at Ellis Island, Tuesday, December 13, 1910. They had sailed aboard the U.S.S. *George Washington* from Bremen, Germany. With the help of mutual Hungarian-American friends, Elie Rodulescu, Mihaly and

Maria Szegedi, the Johanns migrated to Lawrence County, Pennsylvania for "about one year."[4]

Zita was seven when the family moved to 401 East 58th Street in New York City from Pennsylvania. The following year in New York City, Wednesday, March 6, 1912, the third child was born to the Johanns. She was named Agatha. "Aggie" would later marry Elwood Whitney, who later became known as an advertising executive in New York City, December 22, 1932. Their marriage ended in May 1938. Agatha Johann Whitney had no children.

Agatha Johann Whitney followed Zita in death Thursday, December 15, 1994. Zita's middle sister, Magdalena ("Maggie") Johann (born in Deutschbentschek, Hungary/Romania), passed away Friday, August 16, 1963, in Southampton, Long Island, New York. Her second husband, John V. Tarleton, survived her. They also had no children.

In October 1930, Magdalena (Zimmermann) Johann married Antonio Fernandez and gave birth that same year to a fourth child, Remedios Maria Fernandez. For purposes of record, Magdalena (Zimmermann) Johann had divorced Zita's father, Stefan Johann.[5]

When we started talking about friends, Zita revealed that she had made many friends down through the years. She said that her chiropractor was among her friends. There were some pictures positioned around the living room including one of an actor, Richard Kiley. Recognizing who he was, I asked Zita about Richard Kiley.

> Well, we are good friends. He first came to visit me when he was a young man from Chicago, like you. He was already out here in New York acting in the theater and appearing in television. He wanted to learn more of how to maintain the craft of acting. He is an ambitious and intelligent performer. We'd enjoy sitting around encouraging each other with pep talks. I went to the opening night of his *big* play, *Man of La Mancha* in New York City. He didn't know that I was there until after his performance. He is a gifted actor with a remarkable voice. We had spirituality in common. I am proud of him. His two sons, when they were children stayed here for a while. I remember one evening, Richard Kiley and I took an oath, right here in this living room that neither of us would write our memoirs. Why? We felt that there may be too much or not enough to tell, nor did we care. I don't see him as often anymore. He is a busy actor. When he is not working, he spends time with his

family.[6] Rick, I know how important this is to you. It's also important for me to have you here. I appreciate that you came all the way from Chicago to see me. So, I mustn't let you down.

Zita requested that I keep control of my tape recorder. She asked this for purposes of personal editing, "saving tape" and for taking breaks. When I asked about her family, she suggested that we take a break and enjoy her southern porch. Zita went back to the kitchen to pour us both a glass of apple juice. On our way out to the porch with apple juice in hand, Zita said, "You may bring your writing tablet along. You won't need a tape recorder for this."

CHAPTER 3

The Intermission

As we got comfortable on the porch, Zita said:

> My last husband was from Chicago. I've been there. I toured there on stage over the years. It's a pretty place. But, I've always considered myself a New Yorker at heart. An actor friend of mine, Rollo Peters, was one of the first New Yorkers who came up to Rockland County and bought a house up here. And then the rest followed. Rollo was the first actor that I had a crush on seeing him play Romeo.

With her friend Rollo Peters. PHOTO COURTESY OF ZITA JOHANN

As it happened, Carl Markham had been looking for a house for me. We drove around one day and when I saw this house from the road, I said, 'That's it! I'll take it.' He said, 'Zita, you don't want a house like that. It's terrible. Wait until you see the inside. It is awful.' I had to spend a fortune to get it together. It took years before I moved into it! By that time it was worth moving into. Rollo Peters was known as a designer too. He did a lot work for people out here including me.[1]

I'm afraid it is falling apart again…I love the seasons. I love where I live and sitting here on the porch sharing today and finally having you here, my dear. Where do we go from here?

Smiling, I thanked Zita for her comment and asked her about her porch. She said:

The porch is an addition that was put on at the beginning of this century, long before I got here. The previous owner of the house was married to a southern lady and she wanted a southern porch. When a producer friend of mine, Herman Shumlin, had come from New York to see me. He said, "Zita, the front porch has got to go." I said, Herman, I'm not in the museum business, the front porch stays!

For a few moments, we sat in silence. I sensed reluctance from Zita to talk about her family. Instead I asked her how she got the name Zita, she replied:

It's quite simple, really. My father named me by robbing letters from my given name, Elisabeth, to spell SITA. Here, it is spelled Elizabeth. So, here in America, I am Zita.

I asked Zita if she'd rather not talk about her family, it would be fine. She answered:

Well, I don't talk about it, because it is all in the past. But, I'm telling you, aren't I? You're a good receiver. And I admire you telling me about your family. This is *for later* mind you… You said that one of your sisters is involved with genealogy. Well, there is more to genealogy than names and numbers, in my opinion.

Zita asked, "Would you like to talk about your family?" For nearly the next half hour we did. Soon to follow, after a bit of a stutter and a sip of apple juice, Zita looked me straight in the eye and said:

> Look...I came here from Hungary. It was my sister, my mother, and my father, and myself. But I never got to know my father [long pause]...Looking back on them is hard for me. What I do remember about my father was that he was a strapping man with dark hair. I remember him mostly with a big mustache. He had a strong presence, very astute, much like the Hussars captain that he once was under Emperor Franz Joseph I of Austria-Hungary.[2]
>
> A lasting memory that I have of my father is when he took us all to Coney Island for a day. I loved the ocean. That was a good time. I adored my father. Soon after that, he opened a restaurant, a delicatessen rather and later he was gone. It is my understanding there are other branches growing on my family tree. Some are just sprouting. It is an ordeal, as you heard when my sister phoned earlier. Anyone in my position would not subject <u>any</u> child to *negative forces*. I'll remain here for as long as God wills. I see good things for you. With the baptism that you are contemplating, by what you've already told me; what are you waiting for? You'll know when you are ready. You would please yourself and your parents by being baptized. You will find comfort there. Study. Life is study, really. Never dive too deep. But always stay tuned to God. It sounds to me that you have the fundamentals down. So, where were we? Oh yes, my father...My father deserted us when I was fifteen. I never saw him again. I loved my father. It's always been hard for me to cry. So there we were, my sister and I, the baby sister, and our mother, all on our own. I was forced to go out and look for a job, and I did, legitimately! My mother was against my being an actress, you see, and I had to stand my ground with her. She worshipped money. It was her greed that helped to destroy her marriage to my father. She let money control her life. I've had this thing about money since and the effect that it has on people.
>
> My sister, Maggie [Magda], was the more fortunate one, I thought. Our mother discovered that my sister had a talent for artwork. Maggie met a sailor. They eloped. She [at 23] *could*

afford to leave. She had established herself as an artist and sold her work for money. After the romance was jilted, our mother had the marriage annulled.[3]

With her second marriage, Maggie found love in her life. Maggie tried later to control my money. I wouldn't allow it. I stayed independent of them all. I wanted to be left alone. Maggie died before our mother. None of us [sisters or mother] had much in common.

Our mother had already started Aggie in dancing classes. My sister wasn't similar to me, not quite eighteen when she appeared in her first Broadway show (as a dancer) with the Albertina Rasch Ballet company. She really wanted to be an actress. After I began making money, I left too. So, our mother was left with our baby sister [Agatha].[4]

Aggie thought that she was suddenly going to become this big star, you see. She was overheard touting herself in public as "the sister of Zita Johann." That wasn't bothersome to me, however, I personally felt that she needed to have her own identity. She did appear in some more shows, but it was apparent that she didn't have the talent to make it as the actress *she* wanted to be.

But Aggie had done something that I had *not* early on. She got involved with a young man. She was living in an unfortunate situation. I felt that she needed to have a better sense of responsibility and independence going for herself. She agreed with me. So, with the help of my ambitious and sensible friend David [Hertz, a magazine editor and], a playwright, we found her a clerical job and soon a place of her own. Aggie liked David more than I realized at the time. She was getting along fine until she learned that David left for California.

In the fall of 1932, Zita had returned to New York for the wedding of her sister Magda to businessman, John V. Tarleton. Zita currently had appeared in her first Hollywood movie *Tiger Shark*. By that time, Zita's mother had married Antonio Fernandez. Zita said, "He was a Spanish gentleman, a good ol' chap who I felt sorry for in a way. And, she [Zita's mother, Magdalena] had *another* child late in life."

When I saw Aggie, she had a begrudging attitude towards me, as if I had something to do with David leaving. I couldn't cure her wounds. But I simply told her the truth…that David had married a girl in California. That's when I put a down payment on this house. I was in search for one. I planned on moving into it sooner, but life took me in other directions, as you'll find out.

Then I returned to California to settle my contract with RKO Pictures. I agreed to appear in five other pictures. It

Zita with her sister Agatha Johann during the late 1950s. PHOTO COURTESY OF DAVID MAROWITZ

wasn't easy. So, my agent, Leland Hayward, found work for me at Universal when I returned to California. However, *The Mummy* was my only legitimate picture with Universal. And it wasn't my first experience at that studio. We'll talk more about that when we go back inside.

Agatha Johann married Elwood Whitney in December 1932. Their marriage lasted several years. During their marriage, Agatha had sights on becoming a musician. She had aspirations of someday working as a violinist with the New York Philharmonic.

> I'm sorry to say that Aggie wasn't a success with that either. She had serious emotional problems. It took years of treatment to keep her stable. She fights an unbelievable fight within herself to stay well. Eventually, I became her legal guardian. I took care of her for a while when she lived here with me. It was worse when she'd come here sometimes with my sister. Everything was wrong and she'd go into these tantrums. I remember during one of her frightening tantrums, she destroyed our father's violin that I was teaching her to play. My biggest concern regarding my sister was that she could possibly hurt herself or someone else threatening to drive when she couldn't. Later, the courts ruled that she was no longer able to live in society. Then, I had to have her committed to a psychiatric hospital. You heard the phone ring. She phones me almost daily from the hospital and expects for me to see after her and let her live here again. I couldn't have her living here. I'm much too old to look after my sister. She is safer where she is now. She is in an excellent hospital and receives excellent care.

When I asked Zita regarding the last time she saw her mother, she said,

> Probably after she left her second husband. She phoned me and asked me if I would give up one of mine. I don't know what kind of mother she thinks she was or if she really ever cared? What an impostor she turned out to be. Can you believe me? We all have things in life to live through. She died. It's getting a chilly out here. Shall we go back in?[5]

As we went back inside, Zita turned towards a window. She held the palm of her right hand out to command silence. She paused for a moment and spoke:

> On the positive side, look to the number nine and to the east throughout your life. On the negative side, I see there is going to be a catastrophe (explosions) in the East. Yes…I don't know when exactly, but I will not be alive when it happens… you will. [Zita's premonition struck a personal chord the morning of September 11, 2001, or 911.]

Zita excused herself to the kitchen to make some coffee. When she returned to the living room, she read me a poem. She said, "I am a Thursday's child. Which day of the week you were born?" I replied, 'Yes. Tuesday.' She proceeded to read the poem, "Monday's Child"…

> *"Monday's child is fair of face,*
> *Tuesday's child is full of grace,*
> *Wednesday's child is full of woe,*
> *Thursday's child has far to go,*
> *Friday's child is loving and giving,*
> *Saturday's child works hard for his living,*
> *And the child that is born on the Sabbath day,*
> *Is bonny and blithe, and good and gay."*

CHAPTER 4

Broadway and Hollywood

As Zita served me coffee and another piece of pie, she was as anxious to talk as I was anxious to hear about her introduction to the stage. When Zita studied dramatic literature in high school, her English teacher, Miss Lydia Adele Carll, took special interest in her pupil by taking her to Broadway plays. One such play was "R.U.R. (Rossum's Universal Robots)" with Zita's stage idol, Basil Sydney. She was fascinated with theater and believed, she could "do *that!*" Zita was enrolled to the Alviene School of Theatre Arts. However, her physical appearance at the time was not that of a Broadway star. As she remembered:

> Here I was this teenage girl and people were mistaking me for a boy. Well, I didn't dress feminine and I wore my hair short, you see. I didn't care for having hair long and having it pinned up like many of the other girls did.
>
> So, it was Miss Carll, my English teacher, at Bryant High School on Long Island, who became my mentor and my friend. I have her to thank for teaching me how to work on developing my craft. Miss Carll introduced me to society. She groomed me, basically, chose the right clothes to wear, how to wear my hair, how to serve tea, so on and so forth. But, I never much cared for tea. I preferred coffee, although, now my doctor doesn't advise it [laughing].
>
> Yes…I wish Miss Carll was sitting right here so I could tell her how much she meant to me. Her influence is what made me who I am. So, once I got started on my way, God followed. I owe most everything to Miss Carll.[1]

It was the summer of 1922. I was soon to be eighteen when I went on that first audition [held under the auspices of the theater actor, Basil Sydney]. The curious thing was that my mother by this time was reconciling to my being an actress, so she bought me some fancy dress, a *terribly* fancy gray chiffon robe! That's what she thought I should go looking for a job in. Somebody had given me a navy blue taffeta dress that I liked, closed in at the waist, a nice comfortable dress. Anyway, I put on the gray dress one day and started to walk on 89th Street up to 129th Street to apply for a job in a stock company there. In the middle of my walk, an inner prompting said, 'Go home and go downtown.' I followed that inner prompting, but changed to the blue dress. I heard that the Theatre Guild was looking for people. I thought if I could become one of the extras, I could make thirty-five dollars a week! That's wonderful…that's why I was going downtown, to apply at the Theatre Guild as an extra in my navy blue dress.[2]

So, when I reached 42nd Street, there was Basil Sydney, my idol standing next to me on the street as we entered the same building. I had never been that close to an actor before. I was dumbfounded! Then we got into the same elevator. We called our floors. He and I said, 'Eight please!" (He told me later that it was my voice he heard.) When we got off the elevator, he went into the inner office and there was a room full of applicants…full! I was the last one. It didn't seem like the part I was aiming for as understudy. I didn't carry a purse, nothing. I just looked like little Essie in the Shaw play. I just carried a small change purse. Finally, the stage manager, Philip Loeb said, 'Come on in.' When I stood up, all my pennies and nickels fell on the floor and I had to pick them up. Then I saw Basil Sydney and the theater producer. They talked to me a bit, then told me I had to read. All right. I made a date and I read…and I read…and I read on the stage!

As soon as it was over I GRABBED my hat because it was a-c-r-o-s-s the other side of the stage and ran out and down the street [laughing]! Philip Loeb had to run after me…and down the street, because Mr. Sydney wanted to see me.

When we got back, Mr. Sydney said, 'Have you done much reading?' I said, 'Not very much.' He said, 'You've read very well. I want you to read Consuelo.' I thought, Oh, boy! If I could understudy Consuelo in *He Who Gets Slapped*, that's great! I was up on the plays. Naturally, I had read them, *He Who Gets Slapped*, *The Devil's Disciple*, and *Peer Gynt*…read all three.

A few days later, I read for Consuelo and I wound up getting the three parts: Essie, Consuelo and Solveig in *Peer Gynt* at one hundred dollars a week [laughing]. I was sending the money that I made to Miss Carll, because I could not trust my mother with the money. And that was my first job, and we toured with

Zita Johann's theater idol, producer/director/actor, Basil Sydney (1920s).

all three plays for just over a year. And Basil Sydney was such a tremendously nice person. I can't begin to tell you. And he wasn't on the make or anything like that...none of the things you hear about. He was just a tremendously nice person. When he discovered that I had the seventh dressing room (you get them according to your salary, and a hundred dollars was a low

Theatre Guild production as Consuelo in He Who Gets Slapped *(1922)*.

Theatre Guild production as Essie, in The Devil's Disciple *(1922).*

salary), the next thing I knew, I had the third dressing room. But he and Arthur Hopkins were the great, great, great, people in my life, and Miss Carll, of course, in school who gave me the first vocal point of view and so on and so forth. I suggest that you read my articles when you have time. There's a basic resume there too.[3]

Theatre Guild production as Solveig, in Peer Gynt *(1922).*

In the spring of 1924, Zita Johann, appeared in her first Broadway production, *Man and the Masses (Masse Mensch)*, written by Ernst Toller. Also in the cast was the American-Czech stage star, Blanche Yurka. Zita Johann and Blanche Yurka became acquainted during a run of thirty-two performances at the Garrick Theatre. It remained the home of the Theatre Guild until 1925.[4]

Dawn, a play written by Tom Barry, opened in fall of 1924 at the Sam H. Harris and Eltinge Theatres. Zita Johann had a starring role. The play, which ran fifty-six performances, did not attract much attention, nor did two other plays that Zita's friend Alan Brock once mentioned in print, *Romany Rige* and *Junk,* with Sydney Greenstreet.

In the spring of 1925, Zita became the star of *Aloma of the South Seas*, written by John B. Hymer and LeRoy Clemens. Zita played *Aloma*, a third

Backstage at the Garrick Theatre, first home of the Theatre Guild (1924).

in a strange succession at the Lyric Theatre. It was during this engagement that a combination of brown body makeup and the electric fans in the tropical scenes almost ruined her health. She had to take some months off to recuperate.

In June of 1925, Zita took part in the *Grand Street Follies*, the fourth in a series of eight popular editions of the intellectual comedy-variety

Zita's first Broadway play Man and the Masses *(1924).* PHOTO COURTESY OF RICHARD FINEGAN

venues. It was produced by The Neighborhood Playhouse, located on New York's East side. Zita said of the experience:

> I thoroughly enjoyed each and every minute of that production. We were all fine entertainers. The production was smart, fresh, innovative, and exciting. It was *that* show which gave me

Zita as a gypsy in Romany Rige, *an Off-Broadway play (1924)*. PHOTO COURTESY OF RICHARD FINEGAN

> incentive to continue working in the theater, *you see*, because we learned so much from each other. And that, in my opinion, is what this business is about.[5]

From its debut in 1922, at the Neighborhood Playhouse, the *Grand Street Follies* was hosted under the auspices of entertainer and choreographer, Albert J. Carroll. After the fifth edition of *Grand Street Follies* in

Briefly in Aloma of the South Seas *(1925)*.

1926, the Neighborhood Playhouse closed in 1927. Later that same year, the sixth edition was transplanted to the Little Theatre (known as the Winthrop Ames Theatre).[6]

Maurice V. Samuels' play, *Drift*, at the Cherry Lane Playhouse, lasting two weeks, came next. After that, the Theatre Guild took Zita back for *Merchants of Glory*, written by Marcel Pagnol and Paul Nivoix.

Zita Johann in Grand Street Follies *(1925).*

In January 1926, Zita played the character Kruna, in Franz Werfel's, *The Goat Song*, in worthy company. The cast of characters, all who played Serbians included, Edward G. Robinson, the illustrious acting couple, Alfred Lunt and Lynn Fontanne, and Blanche Yurka.

Zita moved on to play a season of stock in Washington DC. Upon her return, she tried out for Edward Goldsmith Riley's *The Claim* in Union

Zita Johann as Kruna in Franz Werfel's The Goat Song, *one of the Theatre Guild's first productions in their new theater (known today as The August Wilson Theatre). Zita co-starred with Edward G. Robinson, Alfred Lunt, Lynn Fontanne, and Blanche Yurka (1926).* PHOTO COURTESY OF RICHARD FINEGAN

Hill, New Jersey. Due to legal complaints by the playwright, his play was never produced.[7]

George Agnew Chamberlain's *Lost* opened at the Mansfield Theatre in the spring of 1927. Zita Johann was in the cast. However, she fell into a disagreement with the producer over the choice of music for interpretation of her part. Consequently, she agreed to disagree and was asked to leave. Subsequently, Eva Le Gallienne's esteemed Civic Repertory Theatre acting company was sending *The Cradle Song* on a national tour. For the tour, Zita replaced Ria Mooney, who had replaced Josephine Hutchinson (in the part of Teresa). The tour began in Hartford Connecticut, September 5, 1927, and ended in California in July 1928. Zita remembered:

> This is where Universal comes in. While I was in California touring in *The Cradle Song*, the mensch, the elder Laemmle, offered me a five-year contract. I told him that I would do it, *that was*, until I got to Cleveland and fate took the upper hand. I broke my word to Mr. Laemmle and I was sorry that I did. However, this is where Universal goes out…for now.

It was upon her return from *The Cradle Song* tour when Zita signed for a special production of *Rope* in Cleveland. It was on the strength of her performance in *Rope* that David Wallace, one of the authors and a member of Arthur Hopkins' production staff, brought the young actress to the producer's attention.

Theater maestro Arthur Hopkins cast Zita Johann as the soul tortured murderess in Sophie Treadwell's *Machinal*. It was a play presented in nine episodes. *Machinal* opened at the Plymouth Theatre, September 7, 1928 running for over ninety performances. It closed November 24, 1928. Mr. Hopkins also directed the play. The play was loosely based on a then current murder trial having gained national notoriety. Ruth Snyder and her lover, Judd Gray, together murdered Snyder's husband. Ruth Snyder was convicted of murdering her husband and later went to the electric chair. Zita's performance as "The Young Woman" made her a Broadway star. Playing alongside her, was a then unknown actor, named Clark Gable (as the lover). Zita mailed the following typed review of *Machinal*, by Gilbert W. Gabriel, to this writer, which appeared in *The (New York) Sun:*

"*MACHINAL*, a tragedy in fine stage clothing with sudden glory for Zita Johann…it gave a comparatively little known actress, Zita Johann, a runway to stardom triumphant…The Zita Johann who bears the brunt of

Zita as Teresa in Eva Le Galliene's national touring production of The Cradle Song *(1927).*

it — and who makes so much of this brunt — is, there's no doubt of it, a magnificent young actress. The movies discovered that fact almost at the same moment when it burst upon Mr. Hopkins, and he must have had a time keeping her east. New Yorkers have seen her in strange outskirt art attempts only. Of late she has been trudging the provinces. Here, at last, she could come home to a play that is worth her tawny, feverishly reaching personality and her rich voice."

This photo of theatre producer and director Arthur Hopkins, was among Zita's cherished possessions in her home. Mr. Hopkins was responsible for giving Zita her big break in his highly acclaimed drama Machinal, *which made Zita a Broadway star.* PHOTO COURTESY OF DAVID MAROWITZ

The casting of Clark Gable as Zita's lover in *Machinal* had everyone in the New York theater baffled. Zita said, "No one had ever heard of Clark Gable." She remembered Clark Gable, in a published 1974 biography written about the actor, this way:

> *"I was worried about the part and I needed men to support me — big names. I told Arthur, and he said, 'Don't worry. I'll get you the proper men.'... Then he came and told me 'I've got you a Woolworth Romeo.'..."He was very good in the part...gave me complete support. He didn't have ups and downs; he knew his lines and didn't make mistakes...He did have impact, but no impact for me. We were on good terms. I liked him. Sometimes he walked me home, but to the door. I didn't even go out to supper with him. But he was genial. He was affable, lovable. Nice...Bemused is the word for him, Bemused."* [8]

Zita Johann and a then unknown Clark Gable in a scene from Sophie Treadwell's Machinal, *which ran 91 performances at New York's Plymouth Theatre during the fall of 1928.* PHOTO COURTESY OF DAVID MAROWITZ

Stage publicity photo of Zita Johann (circa 1931). The inscription reads, "To Mommy with a 1000 bushels of love from your Zita." PHOTO COURTESY OF DAVID MAROWITZ

It was during Zita's successful run in *Machinal* when she met Jacques Haussmann. through her sister, Magda. He was later known as the theater producer, writer, and eventually Academy Award winning actor, John Houseman.

In 1929, soon after her Broadway run in "Machinal," Zita, now twenty-four, was offered a motion picture contract with Metro-Goldwyn-Mayer

Zita Johann in The Lake *(1930), the play that she (under the pseudonym Joan Wolfe) and first husband John Houseman wrote together, She appeared in the play with her actor friend Alexander Kirkland, at the Berkshire Theatre in Pittsfield, Massachusetts, where it was previewed. Zita said, "The play was a consequential failure."*

studios in Hollywood. The art of movies was a new dimension from "the native drama" where Zita first made her mark with audiences.

> It began as an interesting medium. I hadn't yet married Haussmann when I first returned to Hollywood [in February 1929]. My mother insisted on going. I really had no choice but to bring her. I wasn't married, even though that wasn't a prerequisite in Hollywood, but I'm sure you understand. I was a good girl.. Irving Thalberg, at M-G-M offered me a contract with script approval, which is unheard of these days. Let's start with my resume and articles and we can work from there [she laughs]. So, they offered me two or three roles, none of which suited me, and two or three directors, none of whom suited me. I didn't like any of the scripts that were being offered. So I did nothing and was paid $27,000 for that. It was easy work, I admit, but my opinion of the motion picture industry wasn't very high. I had respect for Mr. Thalberg, that is why I agreed to come out west, but I refused his contract. And, after six months, I returned to New York.

Zita and her mother, Magdalena Johann, returned to New York from Hollywood in August 1929. Soon after, Zita began spending more time with John Haussmann.

> Haussmann began spelling his last name Houseman after he and I wrote a play together. Alexander Kirkland, a good friend of mine was the director of a theater down in Massachusetts. I starred in it. The play was called *The Lake* and it was a consequential failure. If you ever come across the name Joan Wolfe associated with the writers of the play [as she points to herself], you can say that you knew her. That was me! I noticed once that he [Houseman] was walking around in his pompous manner and I asked him, 'Why do you look down your nose at the world?' Well, that shook him out of it for a while at least until we were married.

Saturday, October 5, 1929, Zita Johann and John Haussmann were married. It was for both their first marriage, lasting roughly three years before they separated and later divorced.[9] Haussmann, was an exporter of wheat with the Oceanic Grain Company. He was also an investor in the company when I married him. Then along came the stock market crash [twenty-four days later]…I saw it coming, and he didn't have a dime. He had first become a citizen in London, where I've visited. His mother was from Wales. So he gave his last name that English spelling, and I encouraged him to consider work in the theater.

Zita Johann as Natascha in the 1930. Russian drama, Troyka. PHOTO COURTESY OF RICHARD FINEGAN

During the first two weeks of April 1930, Zita starred on Broadway in the play *Troyka*. Adapted by Playwright Lula Vollmer from the Hungarian Imre Fazekas, this harrowing story exhibited Russian drama. Zita's quiet performance as Natascha brought "intelligent presence" to the character, much like she did with her character in *Machinal*.

Subsequently, the theater producer Jed Harris, successfully produced Anton Chekhov's *Uncle Vanya* for Broadway, The play opened at the Cort Theatre on April 15, 1930 and ran until July, with ninety-six performances. The cast included Lillian Gish, Walter Connelly, Osgood Perkins and Joanna Roos as Sonia.[10]

Zita replaced Joanna Roos as Sonya in Anton Chekov's Uncle Vanya *when it toured in four cities in the fall of 1930.*

Zita Johann as she appeared in a scene from Tomorrow and Tomorrow *with Herbert Marshall. The Philip Barry play toured in seven cities over a seven-month period in 1931.*

Beginning the night of September 22, 1930, at the Booth Theatre in New York, *Uncle Vanya* returned for fourteen days before a road tour began with the original cast, with the exception of Joanna Roos as Sonia. Zita Johann replaced the actress from the re-opening through the road tour. Zita shared the following anecdote with this writer after the Chicago opening of *Uncle Vanya* at the Harris Theatre.

> While l was touring in "Uncle Vanya," we went on a four-city tour. After a performance one evening, well, in my hotel room at the Palmer House in Chicago, the telephone rang, which it did quite frequently. *Of course*, I answered it. I remember this as if it was yesterday... The voice on the other end said, "Miss Zita?" I said, 'Yes?' It was a man on the other end *said*, "Al Capone here.... I'm having some trouble. If I offered you one hundred dollars, would you go out with me tonight?" Without hesitating, I said, 'One hundred dollars? Never! And I hung up on him! Needless to say, I was married. But I guess that didn't matter to him. Can you imagine? I wouldn't have gone out with him anyway, but to offer me money? Huh! [laughter] Lordy... Okay. All right! Where do we go from here!?

While Zita was appearing in Philip Barry's play, *Tomorrow and Tomorrow*, he remembered, "Then along came D.W. Griffith, who I called the dean of moviemakers. He made mostly silent pictures, you know *The Birth of a Nation* was one of them."

Fifteen years after *The Birth of a Nation*, Mr. Griffith made his first Hollywood "talkie." *Abraham Lincoln* starred Walter Huston (father of the young fledgling scriptwriter John Huston). Mr. Griffith made a great deal of his early movies in the East and made plans to return there to shoot his next one.

> When talking pictures came in, producers were scared stiff that silent film actors couldn't talk. It put a lot of actors out of work. So they turned to stage actors who had voices. Mr. Griffith cast me in my first picture out here. It was called *The Struggle*. It was shot in the Bronx in five weeks. It was hard work, but I liked Mr. Griffith. He had a heart. We had a wonderful rapport. He was really a man of the theater. The theater is where he got his start and he never forgot that.[11] I played the wife of an alcoholic husband who was played by

Hal Skelly, a fellow Broadway actor. You may look at some of my publicity photos over there. They're from the picture. *The Struggle* went national, but it just *bombed* at the box office. I think it would have gone over quite well today. I think that it's a crying shame that *The Struggle* turned out to be Griffith's last picture. And he never made another picture. Can you imagine that? Where is that book? Let me find it. I feel that it sums things up pretty well. Here it is. I'll read this to you. This would be him [Mr. Griffith] talking…"I know, finally, that because I am a producer of motion pictures, that because I left the old stage for the new one, I am likely to be criticized to my own hurt for the conclusions that I have drawn. Yet I have merely tried to make clear that the arts in form are suspect to a kind of economic and artistic determinism that works ruthlessly to the survival of the fittest."

Movie theatre lobby card promotion sporting the film director's image for The Struggle *(United Artists, 1931), which became Zita Johann's motion picture debut. The movie was shot in the Bronx. Zita liked Griffith from the start and had hoped to continue working with him. However,* The Struggle *opened to scathing reviews. It ultimately became Griffith's swan song.*

Publicity still of Zita Johann from her motion picture debut in D.W. Griffith's The Struggle. PHOTO COURTESY OF RICHARD FINEGAN

Zita joked regarding this pose from The Struggle: *"Oh that? That's how I felt about motion pictures, you see…hemmed against a wall most of the time".*

From left to right: Actors Jackson Halliday, Evelyn Baldwin (who became Mrs. D.W. Griffith, from 1936 until 1947), Zita Johann, and Hal Skelly in a scene from The Struggle. PHOTO COURTESY OF RICHARD FINEGAN

From one of several scrapbooks, I read to Zita a newspaper article quoting her: *"My idea of Heaven is to have all of my plays directed by Arthur Hopkins and all of my films directed by D.W. Griffith."* Zita commented:

> Well, that was my idea of Heaven at the time. [laughing]. Some years ago, I was invited to a [revival] theater out here to see *The Struggle*. So I went. I don't make it a point to see movies that I've been in. But after all of these years, that picture has really stood the test of time. *The Struggle* did bring me *some* attention and after the play "Tomorrow and Tomorrow." And Hollywood was calling once again.

Tomorrow and Tomorrow had a successful Broadway run of twenty-two weeks at Henry Miller's Theatre. Zita remembered:

> It was a smash! To give you an idea of the audience, Noel Coward came back stage after one of my performances. He said that my performance was the best he had seen in a stage actress. And we toured in it, first in Baltimore, then at the Blackstone Theatre in Chicago. We played it in five other cities as well. It toured for about a year.

The cast included Herbert Marshall, Osgood Perkins, Marie Bruce, Eileen Byron, John T. Doyle, and Drew Price. Zita read to me the following un-noted theater review:
"*TOMORROW AND TOMORROW,* with Zita Johann acting holds its audience…Philip Barry's play, *TOMORROW AND TOMORROW,* owed much to Zita Johann…Miss Johann is, in fine, a translucent actress, as an alabaster box in translucent. Set a lighted candle within and it pierces through, clear and gently radiant. Similarly through the envelope of Miss Johann's face and body, by the light of her technical means, glows the soul of the woman she is charged to enact. This translucent quality is gift that the muse of acting — if there is one — seldom bestows. It is essential with the rarefied figures that poets have led to the stage. It is also signal and valuable, essential no less, to the acting of Eve Redman, of Redmanton, which is in Indiana, through Mr. Barry's piece…Miss Johann is the transparency through which she shines."

After completing the seven U.S. cities road tour of *Tomorrow and Tomorrow*, Zita returned to Hollywood with her husband John Houseman where she signed a five-year contract with RKO with <u>no</u> script approval.

Zita had many copies of this photograph from The Struggle *(United Artists, 1931) made to autograph for friends and fans over the years.*

She was "loaned out" to the other studios. Zita Johann appearing in a total of eight motion pictures, six of them were filmed in Hollywood between 1932 and 1934. Zita remembered:

> First, I was loaned out to Warner Bros. for *Tiger Shark*. The director had seen me in *Tomorrow and Tomorrow*. And he wanted *me* for *that* picture. I had no idea who Howard Hawks was then.[12]
>
> As you know, having seen *Tiger Shark*, it was Eddie's [Edward G. Robinson's] picture! Eddie was a ham, but he was one of the great actors, even then. He didn't like the idea that I was being photographed more than him in one scene and complained to the director. Eddie was original. He was from Romania. We had worked together before, so we were already acquainted.
>
> So, every time I had off from *Tiger Shark*, Warners supplied me with a car and driver. I had no car and I made that a condition, and so on and so forth.
>
> I didn't have script approval in the RKO contract and I said that to them in the New York office. I told them that I was afraid that they were going to put me in *Thirteen Women*. I noticed they had just bought it. They said, 'That! We couldn't afford to put you in that, not at your salary!' I said, all right, my salary will protect me. Anyway, I was constantly worried while I was making *Tiger Shark*.
>
> So, every minute I had, I ran over to RKO to find out what they were going to put me in. Well, they didn't have any idea. They had some crazy idea about a melodrama on a train. Finally, I got nowhere! They didn't know what they were going to put me in, but I had my suspicions. Then, we were over at Catalina Island winding up the picture *Tiger Shark* with location shots.
>
> Then, I got the script from RKO, *Thirteen Women*And on page 23, I remember that exactly, it stated, "She raises her arms in a take-all gesture and breathes a little." I said, 'I don't know how to do that. I can't play that part.' Well, Houseman was in a rage! I had to do it! After all, I was under contract. I was making the thousands of dollars and he [Houseman] was on the set all the time learning the business. I made that a stipulation in the contract. But Houseman was sure that I had

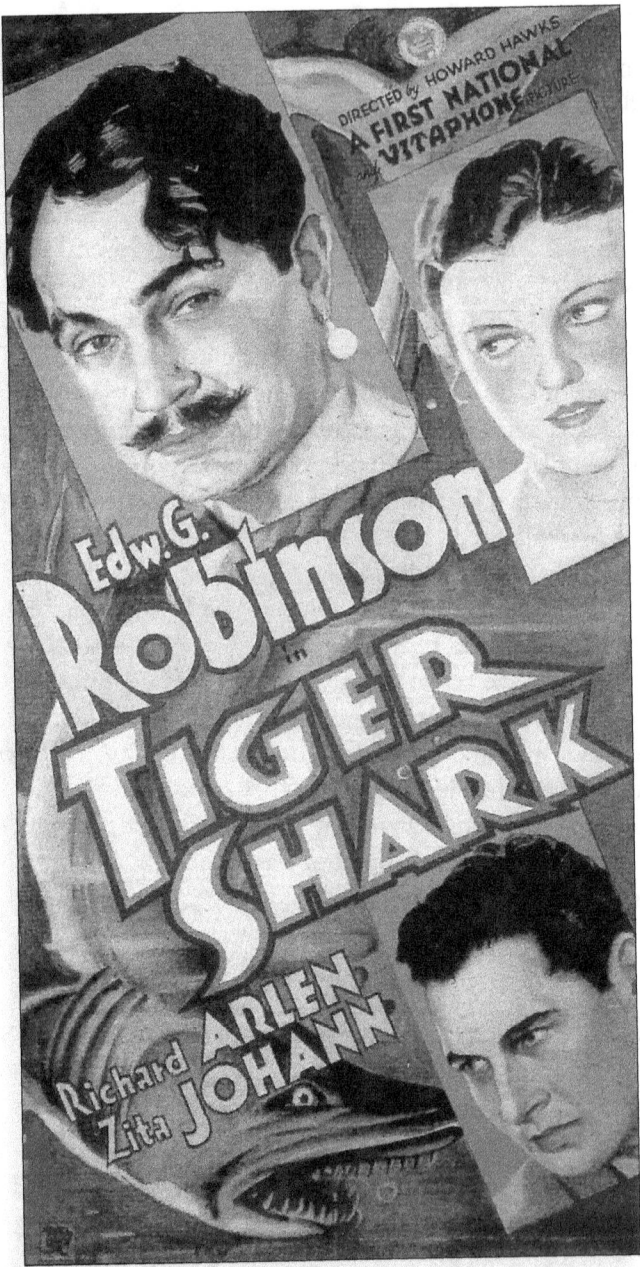

Movie theatre poster art depicting characters from Tiger Shark *(Warner Bros., 1932). This was Zita Johann's first Hollywood movie. Director Howard Hawks starred Edward G. Robinson, Zita Johann and Richard Arlen, who was loaned out by Paramount Pictures to play Pipes Boley.*
PHOTO COURTESY OF ZITA JOHANN

to make that movie. And, I was sure I wouldn't. The Monday after I finished *Tiger Shark*, I was supposed to start on *Thirteen Women* and Houseman was up and ready in his most pompous fashion to go to the studio and I said, I'm not going! He scolded me, "WHAT ABOUT MY MOTHER?" That characterizes it [laughing]! Do you see? I said, 'Well, she'll have to

In character, Mike Mascarenhas (Edward G. Robinson) and Quita Silva (Zita Johann) in a publicity pose from Tiger Shark *(Warner Bros. 1932).*

go to work the way I had to go to work, not the way that you have to go to work, because you don't work!' He was in a rage with me after that. I must tell you, after being released from that prior contract with M-G-M, my agent told me that they wouldn't have me back…[laughing]. So I went back to New York for a while.

Left to right: Edward G. Robinson, Zita Johann and Richard Arlen in a scene from Tiger Shark *(Warner Bros., 1932).* PHOTO COURTESY OF RICHARD FINEGAN

When I returned to California, then again from Universal came *Laughing Boy*. It was a great script. John Huston wrote it. Great, great, script! Superb…better than the book! When I met the author I practically told him that the script was better than his book![13] So I would be making tests. I was being paid and testing for laughing boys every day.

They couldn't find a laughing boy. Finally, I thought of Humphrey Bogart. He wasn't a star yet. So I called him up, found out where he lived and said, look, would you mind terribly if I mentioned you for *Laughing Boy*. We are having a hard time. He said, 'Oh please, please do!' I did. And you know they wouldn't think of it. They wouldn't take him on. When John

Zita in test make-up at Universal Pictures (1932) for the movie Laughing Boy. *Director William Wyler and producer Carl Laemmle Jr., chose Zita Johann for the part of Slim Girl testing her with many laughing boys for months hoping to find the male lead. Wyler ultimately canceled the project. Laughing Boy was never made by Universal. It was during this experience when Zita met the screenwriter John Huston.* PHOTO COURTESY OF ZITA JOHANN

Huston was up here some time ago we went over to Burgess Meredith's for dinner. I told them that if they had taken Humphrey Bogart on, they would have had a great picture. But he wasn't a star yet, you see.[14]

Zita's lifestyle was far from the typical Hollywood glamour. By nature, she was basically a Homebody, not the "enigma" she was touted by in the press. She loved the arts, and she painted canvases as a past time. She learned to play her father's violin, which was given to her by him.

I really didn't care about what people were writing about me. To me, understanding one's self is absolutely necessary before you can understand another. You asked me earlier how I came to be in *The Mummy*. Well, I felt that I owed Universal because I virtually got paid for nothing testing laughing boys. So I told Universal that I would appear in *The Mummy*. The attorney with whom I was signing the contract said, 'Miss Johann, you aren't going to make this picture are you? You're not serious [laughing]?' I said, yes, I think I should. So, that's why I did it.

This is where Houseman's friend, Eric, comes in. I had to import Eric from New York to the west coast. That was *horrible*. As Ruby Holloway, my secretary said, 'They give me a pain in the neck. They walk out on that beach all day and then they say to each other, [Zita laughing] 'Are you tired old chap? Well you were under those lights all day.' In Hungary, wives are submissive. I was that with Houseman and I allowed him to dominate me until I called the marriage off. And this is where Houseman and his friend were told to leave…Out! I said to them!

Universal Pictures publicized *The Mummy* as "*The Strangest Love Triangle Ever Filmed.*" Originally titled, *Cagliostro*, the story was reworked by Richard Schayer and Nina Wilcox Putnam. An uncredited John Huston contributed bits to story editing. *The Mummy* co-starred David Manners, Bramwell Fletcher, Arthur Byron, Edward Van Sloan, and Noble Johnson.[15]

Zita's memory of appearing in The Mummy wasn't a rewarding experience. According to her, an impetuous working relationship ensued between her and the director, Karl Freund, resulting in unsatisfactory working conditions. She remembered the experience well.

Well, the HOURS!...and *Freund* (in German) is suppose to translate to be *friend*...suppose to be! What an amateur he was. In the scenes with the outfits (sleek gowns and all), that I wore, he [Freund] wouldn't let me sit down between takes! I even offered to take them off between takes and put them

Movie theatre poster art from The Mummy *(1932), the motion picture that Zita Johann will be best remembered for. She co-starred with Boris Karloff.* The Mummy *was filmed at Universal Pictures under the direction of Karl Freund.*

back on when I was called back on the set. He would not hear of that! And the so-called "slant board" was unavailable to me. Then he wanted to shoot a scene with me partially nude. I told him that if he could get it past the censors, it would be fine with me. Well that made him furious, you see. He wanted me to be furious.

Freund was known for numerous takes before arriving at a print. One of the first scenes that Zita remembered as "pure labor" was the human sacrifice scene with her and Boris Karloff.

> I was as cold as ice lying on that slab, and I had to lie on it for days! Everyone but Freund was good to me. Boris Karloff was always a gentleman. He was a tremendously nice person. I was thrilled to know that I was also working with Arthur Byron, a veteran of the stage, and my friend David Manners.

Movie theatre lobby card featuring the sacrifice scene from The Mummy *(Universal, 1932; A Realart Re-release). Ardath Bey's words to Helen were, "You shall dawn anew in the East." Zita said that she had to lie on that slab for days. It was pure labor."* PHOTO COURTESY OF ZITA JOHANN

We appeared together years before in *He Who Gets Slapped* at the Theatre Guild.

Having my cook, who was also my driver Sasha, and Ruby, my secretary around…all of these people were positive influences during the making of that picture. I didn't get to "*know*" anybody else, really. Because everybody was so busy, as was I.

The cast of The Mummy *included (from left to right) Arthur Byron, Edward Van Sloan, Zita Johann, Boris Karloff and David Manners (who became acquainted with Zita ten years prior to the making of the film. They were both part of Basil Sydney's touring company in Theatre Guild productions in the 1920s.)*

There was a time when the front office got word that there may be some problems on the set. So, Carl Laemmle, Jr. introduced everyone to his brother-in-law, Stanley Bergerman, who was the associate producer. We were to report any grievances to him. This seemed to ease *some* tension on the set. Stanley Bergerman was always kind and attentive, but he was not always present.

Then, on the Saturday night before the finish of the picture, in the scene in which Boris Karloff showed me my previous lives; I suddenly went out cold (in real life). To all intents and purposes, I was dead!

It was the crew who prayed me back. It took them an hour for God to hear them [as she giggled]. When I came back, naturally, it was Saturday night about eleven o'clock. We couldn't get a doctor, nothing. You see? (The doctor whom I saw later at the hotel told me that I might have suffered a mild heart attack on the movie set.)

Left: Producer and General Manager of Universal Pictures, Carl Laemmle Jr. (seen here in 1931), best known as "Junior." PHOTO COURTESY OF UDO BAYER. *Right: Stanley Bergerman in 1929. He was a producer at Universal Pictures from 1929 through 1935, brother-in-law to "Junior" Laemmle.* PHOTO COURTESY OF STANLEY BERGERMAN

So I had Sunday to rest up. When I got back to the hotel, I got my own doctor and so on and so forth…And Monday, I was on the set to play the Christian Martyr.

And I noticed when I walked on to the set that everybody, especially Freund, the director was behind bars. Do you see? Everybody was protected. E-v-e-r-y-b-o-d-y! And I just blindly walked in through the door of an enormous cage with three lions on huge, high pedestals. Do you see? And Ruby said, "This you are NOT going to do. You are not going to go in there!" I said, Ruby, they saved this for the last day and I'm getting paid. I go in. I was beyond fear. Do you see? That passing out and going on to the next whatever, it is, the hereafter. That just left me so oblivious to everything. So it was a blessing! It enabled me to get in there and face those lions. That's the old story. Don't ever show a dog you are afraid of 'em because the dog catches your fear and he attacks because he is afraid. The terrorists are scared stiff of tomorrow, so they blow up every-

Scene from The Mummy, in which Ardath Bey (Boris Karloff) begins to tell Helen Grosvenor (Zita Johann), the story of their forbidden love in Ancient Egypt as it became depicted in the pool sequence. PHOTO COURTESY OF ZITA JOHANN

thing!…Anyhow, back to the lions. I was beyond fear with the lions. So, I walked into the lion's cage. The trainer with his chair was way at the other end, more than 100 feet away, And I just walked in and I'm sure the lions said, *'Those bones! Who needs 'em?* [laughing]!' I didn't have sense enough to be afraid.

What I realized was that, director Freund sat, <u>behind those bars!</u> And everybody else, the cameramen, everybody was protected with these thick, thick bars! And I walked right passed… and that was the end of that picture. That's the anecdote. What else do you want [laughing]?…Let's let it go at that one!

Quoting Zita, "That picture was taken to show more pleasant relations, a meeting of the minds, if you will. As you see, we are dining together, Freund and me. The gentleman standing there was my personal chef, Sasha. I hired Sasha in California and he later came with me to New York. That picture was taken strictly for publicity purposes. Stanley Bergerman, did a super job seeing that we were all at ease later on the Mummy set." PHOTO COURTESY OF ZITA JOHANN

There were six lives illustrated in the original movie. Four past lives were cut in the final print of *The Mummy* that no one sees; a Madame DuBarry, a medieval noblewoman, a Barbarian Queen, and the Christian martyr. Zita said, "The only two left were the Egyptian Princess and me, the Twentieth Century ancestor."

Im-Ho-Tep awakens the Princess to other past lives as depicted through a mirror in scenes deleted from The Mummy *(Universal, 1932). It was this scene of which Zita said, "...I suddenly went out cold."* PHOTO COURTESY OF ZITA JOHANN

Zita continued:

> Carl Laemmle Jr., I think, was one of the nicest gentleman that I've ever met anywhere. He was a thoroughly nice, warm person, very courteous, everything! I can't say enough nice things about him. In as much as my scenes being cut away, I can't say that I would blame him, nor could I tell him how to run his business.
>
> Further down the road, after I heard that the Laemmles were selling Universal, I phoned Carl Laemmle, Jr., but I was unable to reach him. Several days later, we heard from

Eighteenth Century "Madame du Barry" was one of four incarnations deleted from The Mummy *(Universal, 1932).*

A Thirteenth Century Noblewoman from The Mummy *was another.*
PHOTO COURTESY OF ZITA JOHANN

An Eighth Century Barbarian Queen deleted from The Mummy *(Universal, 1932).* PHOTO COURTESY OF ZITA JOHANN

Zita Johann said that after the final cuts were made to The Mummy *film footage, "The only two left were the Egyptian Princess..."* PHOTO COURTESY OF ZITA JOHANN

"*...and me, the Twentieth Century ancestor.*" (The Mummy, *Universal, 1932*).
PHOTO COURTESY OF ZITA JOHANN

Universal, but it wasn't Laemmle. Whoever it was, offered to test me for, *would you believe it*...a horror picture. I said, 'Is this somebody's idea of a joke?" I asked my husband [John McCormick], who was my agent, what the part was. He said, "....the daughter of Dracula." I said to him, 'Hell no! I will not be testing for *that*.' And I didn't.[16]

Zita as Helen Grosvenor in a scene in which Karloff has a hold on her power from The Mummy *(Universal Pictures, 1932).*

Zita Johann wrote in a 1979 Christmas card to this writer..."I wrote to Mr. [Junior] Laemmle as he was passing away. I told him how sorry I was for not making better pictures with him. Later, I received a reply informing me that he had passed away, but he *did* receive my message."

Even before *The Mummy*, I was being asked to do a number of different pictures. I turned them all down. They were second-rate scripts, so apparently Universal made their first rate billing, so to speak, with the horror pictures, but to consign *that picture* to a horror status? And having *that* monster as a director! Forget it.[17]

Publicity photo from The Mummy. *Zita said, "Oh, you like that photo, do you? I like it too, but I didn't like working on that picture."* PHOTO COURTESY OF ZITA JOHANN

The Mummy had its movie premiere in early January 1933. Zita was the most beautiful attraction for moviegoers. She had separated previously from her husband, John Houseman, and was currently involved with scriptwriter John Huston, whom she met on the set of *Laughing Boy* at Universal Pictures. Some forty years later, Zita saw *The Mummy* for the first time.

Another scene from The Mummy *(Universal Pictures, 1932) in which Im-Ho-Tep alias Ardath Bey (Boris Karloff) holds power over Helen Grosvenor (Zita Johann). Inscribed to the author by Zita Johann.*

I never cared to see *The Mummy* until *my friend* insisted that I *do* see it. My television set was broken so she brought me one. I realized after watching it, why I did it after all. I saw it in the same light as I remembered it to be as we were making it. It is in the category that I saw it, when I read it, even though it was later distorted.

The Mummy, in my opinion was not a horror picture, basically, although for box office reasons that was emphasized. Now, it was really a picture about (you might call it) reincarnation and interrelations...international relations, and so on and so forth. It could have been an important picture. But since it was consigned to a horror status...[Universal] they specialized in horror [laughing]. That's the gist of it. I'll tell you this. That was the first time I felt the *Spirit* in a motion picture. It set the mood for that character, you see. Scenes of me with Boris Karloff, where his character is holding power over mine…and particularly that scene of me in the taxi when I am chanting Egyptian. I really WAS Egyptian.

The Hollywood adage regarding bad luck to actors working with animals or children, Zita said, "The dog (Wolfram) was marvelous. He didn't give me any trouble, which is more than I can say about the director, if that's what he wanted to call himself." (The Mummy, Universal, 1932).

The theater, however, is where I related more to the Spirit. I'd pray *every time* before I had to go on. The roles demanded the truth from me as the actress.

A great deal of the time, I would live in the mood of the character that I was portraying. When I portrayed a role I grew into it. When I played a role on stage, I didn't think of my own reactions at all. But when I was studying it, I found that I must see the woman through my own experiences as well as by means of how the playwright saw her.

Motion pictures are splendid for the actress who wants to find out how good an actress she is. But to me, it wasn't that

Of this publicity photo from The Mummy, *Zita Johann as the Egyptian Princess Anck-es-en-Amon said, "It was originally to be a story of reincarnation…"* PHOTO COURTESY OF ZITA JOHANN

Zita said, "I feel that this photo captured the true Egyptian Princess. The other shots aren't as good as this one because it has a mood about it" (The Mummy, *Universal, 1932*). PHOTO COURTESY OF ZITA JOHANN

way. Motion picture acting was more pretending. However, I learned by watching my mistakes and mannerisms in the daily rushes than I have ever learned through any single medium. And I didn't like that.

The trouble with most film directors is that they are quite inflexible in their ideas. Their inability to see my point of view

The Nubian (Noble Johnson) preparing the bath in The Mummy. PHOTO COURTESY OF ZITA JOHANN

in any way makes me equally inflexible. I called myself professionally introspective.

After I'd finish any role, I liked taking long rests. Preferably, I'd stay in the country, away from everything that could remind me of this work. One of the things that I admired about Greta Garbo, aside from my considering her a dramatic actress of the highest order, was that she had her boundaries too, you see.

After Zita left Universal, her agent, Leland Hayward, sent her to Paramount Pictures. Earlier in 1932, Zita was offered the chance to play opposite Clark Gable in *Deported*. Both Clark Gable and Zita Johann turned it down. The following book excerpt may sum up their brief reunion.

Zita Johann and David Manners (Frank Whemple) in a scene from The Mummy *(Universal Pictures, 1932). Zita said, "Here you are. I signed it. I did what you told me to do." Inscribed to the author by Zita and David, May/June of 1982.*

"Typically, Zita Johann recalls meeting Clark at a Hollywood party, the first time she'd seen him since Machinal. "He came very late, dressed informally. He wanted to talk about old times and we went to a room where we could be alone. You know how some men are; they think they have to make a pass — they're almost obligated to. He tried and I got out of it. It was nothing objectionable, but

Another scene from The Mummy, *in which Zita Johann said that she "was Egyptian".*

there just was no attraction for me, or for him. He was really very detached. His wife [then Josephine Dillon] came in and sort of took over." [18]

During Zita's short employment at Paramount, her beauty was captured in a number of publicity photos that include the expertise of Paramount's top photographer Otto Dyar, and Beverly Hills photographer Gonzalo D'Gaggeri, at his Wilshire Boulevard location.

In Paramount's *Luxury Liner*, Zita played opposite George Brent. She was cast as Nurse Morgan in the streamliner melodrama that takes place aboard the *Germania*, which sailed from Bremerhaven to New York. *Luxury Liner* based on the novel *Die Überfahrt* by Gina Kaus.

Paramount Pictures top photographer Otto Dyar, promoted the image of Hollywood's rising starlets. PHOTO COURTESY OF ZITA JOHANN

Zita said, "In some of those poses, like this one, the photographer allowed me some unconventional poses. I took the allowance in heed (circa 1933). PHOTO COURTESY OF ZITA JOHANN

Zita Johann inscribed this Dyar glamour photo to the author, which reads, "To Rick — Do come again. With best wishes, Zita." PHOTO COURTESY OF ZITA JOHANN.

Portrait by Beverly Hills photographer D'Gaggeri (circa 1933). PHOTO COURTESY OF ZITA JOHANN

Another striking portrait of Zita Johann by D'Gaggeri (circa 1933). PHOTO COURTESY OF DAVID MAROWITZ

Movie producer Jesse Lasky, whom she met at a Hollywood gathering through her agent, Leland Hayward, were invited to Paramount. Adolph Zukor, who was the president of Paramount Pictures, was still running the studio then.[19]

However, production chief B.P. (Benjamin Percival) Schulberg was hired by Zukor as general manager of Paramount. (Schulberg first began

Luxury Liner (Paramount Pictures, 1933) was the only movie that Zita Johann made for Paramount. It starred George Brent and was produced by B.P. Schulberg. Lothar Mendes directed it. COURTESY OF ZACHARY ZITO

working for William Fox in the 1920s), had a good supporting cast that included Vivienne Osborne, Verree Teasdale, C. Aubrey Smith, and Frank Morgan (who later appeared as the The Wizard in M-G-M's *The Wizard of Oz*).

Schulberg introduced Zita to the director Lothar Mendes. The two got along so well that Schulberg began production on *Luxury Liner* began in mid-January, 1933.[20]

George Brent was a gentleman most of the time. He was insistent asking the director to do more takes, which lost spontaneity to me, but that was *my* opinion. However, we did have a flexible director. The director and I were able to speak German to each other. I remember when he allowed me to turn away from the camera in a scene in which I had to cry. I was never good at it. It was always hard for me to cry because when I was a child, my mother wouldn't let me cry, you see. In some of those scenes with George Brent, I'd come close to

The first of three montages depicting characters from Luxury Liner *as seen in* Film-kurier, *a weekly German that was published in Berlin between 1919 and 1945 (No. 660, 1933).* PHOTO COURTESY OF RICHARD FINEGAN

real tears [laughing], just out of sheer boredom. My opinion of *Luxury Liner* is that it sailed nowhere. Let's leave it at that.[21]

Nearly three weeks after the release of *Luxury Liner*, John Huston was driving under the influence of alcohol. Zita was with him in the automobile when Huston suddenly struck a palm tree. The impact of the crash sent Zita head first into the windshield. Broken glass marred her

Zita Johann as Miss Morgan, a nurse aboard the Germania, on its way to New York with an array of characters. PHOTO COURTESY OF RICHARD FINEGAN

face. Her career came to a sudden halt. It took nearly four months before Zita could work again. She wrote: "…fractured my hips in the accident. I recovered, but with age, it's been disabling me."

Hollywood motion picture studios were going through some erratic changes. In 1933 alone, both RKO and Famous Players-Lasky (which by that time had became Paramount Pictures) had gone into receivership.

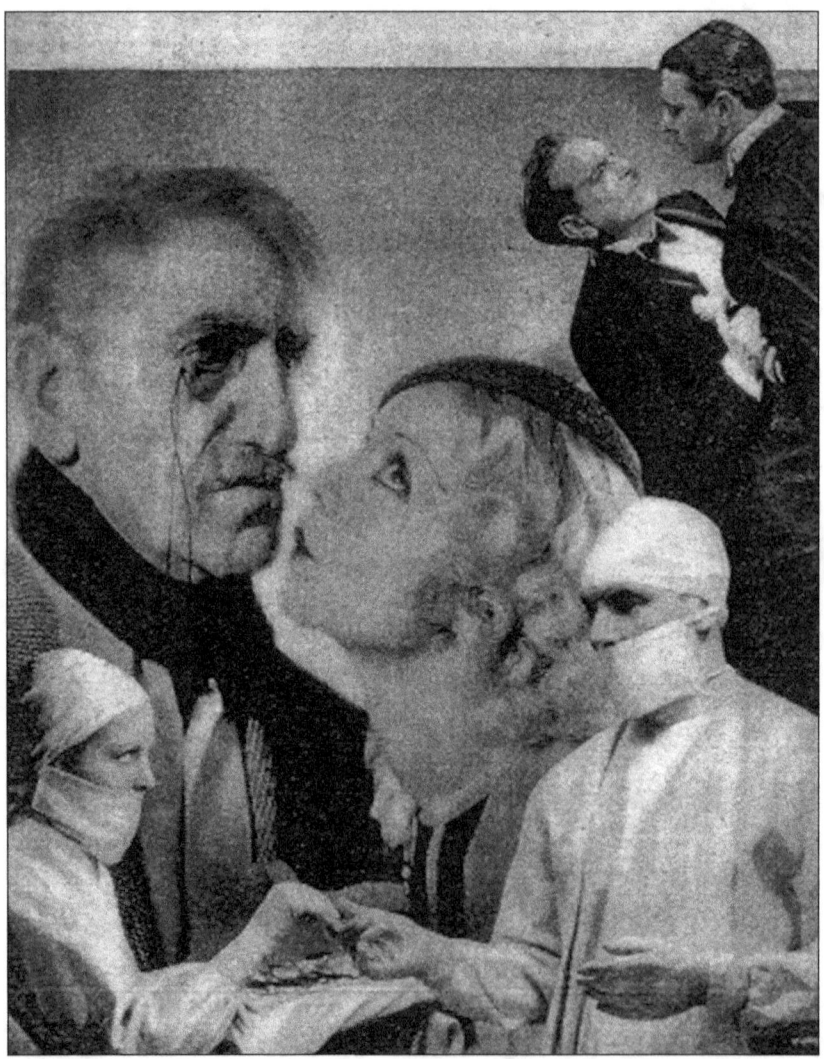

Some of the characters aboard the Germania included, Milli Lensch (Alice White), Edward Thorndyke (C. Aubrey Smith) and Alex Stevanson (Frank Morgan). PHOTO COURTESY OF RICHARD FINEGAN

Joseph Schenck was running the show at Fox Films in 1933 when Myron Selznick introduced him to Zita. Schenck offered Zita a starring role in *The Man Who Dared: An Imaginative Biography*. The working title was *The American*. It was a story based on the life and death of Anton Cermak (Chicago's first foreign-born mayor — his death occurred after an assassination attempt earlier in 1933). Lamarr Trotti and Dudley

Movie theatre lobby card from The Man Who Dared: An Imaginative Biography *(Fox Films, 1933), starring Preston Foster and Zita Johann. Hamilton Mac Fadden directed it.* PHOTO COURTESY OF ZACHARY ZITO

Nichols wrote the screenplay at breakneck speed for the producer, Sol Wurtzel, at Fox. However, the Cermak character's name was changed to "Jan Novak" for the movie. Preston Foster starred.

Zita's priority even before *The Mummy*, was, "Who's directing this picture?" When Zita learned that stage producer Hamilton MacFadden was the director, she remembered:

> I was never fond of close-ups in that picture because I wasn't fully recovered [from the car accident], you see, but my *saving grace*, was that Mr. MacFadden was another flexible

Publicity photo of Zita Johann as Teena Pavelic in The Man Who Dared: An Imaginative Biography *(Fox Films, 1933).* PHOTO COURTESY OF RICHARD FINEGAN

director. He directed the cameramen to "shoot around" me, so to speak. He an experienced stage director, and he had some sound personal advice for me. I was going through my divorce from Houseman at the time, you see. But in getting back...I remember that we had a fine group of actors on that picture. It wasn't the best of times, but I was treated well on that set.²²

Zita recalls the wedding dress and her handsome co-star Preston Foster from The Man Who Dared: An Imaginative Biography. PHOTO COURTESY OF ZITA JOHANN

It is no secret that I was married a few times. They were not good experiences. But if life were like the movies, I would have wanted to stay married to Preston Foster, who played my husband in that picture. As you see by that photograph over there the wedding dress that I was wearing in that scene with Preston was just lovely! And he was a handsome groom. He was a terrifically nice fellow and a finely seasoned actor.

That was a good marriage [she giggles]. But the truth was, it was just a movie, all a make-believe world and we were actors just playing roles. When we met prior to the shooting of the picture. I told Fox that I'd be happy to do it…and *you know* we *did* receive some good notices from it too!

I made another picture right after that. We shot it in a week! That was hard work. I doubt that you've ever heard of it?… There it is, listed right there [as she pointed to her resume], *The Sin of Nora Moran*. It was touted for a while as *The Voice From*

Movie theatre lobby card depicting characters Nora Moran (Zita Johann) and Governor Crawford (Paul Cavanaugh) in The Sin of Nora Moran *(Majestic, 1933).* PHOTO COURTESY OF ZACHARY ZITO

the Grave. Originally, they were going to call it *The Woman in the Chair*. But I politely asked them not to do that because I felt that I did that successfully before on a better stage [referring to *Machinal*]. I didn't want that little picture haunting me. The director was haunting enough [laughing]! But I was able to get through to him.²³

Publicity photo of Zita Johann in the title role from the motion picture The Sin of Nora Moran, *directed by Phil Goldstone.* Photo courtesy of Richard Finegan

September 12, 1933 was the date when Zita's divorce from John Houseman was granted through Juarez, Mexico. Likewise, her relationship with John Huston was over.[24]

Another unfortunate tragedy occurred involving Huston, on the evening of September 24, 1933. He was driving his car when he accidentally struck and killed a pedestrian. A jury would later exonerate Huston.[25]

Movie Poster art from The Sin of Nora Moran *(Majestic, 1933). In the summer of 2000, the UCLA Film Archive announced the movie as one of their preserved films.* PHOTO COURTESY OF ZACHARY ZITO

The Sin of Nora Moran was released December 13, 1933. Zita said, "I wouldn't go see it. I really didn't care to see any of it."

> I spent a lot of time enjoying the weather in Malibu. One morning I got a call from my friend, David [Hertz]. He told me that he'd gotten in as a writer on a picture being considered by Fox, *Grand Canary* [based on the 1933 novel by A.J. Cronin]. I read the script and liked it. Wouldn't you know, my agent called me after that and said Fox would be doing another picture and Irving Cummings would be directing it. That's the one that Warner Baxter was in. I *was* familiar with *Irving Cummings*, and the script, so I did it.[26]

Of all of her co-stars, during the production of *Grand Canary*, Zita's fondest memory was of actress Marjorie Rambeau.

Movie theatre lobby card depicting the characters Dr. Harvey Leith (Warner Baxter) and Suzan Tranter (Zita Johann) in Grand Canary *(Fox Films, 1934).* PHOTO COURTESY OF ZACHARY ZITO

One day, Marjorie and I got into an interesting chat between takes. She learned that I gave readings. So, we arranged to meet where I was staying in Malibu. She brought along her friend, Vivienne Osborne. I had worked with both of them in in a roundabout way, In fact, long ago, Vivienne replaced me on stage in *Aloma of the South Seas*. And I was Marjorie's under-

A scene from Grand Canary *(Fox, 1933). From left to right: Gerald Rogers (Trout), Zita Johann (Suzan Tranter), Roger Imhof (Jimmie Corcoran), Madge Evans (Lady Mary Fielding), Man standing; Gerald Rogers (Steward), (Gilbert Emery (Captain Renton), Juliette Compton (Elissa Baynham), Barry Norton (Robert Tranter), and Marjorie Rambeau (Daisy Hemingway).* PHOTO COURTESY OF RICHARD FINEGAN

study in *As You Like It*, a Shakespearian play with my friend, Rollo Peters. He was the understudy to Ian Keith, who was once married to my friend, Blanche Yurka. Many connected friends have passed on…

Marjorie had been a star on Broadway for many years. She had given up the stage about the same time I was getting started. Then she moved to California, you see.

So, I told the girls that I never made a picture that I was proud of. I turned to Marjorie and said that my objection to Hollywood was that they were manufacturing personalities like *canned goods!* Marjorie was a humorous soul. She suggested that I could remain an unsold tin can in the Hollywood market or make what I could of myself elsewhere. I asked them, who was giving *whom* the reading here?

Barry Norton (left as Robert Tranter), with Warner Baxter and Zita Johann in a scene from Grand Canary, *in which Barry Norton and Zita Johann played brother and sister.* PHOTO COURTESY OF RICHARD FINEGAN

Vivienne loved my Malibu place so much that when I finally left Hollywood, she moved into it. I was only renting it. It *was* quite a beautiful place. But California was not my home.

After reading *The New York Times* review (July 20, 1934) of *Grand Canary* to Zita, she remembered the very first sentence, which read, "Something must have got lost in transit." Zita remembered going to Joseph Schenck's office soon after she finished her scenes in *Grand Canary* at Fox. According to her, *"Yes, something must have got lost in transit there too."*

First of all, the *Hays office* had a field day with that picture before it was ever finished. The Catholic Church had condemned it.[27]

I was considering staying on at Fox for a while longer, but *not* after that one day in Joe Schenck's office after I finished the picture. Joe Schenck was another guy who thought he was

Marjorie Rambeau and Zita Johann from a scene in Grand Canary *(Fox, 1933). Zita recalls a visit from her friend Marjorie that left an indelible impression on them both.* PHOTO COURTESY OF RICHARD FINEGAN

going to marry me. And I wasn't even dating him! I learned that he was a womanizer. He started coming on to me. It was certainly obvious to me *that* day. Well, I told him that his pictures were nothing but rubbish!…And that Hollywood was nothing but a brothel! That was the end. I wouldn't make another picture in Hollywood, and *I didn't*. Then, a little later down the road, Harry Cohn at Columbia Pictures wanted me to sign a contract with him. I brought my friend, David [Hertz], along. Harry said, 'Alright, whose the guy in your life now? I'll sign him up too.' I had already divorced Houseman by then, you see. But David was a friend. I told Harry in German that I saw no future to living in California. I also told him [Cohn] what I had told Schenck. I was fed up with movie acting. I never signed with Harry Cohn, but we had a nice rapport.

Cohen suggested that Hertz go to United Artists, where Hertz befriended motion picture director, H.C. (Henry Codman) Potter. This experience spun a collaborative screenwriting working relationship and friendship between the two men.

So, David [Hertz] got his foot in the door with Harry that day. David so appreciative of my bringing him along that he promised to star me in a Broadway play that he'd written. I knew that David was a talented writer.

By the summer of 1934, Hollywood movie making was going through more financial and socialized changes. Zita's concern was the RKO contract that she remained under. With the help of legal representation, she was freed from that contract once and for all. Zita chose to remain in California for personal reasons.

Joseph Schenck's partners, Darryl F. Zanuck (who had been head of production at Warner Bros. from 1931), Raymond Griffith (a former silent screen comedian who turned to writing and producing at Fox) and William Goetz (associate producer at Fox), helped to found Twentieth Century Pictures in 1933. Schenck himself was the former president of United Artists. In less than a year after the release of *Grand Canary*, a merger with Fox Films and Twentieth Century Pictures resulted in establishing was known as 20th Century Fox Pictures, Incorporated. *Grand Canary* opened in New York City, July 19, 1934. It became Zita Johann's last Hollywood movie

CHAPTER 5

Transitions

Zita returned to New York from Hollywood in 1934. She spent considerable time at her beloved "retreat" at the Adirondacks Mountains. It was introduced to her during her early Theatre Guild days, when seeking spiritual and physical comfort.[1]

> I really wanted to stay in the mountains. I could relax, pray and heal and not fear God. Who was I kidding [laughing]?

Upon return to New York City, in August 1934, Zita met the author John O'Hara. His first novel (later a classic), *Appointment in Samarra*,

Zita at her beloved retreat in the Adirondacks Mountains (1934). PHOTO COURTESY OF DAVID MAROWITZ

had just been published. Before the relationship hadn't gotten too far Zita learned about O'Hara's alcohol addiction She mused, "I should have made an *Appointment with a Psychiatrist!*"[2]

David Hertz kept his promise to Zita. She attained the starring role in his forthcoming play, *Waltz in Fire*. The cast included Osgood Perkins, Douglass Montgomery, Eduardo Cianelli and Morgan Farley. It was scheduled to open at the Masque Theatre, Wednesday, October 31, 1934. However, it closed before it was presented to the public. Zita said, "It became a legal disaster. You can read it for yourself in this article, if you please." After the article was read, Zita said, "That was just another of the many struggles that go on in this business."[3]

> So ends that story... *Waltz in Fire* was never seen. It became *history*. David shelved his play and returned to Hollywood. He was a writer in motion pictures. However, he did write another play in California later. David was a gifted writer and a good friend.[4]
>
> So after the *Waltz in Fire* dilemma, I wanted to go back to work. Orson Welles was a young theater actor and a hell of a nice guy. I would have liked to work with him more. So, I agreed to appear in one of Welles' and Houseman's first productions. The play was called *Panic*.
>
> It had a run over on 45th Street [The Imperial Theatre]... with only three performances. It wasn't well received, probably because of its Un-American leanings. They played it mainly to the press first...And the boys got slapped for it. This came before Orson's *big* radio broadcast [*War of the Worlds*]. You know that later down the road Orson and Houseman, formed The Mercury Theatre. Their business partnership later dissolved along with their friendship.

Soon to follow, Zita appeared in a special nine-performance run in the popular *Seven Keys to Baldpate*, with George M. Cohan. It was based on the novel by Earl Derr Bigger. The Players Club produced the all-star revival at the National Theatre. Aside from Cohan, and Zita, the cast included George Christie, Walter Hampden, Josephine Hull, Irene Rich, Ruth Weston, and Otis Skinner.[5]

During the run of that play, Zita became reacquainted with a former film executive whom she first met in California during the making of

Zita Johann publicity photo marks her return to the New York stage in 1935.
PHOTO COURTESY OF RICHARD FINEGAN

Tiger Shark at Warner Bros.. He was now a theatrical agent and had moved to New York City. His name was John McCormick. He was once general manager of First National Pictures.[6]

Seven Keys to Baldpate became the highest grossing limited engagement of its time. Four weeks after its closing and after a whirlwind courtship lasting all of two weeks, Zita and McCormick were married in New

The cast of the successful George M. Cohan play, The Seven Keys to Baldpate *(New York, 1935).* PHOTO COURTESY OF ZITA JOHANN

York City, July 9, 1935. Mr. McCormick had previously Been married and divorced from movie actress Colleen Moore. In her second marriage, Zita became McCormick's third wife.

During a brief honeymoon in New York, the couple returned to Hollywood, via the Santa Fe Chief, July 15, 1935. McCormick began fortuitously promoting his wife in various Hollywood publications. Zita appeased her second husband with the possibility of resuming work in motion pictures.

> He [McCormick] thought that he was going to sell me back to Hollywood. There were a few scripts being offered and

I read a few. And I continued to refuse them simply because they did not suit me. I didn't want to be in the movies, you see. When you want something bad enough, you're willing to pay for it [chuckling]. Then I learned more about him [McCormick]. His *attitude* was just outrageous. When I would turn down a test, his protest was getting drunk and staying drunk for days. That was only the beginning. I was only going to California for the summers because I wanted to continue to work on Broadway. That's what we did then. Once I decided that I didn't want to live on both coasts, I returned to New York.[7]

Zita's auspicious introduction to radio began by way of CBS and Cecil B. DeMille with *Lux Radio Theatre of the Air*. On the evening of October 19, 1936, *Captain Applejack* adapted from the play by Walter Hackett was broadcast from the Music Box Theatre in Hollywood. Zita played the character Anna Valeska. It was her only appearance on the *Lux Radio Theatre of the Air*. It co-starred Frank Morgan as Ambrose Applejohn, Maureen O'Sullivan as Poppy Faire and Akim Tamiroff as Ivan Borolsky.

Sponsored by Lever Brothers, the makers of Lux Bar Soap, *Lux Radio Theatre of the Air* featured celebrities both from stage and screen. The hour-long program later was moved into adaptations of motion pictures. It became the most popular and longest running anthology series on radio. The first two seasons of the show were originally broadcast from New York via the NBC-Blue network and later in Hollywood by CBS. With a variety of hosts, it's most popular was DeMille, who joined the broadcast's third season in Hollywood, June 1, 1936. DeMille remained with the program midway through its eleventh season, January 22, 1945. The last broadcast of *Lux Radio Theatre of the Air* ended June 7, 1955.[8]

So I made the trip to Hollywood for DeMille, and then another. My sister [Agatha] wanted to visit me in California before I moved back to New York. So, she set sail [in 1937] for California, alone. I wish that hadn't happened. When my sister *did* arrive, she appeared well and excited. She read in the papers that a play starring Walter Huston, written by David Hertz, was being previewed in Santa Monica. So we went. David along with his wife arranged to take us to the theater that night. Well, after a few days, my sister was acting unusual. That's when she suffered the breakdown. I was having a terrible time with my marriage [to McCormick]. I wouldn't call it *marriage*. I'd call it *hell*. Fortunately for my sister, she was moved to a fine hospital in Connecticut after we arrived by train. Unfortunately, she and her husband divorced around this time. She eventually made a life in Connecticut.

Zita and McCormick legally separated April 11, 1938. She charged him with estrangement and filed for divorce. The divorce was granted August 18, 1938. McCormick eventually returned to California, where

Lux Soap Ad (circa 1936). Zita returned to Hollywood in 1936 to appear in the Lux Radio Theatre production, Captain Applejack *for Cecil B. DeMille. She would remain in Hollywood for six months before returning to New York permanently.* PHOTO COURTESY OF JANE E. MOORE

he lived until his death in 1961. Zita's brief summation of her second marriage was:

> He had physically abused and threatened me. He had a serious drinking problem that kept him institutionalized a good part of the time, and for whom I was the wrong sex. So, to get to the end of this California business, I was still a renter at the place in Malibu. I had to return to California one last time for personal reasons, and again after the divorce. I was then able to say, *Auf Wiedersehen* [Goodbye] to Hollywood for good.

In the fall of 1938, after her divorce from McCormick, Zita moved from New York City to the peaceful countryside of West Nyack, New York, located in Rockland County. She moved into her pre-revolutionary Dutch Redstone farmhouse. According to Zita, she moved into her home "at the niche of time." Living in West Nyack was a peaceful change for her. Zita's lifestyle began to shift from the fast pace of New York City. Zita began writing and also dabbled in poetry and resumed painting. She read many books that included children's stories. Later Zita would write book-manuscripts, but none were published. Her love for the theater inspired her to write plays. She also continued radio work.

> When I moved into my home, the "great hurricane" came. I did not see *that* coming [laughs]! Fortunately, this house withstood much water damage. It was amazing. So I looked at it as not only my new home, but as my fortress. After I spent my first winter here, that's when I came up with the name Winter Quarters. When we were interrupted earlier, you asked me when this house became mine. It was 1939. I do remember that precisely.

Zita had other opportunities to continue radio work for the Columbia Broadcasting System (CBS). One such program was "The Winged Victory," written by David Redstone. It was the story of a tyrannical author and his wife. She is torn between her husband and the publisher she really loves. It aired March 6, 1939 on the *Columbia Workshop*. Zita's character was (the wife) Joan. The cast included British actor Donald Bain, Frank Lovejoy, Adelaide Kline, and John Briggs. Brewster Morgan directed "The Winged Victory."[9]

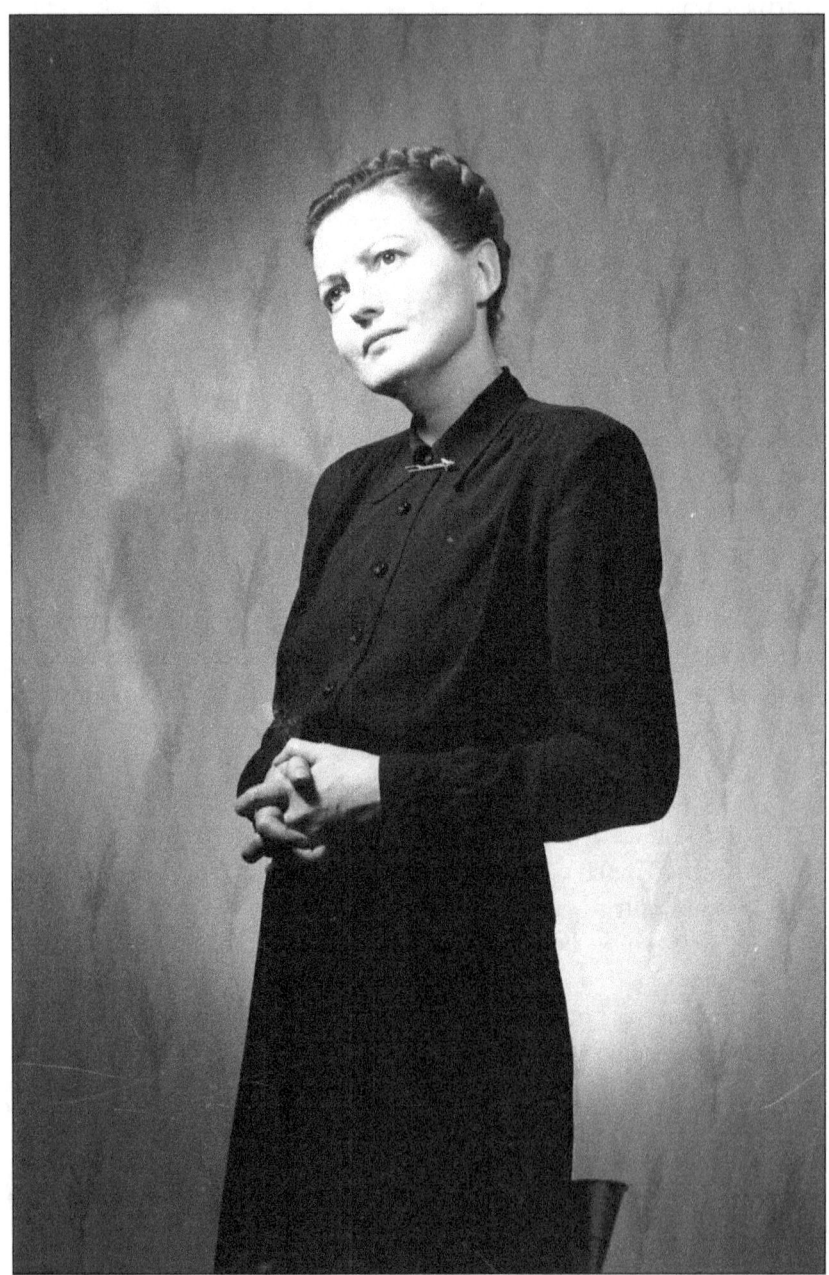
A candid portrait (New York, 1938). PHOTO COURTESY OF ZITA JOHANN

I enjoyed radio. Working on radio wasn't as easy as one would imagine it to be. It was work like anything else. Back in those days there was a popular radio show called *"John's Other Wife."* I worked on that for about a year. I worked on several others. One of the benefits of working on radio was the wonderful reunion with old friends. But these were not the greatest times to live through. I'd been away from the stage for several years and wanted to do another play.

Long before The Actors Studio, there was only the acting teacher, Lee Strasberg. In 1939, he directed Zita in Pearl S. Buck's first play, *Flight Into China*. It premiered at the Paper Mill Playhouse up in Milburn, New Jersey. Zita remembered:

> If you're not familiar with Pearl S. Buck, she wrote the novel, *The Good Earth*. It won a Pulitzer Prize and M-G-M based a motion picture on it and made a fortune. I received top billing in *Flight Into China*. Uta Hagen and Jose Ferrer were in it. The enthusiasm was gone after a two-week run. We couldn't believe it! But seriously, I saw it coming…World War II. It had just started in Europe. It was a time of terror.

Andrew Rosenthal, a twenty-one-year-old British playwright, wrote his first play, *The Burning Deck*. Jack Small produced it on Broadway. Zita was cast in the role of Nina Brandt. Her director friend, Robert Milton, staged the play.

The Burning Deck opened at Maxine Elliott's Theatre, March 1, 1940. The play ran three performances. *The New York Times* theater critic, Brooks Atkinson, said in part: "If Mr. Rosenthal's writing is uncertain, so is the performance, which in general lacks definition. Zita remembered:

> So, I decided to back away from the stage for a while. So, I was fortunate to do some more radio work. Several years after Houseman parted with Orson Welles, Houseman was working with the composer, Virgil Thompson, for CBS radio. So, Houseman called me up to say that he was producing a version of Euripides' *The Trojan Women*. So I said that I would do it. I was determined to have him pay back the money he owed me.[10]

Between the months of February and November in 1941, Zita could be heard on the radio program, *We Are Always Young*. The cast included Alexander Kirkland, William Janney, Jessie Royce Landis, Mona Moray, William Harrigan, Joe Laurie Jr., and Jason Beck. Robert Lewis Shayon for whom Zita had a great deal of respect, was the program's producer and director at WOR in New York City. Zita remembered, "Robert Shayon is a very smart and kind man who never forgot where he came from. We both shared rough starts in this business as many of us did. However, he looked at it all objectively." [11]

Zita was at a crossroads in her professional and personal life. During her radio work in New York City, she met Bernard Edward Shedd. Shedd was and had been vice-president and secretary of the Commodity Research Bureau (CRB) from its founding in 1934.

Zita and Bernard E. Shedd were married. A traditional wedding ceremony took place at her Winter Quarters home in West Nyack. The event took place, Friday, April 18, 1941. Zita recalled, "We planned the wedding together, but I made the guest arrangements." Among the guests were Rollo Peters, Arthur Hopkins, Henry Varnum Poor and his wife, novelist and playwright Bessie Breuer, playwright, Maxwell Anderson and his wife, Gertrude Higger, filmmaker and movie critic, Pare Lorentz, and his wife, Elizabeth Lorentz, Agatha Whitney Johann and actor Alexander "Billy" Kirkland (who married Gypsy Rose Lee in 1942).

Justice of the Peace, T. Gerard Baker performed the ceremony. Magdalena Johann Tarleton, Zita's sister, was maid of honor. Bridesmaids were actress, Sheila Bromley and Big band singer, Mildred Fenton. Maurice Berck, Mr. Shedd's friend and physician was the best man.

Eight months later, December 7, 1941, United States involvement in World War II officially began with the Japanese invasion of Pearl Harbor. Six months later, in the summer of 1942, Zita Johann made her final Broadway appearance in *Broken Journey* written by the aspiring British playwright, Andrew Rosenthal. It opened June 23, 1942, at Henry Miller's Theatre.

> Nearly three weeks of performances was better than three days! Arthur Hopkins (God love him!) directed "Broken Journey." He [Hopkins] was sure that we'd have a longer run. I felt that I was leaving Broadway on my own terms. It was time to move on. Soon after that, I became involved with community events in Rockland County.

Rockland Riot was a twelve-act celebrity, one-night only, stage variety show. It was presented August 22, 1942 at the Clarkstown Country Club in the South Nyack outdoor theater. Kurt Weill and his wife, Lotte Lenya, were part of the large celebrity cast.[12]

In one of the acts, Zita played a scene as Queen Elizabeth in Maxwell Anderson's *Mary of Scotland* with Helen Hayes. Zita remembered it all too well:

> I enjoyed *all* but the mosquitoes [she giggles]! We had three thousand people there and suddenly, *out of nowhere*, it became the 'mosquito riot.' Mosquitoes, hordes of them…they came from e-v-e-r-y-w-h-e-r-e! As they say in the business, *the show must go on*. Well, it did. And did you know, it was artistically and financially a success!

Bernard Shedd enlisted in the army, November 13, 1942. Two months later, Zita joined the women's war auxiliary organization of Rockland County. Women were required to enroll in one of the several courses sponsored by the United States Office of Education. Zita later resigned

Edith Atwater and Zita as they appeared in Andrew Rosenthal's Broken Journey (1942). This was Zita Johann's last Broadway play. Arthur Hopkins directed it.

from the Women in Industry Committee in order to take a welding course. Women's roles during and after the Second World War changed the social status and working lives of women in many countries. Zita recalls:

> It was great training and had a *positive* effect on so many of we women, me included. It gave to all a truer understanding of community at work, not only in Rockland County, but all over the world in our troubling times.

Ed Wynn, Helen Hayes, Zita Johann (as Mary Queen of Scots), Larry Adler, and producer Bernard Shedd (in background). Rehearsals for one night variety show Rockland Riot *(1942).* PHOTO COURTESY OF DAVID MAROWITZ

Zita entered Camp Shanks Military Installation in Orangeburg, New York, March 2, 1943. She became the chief entertainment director. Her job was to recruit stage celebrities to head programs and cull local talent from the soldiers stationed there.

Later that year, Leland Hayward dismantled his talent agency to become a Broadway producer. Zita found another agent, Stephen Draper. Zita remembered:

Portrait (circa 1940s).

I am grateful to have had Stephen as my agent, when Arthur Hopkins called up and wanted me to star on his radio program, I was elated! Of course I would do it. No question! I did a couple of them in fact. "Machinal," I reprised that role. That was with Sidney Blackmer and Hal Dawson, who was one of the original cast members from the Broadway play. The other was *A Bill of Divorcement* with Edgar Stehli. He was a lovely Frenchman and a fine actor. In fact, he appeared in my first acting job, *He Who Gets Slapped*. And here, after so many years, we were together in my last professional acting job.[13]

By 1945, Zita Johann had appeared on the stage over 500 times, was a Hollywood movie star, a radio personality, and had thousands of fans all over the world. In the fall of 1945, Bernard Shedd returned home from the service. During a telephone conversation with Zita in 1988, she talked to me about her last marriage:

Honestly, he [Shedd] as many men in service came back a changed man. I'll tell you politely that I don't want to be bothered. But, what I *will* tell you is that he became infatuated with

(Unknown origin)…the play may have been presented in Rockland County during the early 1940s. PHOTO COURTESY OF DAVID MAROWITZ

the military and all of his military cronies. After the divorce, he went to live in Europe. The marriage was over [in the late 1950s]. Lately, people have been calling to tell me that he passed away. They are also calling to tell me that Houseman has passed away too. That's all in the past. I don't want to be bothered.[14]

At the age of sixty-five and twenty-seven years since her last appearance, Zita returned briefly to the stage. She portrayed Christian Scientist founder, Mary Baker Eddy, in the play *Battle for Heaven*. This spiritual revival premiered Wednesday, October 8, 1969, at the Elizabeth Seton College. The Seton Players in Yonkers, New York produced it. Zita's performance was considered a "magnificent performance radiating inner light." Zita's friend of over forty years, Alan Brock, made her performance possible. Brock also appeared in the play.[15]

The Mary Baker Eddy character made a personal impact on Zita. she staged her own one-night production for a Rockland County benefit. *Battle for Heaven*, the three-act play ran three consecutive nights beginning October 8, 1969.[16]

Of her portrayal of Mary Baker Eddy, Zita said, "I put off writing my book to study this character as thoroughly as possible. I was already familiar with the person." The following was written by Zita and used for the play.

"Dead am I?...
To Whom It may concern.

Since Mrs. Eddy is watched as one watches a sick person or a criminal. She begs to say in her own behalf that she is neither. Therefore to be judged by either a daily drive or a stay at home is superfluous. When accumulating work requires it or because of preference to remain indoors, she omits her drive. Do not strain at gnats or swallow camels over it. But try being composed and resigned to the shocking fact that she is minding her own business and recommends this surprising privilege to all her dear friends and enemies. And that my dear Calvin is that what Mark Twain doesn't realize — and this I shall point out clearly in my reply — what he doesn't realize and what causes him to so grievously misinterpret my purposes, is that the powers of evil have from the very first sought to destroy these truths, which have been revealed to me. I have had to fight evil with every weapon at my command and if from time to time, I have seemed ruthless and despotic, I have done what I have done to free those less blessed with divine guidance — and to help them along the way to truth with greater ease and rapidity — to the end of time. What of that? That is why I'm so impatient."

CHAPTER 6

An Awakening

Zita found a new sense of awakening far from the world of acting. She spoke about the catalyst for the awakening that changed her life in 1944. In New City, near Maxwell Anderson's home in Rockland County, came the opening of a school for the children of artists, writers and actors who lived in the neighboring vicinities. Maxwell Anderson, Burgess Meredith, Helen Hayes, screenwriter/playwright Ben Hecht and costume designer Millia Davenport sponsored it. The school was open to all children in the vicinity with talent. There were also courses for adults interested in writing, drama, music, painting, dancing and gardening.

My friend Lotte Lenya…if you haven't heard about her, you will in time. We were good friends. She used to visit here frequently. She has recently passed on. I still expect to hear the sound of her footsteps upon my porch. I always knew it was Lotte by her walk. She'd always tell me in German as she was leaving that if I taught her how to act, she would teach me how to sing. She was a superb singer. Her husband was a composer. Singing is what Lotte was known for. Anyway, Lotte and I were among the teachers at this school. We started with eight pupils. It was "Mab" Anderson [Mrs. Maxwell Anderson], who came up with the idea for this new type of school through Mab's extremely talented young daughter, Hesper. So, Mab Anderson and Mrs. Henry Varnum Poor [Bessie Breuer] were among others on the board of directors. I stayed until the day the bomb that fell on Hiroshima. I was in a state of shock. A doctor friend and his wife dropped in here and said, "Isn't it wonderful." I said, 'No. It's horrible!' They said, "What do you mean? It's great!" So I said, 'What's so great about it?' They answered, "Well look at all the leisure we'll have. This will create this energy." I said, 'And what are we going to do with it?...And what ARE we doing with it?' Oh boy. I couldn't understand that attitude at all. Now, I think that we are taking the horror of our time in stride, so to speak. It is a time of terror today.

So, I took some time away from things, to recharge, if you will. I'd sit out there on my porch watching the school buses

Zita Johann and her friend Lotte Lenya (West Nyack, New York, 1939).

transport the children in this community to and fro. They <u>are</u> our future, like it or not. Starting this work with children inspired me in other areas working with children. And with this inspiration, instilled the power of the Holy Spirit with all of these children. I felt love for all of them.

I had uneasiness for years that something dreadful was going to happen here. God forbid...and unfortunately, a tragedy occurred further down the road. There came a deadly school bus crash here in Rockland County. It killed several children and injured many others. It was a sad time for everyone.[1]

Zita's newfound independence allowed her to self-actualize the ability to indulge in what she found truly passionate. It was through her church, St. Margaret's of Pearl River that Zita gained this other love. She began working with children who had developmental disabilities. She first became a religion instructor at Letchworth Village in the Hudson Valley.

Subsequent to her job at Letchworth Village, Zita also began working with a group of children at St. Agatha's Home for Children in nearby Nanuet, New York. She also worked with children from St. Dominic's Convent at Blauvelt. Her technique? Tender Loving Care. She specifically remembers one child who made remarkable progress.

> You can't help but fall in love with children when you work with them. They really have so much to give. They have their own wonderful logic.

Her first charge was a boy who presumably could not hear. Zita smiled remembering an error the child made in his preparation for the communion examination...

> Instead of saying, 'Give us this day,"Tony kept saying, 'Give up the stage.' He finally got it right and passed the exam. As it turned out, he can also hear.

She found that her work with children was more rewarding than her former acting career...

> I couldn't dedicate myself to being an actress the way I should have. In acting, sometimes you have to lose yourself in the role you're playing to find yourself. I think I've found myself in my work with children. Then along came that marvelous Rodgers and Hammerstein musical, *The King and I*. One song in particular became a favorite for the children, "Getting to Know You." I consider it my own for teachers and parents. The children loved it!

Zita's pre-revolutionary home in the woods became the after-school haven to a bevy of excited neighborhood youngsters. There they could romp in the woods and play with Zita's magical tape recorder or simply snuggle into one of the overstuffed chairs for a quiet nap. Zita said:

> I've been doing this for nearly forty years. The children have been coming over to have fun. I had some of them as students in personality development and acting. They began bringing friends over and it soon became a regular thing. We would play games and discuss things and all had a great time. Then suddenly I realized I had the perfect children's television show taking place daily in my home. We often played a game where I would read a story to the youngsters and then we would discuss it, to find out the 'whys' of life. The game had all the ingredients of a good show.

By the early 1970s, there were plans for a children's television show that was originally called, *The Children's World*. It was later re-titled, *Zita and Friends*, before the pilot was to be filmed. The program would involve the ethics and values contained in a tale or fable read by Zita as a take-off for discussion. The program was based on a concept that would allow children to stretch their imaginations and express their thoughts. They would be using local children of grade school age. Most of them were after school friends.

Unfortunately, the project never materialized. In addition to all of this, Zita became involved in training young aspiring actors for the theater. She said:

> What I am doing is my way of paying back the good that was brought to my life. They are all young people aspiring to the theater. I am teaching them to plant themselves firmly so that they may take off. I call it personality formation. Each person is different. You cannot have an overall formula. There are the basics though, body and voice. I loosen them up with yoga, and give their voices a resonant and soothing quality. Then I have them practice Oriental chants.

Are her students talented?

> Great talent, no matter where you are, is scarce. But the training they get here is useful. They learn to plug into the theater of the spirit. A lot of people want to become actors

to get away from themselves. Well, it's healthier than liquor. I had an eight-year-old boy here who could barely talk. Now, at thirteen, he's doing Shakespeare. I didn't see any talent in him at first, but I got him over the bridge.

Was his mother satisfied?

I asked her and she said, "Satisfied, he's a different kid!"

Zita felt that if a student didn't have any talent or if they appeared "*uppity,*" she would tell them not to come back:

> It is not honest to pat them on and if they come to me under the influence, they are told not to come back until their heads are clear.

Zita had strong empathy for the young:

> I think that they are terrified of the world, what with the nuclear weapons and all. I think that was what the LSD was all about in the 1960s, a search for the self, the real you.

Zita, who never had any children of her own, said:

> We can't pay enough attention to children. We're going out and they're coming in. We've got to face it, we've left them a lousy legacy, a bankrupt world.

Zita believed in giving children a solid sense of values, which juvenile delinquency may be prevented. She said of children generally, "They <u>need</u> values to function."

CHAPTER 7

Crescendo

When it came time to leave, we parted with a warm embrace. Zita said, "Rick, it has been such a pleasure. Thank you and please do come again". I always had a sense of knowing that I would someday return. As I pulled away, there stood Zita on the front porch, waving goodbye with her beloved canine Peanuts. To this day, I feel a little bit of that house and Zita came with me.

Zita wrote the following letter, May 30, 1982:

> Dear Rick,
> Thank you for returning the photos — but I'm sorry you had to go to the trouble and expense. I want to leave them in their protective shields. They are so beautifully mounted. Forgive this delay in writing you, but shortly after you left I had a call to read the script for a movie. I casually said I'd be glad to… It's a low budget picture but has something for me to say…I enjoyed your visit and hope to see you again! With all my best wishes and love Always, Zita. Do come again — soon. P.S. And how did the photos you took turn out? May I see one? Send me a copy please in your next letter. Z

The "low-budget picture" that Zita wrote about originally began filming in 1983 by the independent filmmaker, Brett Piper. However, Zita's participation in the movie took place after Sam Sherman, an exploitation film producer and director, and friend to Zita collaborated on the project. Mr. Sherman re-shot and re-titled the movie, *Raiders of the Living Dead*. Zita later told me her reason for appearing in Sam Sherman's production:

> Sam's father and I went back many years. I did the movie as a favor to Sam's father. That's basically why I did it.[1]

On her 79th birthday, Zita received a transcript of our interview. We spent the better part of that evening by phone proofreading and editing that particular story.

Zita and I continued to stay in touch over the years. We always cared about where life was taking us and continued to encourage each other.

> As you know, I've written a few books. There is one in particular that I would like to have published. I'm preparing to send it out. Wouldn't it be nice if our books were published at the same time?

Zita's news was exciting, however, her book, *The Unknown Country*, was never published. Soon before Christmas of 1990, Zita sent me her unpublished play entitled, *And Then It Was Morning*. In the package, she wrote the following memo:

> Dear Rick, Good luck with this. If you receive *The Sunday New York Times* you may have seen the ads for my book, *The Unknown Country*. Panda Press is publishing it. I'll be on the market in a couple of months. Again, Good luck, Zita.

Left: With the author at Zita's home in West Nyack, New York (May 2, 1982). Right: After receiving copies of the pictures Zita wrote, "Thank you for the photos. They were well done. I do like them." PHOTOS BY THE AUTHOR

When I telephoned Zita to thank her for the gift, she said:

> The play, I worked on for a long time. And since you do have the patience of Job, my dear, this can be a useful tool in your writing someday.

In what became our last phone conversation, which took place May of 1991, Zita told me:

> Rick, I'm going into the hospital for some tests. I've had some difficulty walking lately and the doctor wants to admit me. Call me in a couple of weeks and we'll talk more.

Two weeks passed. I telephoned Zita but could not reach her. This continued for months. Finally a friend to Zita who identified herself as "Sue," answered Zita's phone in December 1992. Sue told me that Zita had entered a nursing home "last June." She also suggested that I write to Zita and the mail would be taken to her. After writing to Zita, I received a letter from Mr. Martin Kauder. He wrote that he was a trusted friend to

Left: Portrait, 1982. PHOTO BY THE AUTHOR. RIGHT: *This is the 2002 DVD release promotional jacket for* Raiders of the Living Dead. *The 1986 movie that was directed by Samuel Sherman featured Zita Johann, in what became her final movie appearance, her first in some fifty-plus years.* FROM THE AUTHOR'S COLLECTION

Zita for many years. Mr. Kauder asked in the letter that if he could be of assistance to telephone him. I phoned Mr. Kauder. He told me:

> I'll never forget the day, thirty-seven years ago, when I met Zita Johann. She pulled up in front of my store with her husband in that old '38 Chevrolet during a storm. I welcomed her in. I've known her since. She is a dear person with a great wit and great sense of humor and intuition. Unfortunately, Zita is not well. Some days are better than others. Physically, she is fine. But her mental state is challenged at times. She turned 89 recently. I feel that we are not going to have her around much longer. There's a small group of friends who visit Zita. I do know that Zita will be pleased to know that you have asked about her. I will keep you informed. It's been a pleasure talking with you, Mr. Atkins. Keep Zita in your prayers, as we all will.

Thursday, September 23, 1993 I received the fateful phone call from Martin Kauder. He said:

> Mr. Atkins, I have sad news. Zita came down with pneumonia in the nursing home and had to be taken to Nyack Hospital, where she passed away. We plan to deposit her ashes near the home of a friend.

I asked Mr. Kauder if he was aware that Zita wished her ashes to be scattered beside her home. His reply, "Oh, I wish you hadn't told me that. I was directed to deposit her remains where I wished. We plan to have them scattered in Nanuet. As I thanked Mr. Kauder for his calling me, he said:

> I had to sell her house because of the surmounting costs incurred at the nursing home for Zita's care over the past two years. I know that your friendship with Zita meant a lot to the two of you. She was a dear friend to me for many years. Let's pray that her spirit of goodness will continue to serve us all.

After the phone call, a profound sadness and curiosity remained with me for a long time. I felt close to Zita. She had a way to make everyone feel close. Zita was my friend and a confidant who cared, but also had a good sense of optimism and intuition.

Zita outlived most of her acting contemporaries with the exception of a few, one of Whom was David Manners, Zita's former co-star of stage and screen. He survived her by five years. Through this writer, in 1982, David and Zita were delighted to be corresponding again after an absence of many years. Two special photos autographed by both marked that occasion.

David Manners later wrote to me the following:

> Dear Rick…You don't need to be caught up in the appearance of Death of friends — You don't need to feel loss. What has gone is naught —but the shell — or cocoon. That which moved the body and spoke through the mouth — is not lost — can't be — It is the conscious awareness we are and the *action* of the far greater power behind all life appearances. Keep in touch. Love —
>
> David.

Zita was born within the astrological sign of Cancer (a water sign). How interesting having seen all of Zita's motion pictures. She is in death, as she was in most of her movie roles, finding herself surrounded by water.

There is closure for Zita because what was believed to be her final resting place, we now know is different. According to someone known to Zita, her crematory remains were scattered through acreage in Deposit, New York. Zita's spirit, however, lives with those whose lives she touched. Ultimately, closure arrived for this writer as well.

CHAPTER 8

The Reawakening

Five years after my spiritual epiphany with Zita Johann, I found myself reopening the storage box containing all of her material. Much like Zita, an inner prompting had me making a copy of her play. I would finally read it while vacationing in Florida.

The afternoon of November 16, 2005 in Florida was an unforgettable day. Leisure had come, and with it, the opportunity to read Zita's play. In retrospect, I questioned, *why* was it her play that I chose to take with me on this trip after all of these years? It must have been fate. It must have been Zita.

As I began reading the first several pages, my thoughts became distracted. So I placed the manuscript aside. My nearby laptop became my interest. And it was no mistake. I typed the name Zita Johann into the search prompt. The entries for Zita Johann were many. However, when I clicked my first choice entry, I realized I had serendipitously entered a new world.

A website of a young lady, an aspiring actress, by the name of Liesl Ehardt, drew my attention. I thought, who is this? She wrote in her website that she is a cousin to "the former stage and screen actress, Zita Johann." When I read more about Miss Ehardt, I decided to contact her through her website. Zita's manuscript set beside me but I was overwhelmed by what had just happened. I laid the manuscript off to the side again and was in awe.

The mild evening Florida air was welcomed. I was in full view of the evening sky. As I gazed at the bright stars, suddenly off to the right, I saw my first shooting star! Grinning, I said aloud, 'Zita's here!'

Returning inside, I began reading Zita's play more intently. Later, in checking e-mail messages, a reply from Liesl Ehardt had arrived! While reading Liesl's reply, suddenly, I was invoked with memories of Zita and her words, *"for later"* and *"other branches growing."*

Since that fall evening in Florida, a chain of events began. Liesl and I first met in Los Angeles, California in October 2006, after months of corresponding. I learned through Liesl that there were more family members of Zita's family on Liesl's paternal side. Though an aspiring actress today, I found Liesl to be a natural. She hopes to someday work with children much like Zita.

Portrait of Liesl Ehardt, cousin to Zita Johann, and friend to the author.
PHOTO COURTESY OF LIESL EHARDT

From the moment when I looked into Liesl's eyes, I was emotional. Regardless of a lapse in several generations, a resemblance with the eyes between Zita Johann and Liesl Ehardt was incredibly uncanny. I felt that both a reunion with a kindred spirit and a new friendship had occurred. There have been other annual meetings with Liesl since our first, including multitudes of electronic correspondence and many cards and letters.

During this time, I began corresponding and having phone conversations with Liesl's Aunt Jane Moore. Jane has been most helpful in sharing information regarding the Johann family. I am thankful for her friendship.

In one of my previous books published, *Let's Scare 'Em! (Grand Interviews and a Filmography of Horrific Proportions, 1930-1961)*. Included was a brief biography of Zita Johann in which an inaccurate date of death was given.[1]

The death date was listed as September 20, 1993. However, further research by this writer verifies that Zita Johann's journey on earth ended at Nyack Hospital in Nyack, New York, Friday, September 17, 1993. Had I questioned the date at the time when learning of it, I would not have written it. I regret to inform that it wasn't until late 2006 that I learned of my error. Reports that list Zita Johann's death occurring September 20, or September 24, 1993 are therefore inaccurate.

Another special correspondence with phone conversations that cannot go unmentioned began in February 2006 between this writer and Mr. David Marowitz, a good friend of Zita for many years. His late wife, Mildred, also was a friend to Zita.

After these serendipitous encounters, I realized that writing a book was inevitable. However, in order to complete, I knew that the only way for closure was to revisit Zita's West Nyack, New York home if only at a glimpse.

The day finally had arrived. It was September 29, 2009. Sixteen years had passed since Zita left this world. But had she? Many people believed she is still among us. I believe that. This was a day like no other. I took the drive from LaGuardia in a rental car with my friend, Zachary Zito, from Brooklyn, to Spring Valley. The visit to and from our destination was only four hours but seemed like a lifetime.

At one point, Mr. Marowitz took us to his basement where he had a collection of movie and theater memorabilia. Back in a corner, there was an assortment of large 'paste up' photographs of Zita Johann. He offered us our choice of any to take back with us. At the age of eighty-seven, David Marowitz said that he was in the process of eliminating many of his collectables.

Zach and I each chose a photo. Soon I felt an inner prompting as if Zita herself had prompted this decision. I asked David Marowitz if I might have another picture. He said, "Sure, help yourself." I couldn't resist

Zita Johann's former home, Winter Quarters (September 29, 2009). PHOTO BY THE AUTHOR

a classic shot of Zita taken around 1928, at the height of her Broadway stardom. Little did I know what would happen later that day.

After returning to Mr. Marowitz' living room upstairs, we snapped photographs and reminisced. Later, he accompanied us to West Nyack to locate Zita's house on Sickletown road. We were having difficulty locating the address, but learned later that the address had changed.

Finally, Mr. Marowitz suggested phoning another Zita friend who lived nearby, Rosemary Franck. By following Rosemary's simple direction due south, we found Zita's home.[2]

Unannounced, we pulled into the driveway. The home that Zita loved had been renovated and restored. It was spectacular. However, the southern porch where we once sat was no longer there. We noticed unknown persona leaving the house. Had we been there any earlier, we may have been intruding. But suddenly, a girl appeared at the screen door. She said, "Are you looking for directions?" With that, David Marowitz got out of the car, walked up to the front porch with greetings. We all introduced ourselves. The girl's mother appeared. We explained who we were. Her name was Vickie. She graciously invited all of us to come in. We were invited

From left to right: The author with the new owner of Zita's home, Vickie, and Zita's good friend of many years, David Marowitz (September 29, 2009).
PHOTO BY ZACHARY ZITO

The author's friend and east coast host, Zachary Zito.

A gift to the new owner Vickie upon her birthday and Zita's homecoming (September 29, 2009). PHOTO BY THE AUTHOR WITH PERMISSION OF THE SUBJECT

to come in. The warmth radiating through the house brought back many loving memories of Zita. The living room where she once entertained hadn't really changed. The new owners of course, had enhanced the charm, but Zita's presence could still be felt. After a brief time we exchanging phone numbers and addresses and were allowed to snap photographs. Vickie told us that her birthday was that very day. Without hesitation, I

The living room as it appears today where Zita and the author spent a considerable amount of time together. Her spirit resides there twenty-seven years later. PHOTO BY THE AUTHOR

asked Zach to help me with the picture that we had in the trunk of the car. We gave it to Vickie as "it was meant to be!"

She thanked us ever so much and promised that Zita's photo would be framed and have a focal point in the house. It was a serendipitous and emotional day for us all, a spiritual homecoming.

Since the journey back home another portrait of Zita, hangs on the opposite wall of my living room along with the first, to which I said, 'Zita, the journey back *has* been gratifying. The new portrait has a quaint touch. You are smiling and waving, much like you did when I saw you last. What I've learned regarding *"for later"* is that I didn't get to it alone.

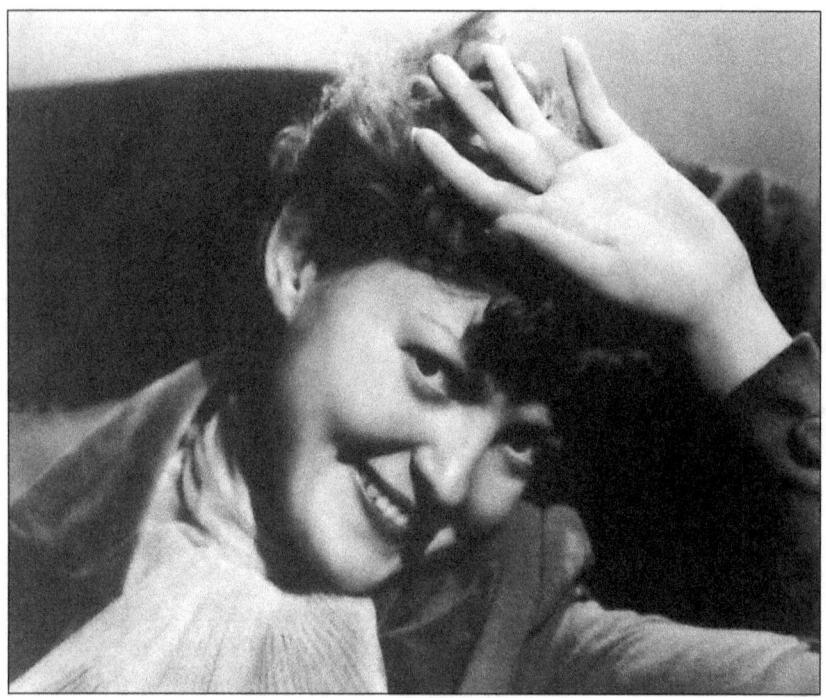

The portrait of closure for the author. PHOTO COURTESY OF DAVID MAROWITZ

CHAPTER 9

And Then It Was Morning
by Zita Johann

Among other unpublished literary works by Zita Johann were, *The Unknown Country* and *After the End*.

The following play *And Then It Was Morning* was transposed in its entirety from the original manuscript written by Zita Johann during the late 1930s through the mid-1940s. In the 1950s, she later wrote a 271-page story of this play that she entitled, *The Sun Is Coming Up!... That's Odd?* Fifty-six pages of that manuscript are missing from its original notebook.

Zita wrote the two-act-play with mindful thought of the characters and of herself, for whom she created a character. Zita based her play loosely on the 1944 existentialist play *No Exit* by Jean-Paul Sartre.[1]

This photo was intended as "an author shot" of Zita Johann, during her writing days. Theater and movies were long behind her (1955). PHOTO COURTESY OF ZITA JOHANN

AND THEN IT WAS MORNING
By Zita Johann

West Nyack, N.Y.

CHARACTERS:

>The Innkeeper
>Mr. Dukely
>Mike
>Mrs. Holloway
>Coco
>Mr. Sterling
>Mrs. Sterling
>Ann Stratton
>Mr. Charles
>Paul
>Mr. Cameron
>Bellhop

AS SOUNDING BRASS
(Late 1930's)

ACT ONE
Scene I

> Scene: The lobby of an Inn. Tables and chairs are comfortably placed. There is a very tall window at the back, hung with red velvet drapes. The sky is always a cheerless grey. To the left of the window is a door to the outside. To the right a bar, partly concealed, an archway at the right leads into the dining room. On the extreme left is the door of the elevator. And above that the desk and a magazine stand.

MR. DUKELY
(Coming out of the elevator)
Damn this place!

INNKEEPER
(Brightly from behind his counter)
It is damned.
(To himself)
Yes. That it is.

MR. DUKELY
(Crosses to the news stand, grumbling)
Everything in its place. Thought there'd be no towels in my room.

INNKEEPER

They were there thought?

MR. DUKELY

What? Oh yes. Six. Counted them.

INNKEEPER

Then you've no complaints.

MR. DUKELY

No. Damn it.
(Pages through a magazine)

INNKEEPER

That's too bad.

MR. DUKELY

I'll take this one. Terrible waste!

INNKEEPER
(Absently)

Yes.

MR. DUKELY

Six towels!

INNKEEPER
(Looking up from his account book)

Oh…How many would you like?

MR. DUKELY

Two's plenty!

INNKEEPER

I'll see to it.

MR. DUKELY

Yes. I was afraid you would.
(Holding up the magazine)
How much?…There's no price marked on it.

INNKEEPER
But there's no charge. I've told you over and over.

MR. DUKELY
Oh…keep forgetting. Can't get used to not paying. Habit. Been paying through the nose all my life. All my life! My life that was. My life on earth. You have to be dead to live on the cuff. That doesn't make any sense…you have to be dead to live.

INNKEEPER
Oh yes. It makes sense. It makes a lot of sense here.

MR. DUKELY
Well, anyway, I'll take this and…

INNKEEPER
You can take as many as you like. Go right ahead.

MR. DUKELY
It beats me. It's not right. It's against all law. It's something for nothing. And that's not right.

INNKEEPER
There aren't any laws here.

MR. DUKELY
No laws! Six towels and no laws!

INNKEEPER
Why are you always looking for trouble?

MR. DUKELY
(Stumped)
I don't know.

INNKEEPER
Then why not stop?

MR. DUKELY
Stop? I can't. No matter what I do or try to think about..it's always there. This..this..thing in me…Aw, hell!

INNKEEPER
It's that way with all of them.

MR. DUKELY
How long does it go on like this?

INNKEEPER
Well…for as long as you're here.

MR. DUKELY
For as long…You mean I'll feel like this as long as I'm here?

INNKEEPER
Yes…just about.

MR. DUKELY
Great! I'll check out. I'll check out right now. Just walk out of the place.

INNKEEPER
But you can't do that, sir.

MR. DUKELY
What do you mean, I can't? Who's to stop me? What's to stop me? You just said yourself there aren't any laws here.

INNKEEPER
That's right. There aren't any laws here.

MR. DUKELY
Then what's to stop me?

INNKEEPER
You.

MR. DUKELY
Me?

150

INNKEEPER
Your former self will keep you here until you find your true self.

MR. DUKELY
Former self? What the hell kind of talk is that? Hell! Maybe I'm not dead at all. Maybe I'm just in a nut factory. And if I am I got railroaded.

INNKEEPER
Well…you do remember how you died, don't you?

MR. DUKELY
I remember that alright…but I don't remember when…how long ago. It's because of that damn clock! It's got no face! There's no time. And too damn much time.

INNKEEPER
That's right.

MR. DUKELY
Former self!

INNKEEPER
It's what you let the world make of you. And this is the place where you can shed that self and all its cares.

MR. DUKELY
Like a snake sheds its skin, I suppose!

INNKEEPER
That's right…and when you've done that you leave here free.

MR. DUKELY
A nut house. That's what this is.

INNKEEPER
For you…yes, I dare say. Go right ahead. Take as many of the magazines as you like.

MR. DUKELY
Yeah. Only now I don't feel like reading. Now that I can have magazines on the cuff I don't want them…Former self! Aw, nuts!
(And he walks off into the bar)

MIKE
(The taxi driver, bursts onto the stage from the orchestra pit)
Hello, pop!

INNKEEPER
Hello, Mike. What's new?

MIKE
What's true?…Now look, pop…get this. I just seen this nail in the road, see. A regular spike. I aimed right for it, see. Well…my front left wheel went over the spike…just as neat. And wadda ya think?

INNKEEPER
What?

MIKE
(With real chagrin)
No flat! No puncture! I couldn't believe it. I got out. I looked. No noth'n.

INNKEEPER
You should know by this time.

MIKE
Yeah…but I'm always hop'n. But noth'n ever goes wrong. It gets on your nerves. That's what.

INNKEEPER
You mustn't let I, Mike. Unless you want to stay on here forever.

MIKE
Me stay on here forever? Oh, no. Not me. I ain't got enough relaxation for that. My old man…he didn't have no relaxation neither. Runs in the family. That's why I become a hack. So I could keep go'n…Oh, almost forgot. I got a call from gate three.
(He dashes out)

MRS. HOLLOWAY
(Has wondered in from the dining room. She is a woman in her late sixties, frail in appearance but bitter. She alternates between defiance and timidity.)
You haven't had any word of my daughter yet, I don't suppose?

INNKEEPER
No, ma'am. I'm sorry.
(His attention goes toward his account books)

MRS. HOLLOWAY
That's all right. I was just wonder'n. Yes. There isn't any place I could write to? Just to find out, I mean. I waited so long to die so that I could be with her again. And she was so young when she left me. And now I can't find her. I was expecting to see her the minute that I got here… when her child was born…that's when she died. And I had to go on living without her.
(Suddenly strident, demanding the Innkeeper's attention)
Where is she now? Where can she be? How can I find her? Why doesn't somebody help me?

INNKEEPER
(Puts down his pen and sighs)
I wish I could help you…believe me. But there seems to be so little that we can do for each other sometimes. And so much that we must do for ourselves. So much that only we, ourselves, can do.

MRS. HOLLOWAY
Yes.

INNKEEPER
And I'm not very competent, you see. I never was. I was an Innkeeper on earth. And I wasn't very successful. That is, I didn't make any money. I failed, in fact. And died in debt. And I daresay I'll always remember my last wish as I was dying.

MRS. HOLLOWAY
Your last wish?

INNKEEPER

Yes. I wished that I might have another chance. And that's just what happened. When I arrived I was put in charge here.

MRS. HOLLOWAY

H-mm. You had all the luck…you got your wish. They wouldn't even let me bring up her baby…my own daughter's baby. That husband of hers…he took the baby. First he took my daughter away from me…and then her baby. She never should've married him…it's what I told her. She was much too good for him…having the baby that killed her. Yes… he killed her. That's what he did. I know. That's why I've hated him all these years. Yes…and I guess I'll go on hating him.

INNKEEPER
(Just shakes his head sadly)

MRS. HOLLOWAY

Well, why shouldn't I hate him? After what he did. You got your wish. I didn't. And I wished for years…just to be with my daughter again. I was expecting to see her the minute I got here.

INNKEEPER

But she died a long time ago.

MRS. HOLLOWAY

Yes…and why couldn't she have waited…the way I did.
(Suddenly grasping at hope)
Maybe she's at one of the other places around here —

INNKEEPER

Mike's inquired at all the other Inns, ma'am.

MRS. HOLLOWAY

Well, where is she then?

INNKEEPER

She's probably gone on…into the future.

MRS. HOLLOWAY

The future? But why should she? What kind of a future can there be for her? For me…for anybody —

INNKEEPER

That depends, ma'am…

MRS. HOLLOWAY

Depends?

INNKEEPER

Upon ourselves.

MRS. HOLLOWAY

If it wasn't for that husband of hers —

INNKEEPER

She must've loved him —

MRS. HOLLOWAY

Loved him! He was no good. Just like her father. He was no good…So my daughter was all I had to live for. And now —
(She lapses into hopeless preoccupation)
(The sliding door of the elevator has opened with a clang)

COCO

(Emerges. He is a former circus clown, and on this occasion is dressed in his newest improvised costume. It is the failure that haunts him. Right now he has something to display. A new act, just conceived, and for which he must have an audience. He gestures with his left forefinger for the attention of his friend, the Innkeeper, then bows formally to his audience of two and eases immediately into his act. At the conclusion of his performance he looks apprehensively at the Innkeeper)
No good, huh?

INNKEEPER
(With deep regret)

No good.

COCO
(Utterly dejected, sits in the nearest chair)
I thought it was good. When I was downstairs I thought it was good…
I worked hard on it.

INNKEEPER
I know you did.

COCO
It wasn't funny?

INNKEEPER
(Wishing he good be less honest)
No. It wasn't.

COCO
Maybe it's my make-up…

INNKEEPER
(Can only shake his head)

COCO
I know. I lost it. I lost it and I can't seem to find it again.

MRS. HOLLOWAY
Oh…you've lost something too?

COCO
Yes, madam.

MRS. HOLLOWAY
I know how you feel. You see I lost my daughter. Yes…
(Giving in to her need to cling)
What is it you're looking for?

COCO
Laughter, madam.

MRS. HOLLOWAY

Laughter! Well…that should be easy. It seems to me people laugh quits a lot. Too much sometimes. When there wasn't even anything to laugh at. But come to think of it…I haven't heard anybody laugh in this place.

INNKEEPER

They don't laugh easily. Those who come here. It's only when they laugh that they're ready to leave.

COCO

It's laughing that frees people. That's my belief…the only one I've got.

INNKEEPER

One belief is all a man needs…if —

COCO

That's right! That's all I needed…while I was successful. When they laughed. But when they stopped laughing my belief and my failure didn't mix very well…I remember…I had worked for a long time on a new act. Then one night…I'll never be able to forget that night. It was in Austria…where they knew how to be gay and how to laugh. It was there that I tried out my new act…It was to have been the most memorable night in my career. I had the good wishes of my friends and the envy of my rivals to insure my success.

MRS. HOLLOWAY

Yes…I used to take my daughter to the circus. Every year. She liked to laugh my daughter did. She liked peanuts and popcorn…yes.

INNKEEPER
(Even though he's heard Coco's story before)
And what happened on that night, Coco?

COCO

Nobody laughed.

INNKEEPER

Nobody at all?

COCO

Not even the children. There was only that hollow silence. I stood there. The glaring lights like fingers pointing at me. I felt trapped. Trapped by the lights. Trapped by the silence. Unable to move. It was like being in the middle of a terrible dream. I remember telling myself that I must be dreaming. I waited for the relief that comes with waking…

INNKEEPER

But you didn't accept that as final, did you?

COCO

No, the next night I worked the new act again. I tried even harder. Yes… and the same hollow silence greeted me. The same silence. And then that other silence. That silence of pity from the others in the company. They looked alarmed when I came off. Then they turned their heads away…busied themselves with fixing their costumes, their make-ups. They were afraid. Failure is contagious. They were afraid. No laughter! Laughter was my only reason for being!

INNKEEPER

But your other acts had been successful. Why didn't you go back to them?

COCO

I did. Yes…

(His voice becoming a shrill)

I went back to my old acts. My sure fire acts. And even then I went back to my old acts. My sure fire acts. And even they didn't laugh. Night after night there was always that silence. That hollow silence. Then…all at once they started booing me. They whistled. They threw things…

(He covers his face with his hands to shut out the image)

INNKEEPER

(In an attempt to pull Coco out of his despair)

Oh…Mike had a call. He should be here soon with the new arrivals. Perhaps there'll be someone you know.

COCO

New arrivals? No. No. I've got some work to do. I'd better be going.

(He seems to be incapable of moving)

MRS. STERLING
(Comes out of the elevator. This time, however, the door does not clang. Mrs. Sterling is a sensitive woman who looks about thirty.)

INNKEEPER
Good morning, madam.

MRS. STERLING
Good morning. Have there been any new arrivals.

INNKEEPER
Mike had a call. They should be here very soon.

MRS. STERLING
Oh, good.

MRS. HOLLOWAY
Maybe my daughter —

INNKEEPER
No. Your daughter won't be among them.

MRS. HOLLOWAY
How do you know? She might be.

INNKEEPER
No. Your daughter died a long time ago. These are the newly dead.

MRS. HOLLOWAY
Oh. Well…
(She starts to leave, then says)
No, I think I'll stay. I might miss her. Yes…It's all right if I just sit here and wait, isn't it?

INNKEEPER
Yes. Yes, of course.
(He turns to Coco)
Well, my friend…

COCO
(Has been brooding. He looks mutely at the Innkeeper)

INNKEEPER
You'll get it. You'll find it. Just keep trying. I wish I could help you.
(He gives Coco a reassuring pat on the shoulder, then goes back to his counter and busies himself with his books)

MR. DUKELY
(Has come back from the bar, muttering)
Former self. A nut house.
(He sees Coco)
Oh…and I suppose you still think you're Coco…the famous Coco…just because you look a little like him.

COCO
Yes. I do think…I mean…yes. I am Coco.

MR. DUKELY
Yeah.
(And he walks over to the news stand, again muttering)
A nut house.

COCO
But —
(Left alone and utterly disheartened, he manages to get up and cross to the elevator)

MRS. HOLLOWAY
(Goes to Mrs. Sterling)
Excuse me. But you're waiting for somebody too, aren't you?

MRS. STERLING
Why yes. Yes, I am.

MRS. HOLLOWAY
I've seen you here often, but I always been a little timid about speaking. You've been here a while, I suppose? Before I got here, I mean.

MRS. STERLING
A long time.

MRS. HOLLOWAY

I would've come sooner myself. But I had to wait. And now she's gone and I can't find her. Who is it you're looking for? If it's all right to ask.

MRS. STERLING

Anybody.

MRS. HOLLOWAY

Anybody?

MRS. STERLING

Yes, anybody. Anybody who can bring me some news of my children. It's been so long since I've had any news.

MRS. HOLLOWAY

Oh. You know where your children are then…but you'd like them to be here with you, of course.

MRS. STERLING

No. God, no! I hope they won't have to come here. If they die happy they won't have to come here. That much I've learned. And if they live happy they should die happy. That's all I want for my children.

MRS. HOLLOWAY

You're a strange mother. You mean you won't mind if you never see them again?

MRS. STERLING

Of course, I'll mind not seeing them again.
(Remembering back)
That's what was so hard. Leaving my babies. I tried to stay. I tried to live. For over a year I fought to live. And I was beginning to win the battle. I'll always remember the day the doctor told me that I'd be able to go home in another month. We were all so happy…Then something happened. At the end of that month I didn't go home. I came here instead.

MRS. HOLLOWAY

Oh, you poor dear…Perhaps you'd rather be alone. Yes.

MRS. STERLING
(Withdrawn, does not answer. And Mrs. Holloway wanders away, back into the dining room)

MR. DUKELY
(At the news stand, to the Innkeeper)
All right! If he's Coco, I'm Napoleon! And who are you?

INNKEEPER
What? What was that?

MR. DUKELY
Who are you?

INNKEEPER
Who am I?

MR. DUKELY
If he's Coco, I'm Napoleon. Who are you?

INNKEEPER
He <u>is</u> Coco. And I? Why…you can see for yourself…
(Putting down his pen)
And you? Who are you?

MR. DUKELY
I'm Napoleon!

INNKEEPER
You can believe what you like, sir. And so can the other fellow.

MR. DUKELY
Coco, my foot!

COCO
(Has been waiting patiently for the elevator. At this point the door opens and he leaves.)

ANN STRATTON
(comes briskly up the steps from the orchestra pit. She is dressed in a heavy uniform, and is a girl in her twenties, a girl with a purpose.)
Room and bath, please. Any water here?

INNKEEPER
Water? Oh, yes.

ANN STRATTON
Good. Then I can really clean up. Oh…I haven't any luggage. The plane was shot down.

INNKEEPER
I'm sorry to hear that.

ANN STRATTON
Been expecting it. Glad it's over. I'd like to send a cablegram.

INNKEEPER
A what?

ANN STRATTON
A cablegram. Don't you have a telegraph office here?

INNKEEPER
Oh. Is a cablegram similar to a telegram?

ANN STRATTON
Huh? Yes. Where can I…have you got a blank?

INNKEEPER
Well…no.

ANN STRATTON
I've got to get in touch with my paper! I'm a war correspondent.

INNKEEPER
Oh…I'd like to help you. But I'm afraid I don't understand.

ANN STRATTON
But it's so simple. This is a hotel, isn't it?

INNKEEPER
Why…yes.

ANN STRATTON
Then let me speak to the manager.

INNKEEPER
The manager?…Oh. Oh, yes. I am the manager.

ANN STRATTON
Oh. Well, let's start all over. From the beginning. I'd like to send a cablegram. It's very simple. And it's very important.

INNKEEPER
Yes…simple things are important…just as to simplify is…

ANN STRATTON
(Out of patience)
A cablegram!!!

INNKEEPER
But there's no such thing here.

ANN STRATTON
Where the hell am I?

INNKEEPER
You're here.

ANN STRATTON
Where's that?

INNKEEPER
Where you are. Now!

ANN STRATTON
I don't get it. Well…I'll go and clean up and puzzle it out. I'm tired… probably all that's wrong.

INNKEEPER
I'll see you to the lift, miss.
(He goes with her)

MIKE
(Comes up from the pit, carrying some luggage)
Whew! What a dame! She was outta that car before I even slowed down…say…take it easy, sister.
(Shaking his head)

MR. STERLING
(Distinguished looking and in his fifties, has come in behind Mike)
Well…Where's the room clerk?

MIKE
Hey, pop! Kinda nervous, ain't-cha mister? Everybody comes over these days is jumpy!

MR. STERLING
Maybe you haven't heard. But there is a war going on.

MIKE
Don't mind me, mister. I ain't sensitive. Been hack'n too long. You meet all kinds that way. There's been wars before. I was in the last one. But Gee! People wasn't jumpy then like now. Now it's terrible.

MR. STERLING
The last was! This one's insidious…go out with everyone waiting… waiting for the thing to go off. It could mean the end.

MIKE
Of the world? Gee! I guess we/re lucky then…here I mean.

MR. STERLING
Lucky? Here? I don't —

INNKEEPER
(Has returned)

Sorry to have kept you waiting. But the young lady…it's a good sign when they're like that. It means they're beginning…

MR. STERLING

My name's Sterling. I have a reservation.

INNKEEPER

Names don't matter here, sir.

MR. STERLING

Oh…they don't, eh? Well, what about my reservation?

INNKEEPER

We've plenty of rooms, sir.

MR. STERLING

Well, I'd like a corner room facing south and east. I like the sun streaming into my room.

INNKEEPER

The sun…Oh. But there isn't any sum here.

MR. STERLING

D'you mean to say I've come out of season?

INNKEEPER

Out of season? It's always the same here, sir.

MR. STERLING

D'you mean there's always that haze?

INNKEEPER

Ever since I've —

MR. STERLING

Yes. Well, look here, my good man, if the sun never shines how is it the delphinium do so well?

INNKEEPER

Oh. So you're one of those who see them.

MR. STERLING

See them? D'you think I'm blind? Acres and acres of them. Miles, I should think. Do they grow wild here?

INNKEEPER

They seem to I'm very glad that you noticed them, sir, very glad for you. It's very few that see them…especially when they first get here.

MR. STERLING

Something peculiar about this place. Whatever made me come here.

INNKEEPER

You'll realize that in —

MR. STERLING

Who's that woman? Looks like someone I know.
(He looks again at Mrs. Sterling, bewildered)
Incredible. It can't be.

INNKEEPER

Sterling, you said was your name?

MR. STERLING

Right…Now if you don't mind I'd like to go up to my room.

INNKEEPER

(Is puzzled. He rings a tiny bell and a bellhop appears.)
We'll be having tea here very shortly, sir.

MR. STERLING

Oh, good. A spot of tea's just what I need.

BELLHOP

This way, sir.
(He picks up the bags. Mr. Sterling follows him into the elevator.)

MRS. STERLING
(Has been watching and listening all this time and is now in a state of suppressed agitation)
He didn't know me. I'm his wife…his wife once removed. I was his wife until I died…and he doesn't know me.

INNKEEPER
He's confused still. Just as you were when you —

MRS. STERLING
How changed he is. I haven't grown any older. And he has. I hardly knew him!
(As though she'd become suddenly aware of him)
Oh, thank you. I'm frightened. Do you know that? I'm frightened.

INNKEEPER
I know. You've waited so long.

MIKE
(Is back)
Say, pop…I got a fella out there…he won't come in.

INNKEEPER
Why not?

MIKE
He says there must be some mistake. That's all he keeps saying. Ever since I picked him up at the gate.

INNKEEPER
His record in order?

MIKE
Oh, sure. I checked. Don't I always? This is where he belongs all right. But he won't believe it.

INNKEEPER

Poor chap.
(He has come to the edge of the stage, reaches an arm down to the man in the pit.)
Come, my good man. This is your destination.

THE MAN

No. You do not understand. There has been a mistake. I cannot afford this place. I no longer have the means.

INNKEEPER

That doesn't matter here!

MIKE

(As the man climbs up onto the stage)
Name is Charles. His last name I mean. Odd, ain't it. One o' those foreigners, I guess.

MR. CHARLES

(Is very tired and looks a good deal older than he is.)
Yes…I am confused. And very tired.

INNKEEPER

That's easy to understand. I'll see you to your room. Oh, Mike…order some tea, will you?

MIKE

Sure, sure, pop.
(He goes into the dining room)

MR. STERLING
(Comes out of the elevator)

INNKEEPER

Oh…tea's a little late, sir. But it won't be long now.

MR. STERLING

Quite all right.

INNKEEPER

I don't think you'll need an introduction to the young lady. She knows you too, she says.

MR. STERLING

Oh?

INNKEEPER

Now, if you'll excuse me, sir.
(He gets into the elevator with Mr. Charles)

MRS. STERLING

Eric?

MR. STERLING
(Puzzled)

What?

MRS. STERLING

Eric...You don't know me? I'm your wife. I'm Eva.

MR. STERLING

Eva? Oh, my dear...forgive me. I saw you when I first got here. But, I couldn't...I didn't believe it was possible that you'd be here. How —

MRS. STERLING

I've been here a long time.

MR. STERLING

But you've been...You haven't changed. In all this time...you haven't changed.

MR. STERLING

You're just as lovely as you always were.

MRS. STERLING

Thank you, Eric...you've changed.

MR. STERLING

I've grown older...and you haven't. That's odd. I don't understand.

MRS. STERLING

You will in time.

MR. STERLING

And you don't seem very glad to see me. Well…Can't say that I blame you.

MRS. STERLING

Oh, but I am. I am glad to see you…Tell me about the babies.

MR. STERLING

The babies?…Oh…the boys you mean.

MRS. STERLING

Yes, they're young men now…Aren't they?

MR. STERLING

Oh, quite. Yes. Fine young men. Both in the service now.

MRS. STERLING

The service? Yes, of course. The war. I hadn't thought of them as in the war. Were they ready when the time came?

MR. STERLING

Ready? Yes…of course, my dear. They've had good training…been to the best schools.

MRS. STERLING

That isn't quite what I mean. There's so much I want to know. So much I need to know about them.

MR. STERLING

They're quite well. Were when I left. They've always been in good health. Except for the time when Peter…Oh, well…

MRS. STERLING

When Peter what?

MR. STERLING

Nothing to be alarmed about, my dear. A slight case of flu…and he came 'round beautifully.

MRS. STERLING

He was always so afraid of thunder…did he ever get over that?

MR. STERLING

Oh, yes…he got used to that all right…what with bombs going off…he had to.

MRS. STERLING
(Incensed)

Had to! You're so casual about them…your sons…so detached. You've grown so hard.

MR. STERLING

Come, come, my dear. Let's not quarrel. I've only just got here. And I am a bit tired.

MRS. STERLING

I'm sorry. But I've waited so long for some news. Paul was only seven years old when I died.

MR. STERLING
(Startled by the word, "died")

MRS. STERLING

All this time without any word…not knowing. Are they happy?

MR. STERLING

Happy? Oh…yes…quite…on the whole I would say. Paul is a very brainy chap.

MRS. STERLING

Not all brain, I hope. Not my son. What about his loves?

MR. STERLING

Oh, well…there was one girl.

MRS. STERLING

Was? What happened?

MR. STERLING

Well…they didn't get on too well. She went into the service…and they more or less decided to wait until after the war.

MRS. STERLING

And when will that be?

MR. STERLING

There's no knowing.

MRS. STERLING

Poor darlings.

MR. STERLING

Yes…The young are having a rough time of it.

MRS. STERLING

Oh, I was fairly competent in my day.

MR. STERLING

Of course, you were. You were very competent. You weren't very strong…that was all.

MRS. STERLING

I'd been strong at one time though…quite strong. And I could have been strong again if not for —
(She stops herself)

MR. STERLING

If not for what, my dear?

MRS. STERLING
(Hostile now)
It doesn't matter now. It's too late to matter. Much too late.

MR. STERLING

I'm afraid I don't follow you.

MRS. STERLING

It doesn't matter. Tell me more about Peter's flu. I've worried a good deal about him. I was always afraid he might have inherited my weakness…my illness. He was such a frail baby.

MR. STERLING

He got to be quite a husky chap. Besides there's a cure been discovered…so it wouldn't have mattered.

MRS. STERLING

Wouldn't have mattered? How can you say that? Of course, it would have mattered…a cure you say? A cure that might have —

MR. STERLING

It works wonders…this new drug…absolutely infallible.

MRS. STERLING

A cure that might have kept me alive.

MR. STERLING
(Startled, curbs the lurking guilt)
What? Oh. Oh, yes…but you see —

MRS. STERLING

I might have lived. I was born too soon and the cure came too late. And so I died too soon…before my time. Still…I could have…the doctor had said I was on the mend and ready to go home the end of the month.

MR. STERLING

Yes, my dear…and then you took a turn for the worse.

MRS. STERLING

Of course, I took a turn for the worse.

MR. STERLING

Why do you say "of course'…and you're so bitter —

MRS. STERLING

Why shouldn't I be bitter? I was robbed of my life.

MR. STERLING

Who robbed you?

MRS. STERLING

How can you say that?

MR. STERLING

This place has had a bad effect on you. Something most depressing about it…something peculiar.

MRS. STERLING

No. It's not the place. This is merely a vacuum through which we must pass. No…it's not this place —

MR. STERLING

I'm afraid I don't understand you.

MRS. STERLING

I needed your help that last month. I needed you desperately.

MR. STERLING

But, my dear, I was with you all the time. As much of the time as I could be. There was my business you know.

MRS. STERLING

Yes…and there was also Melissa.

MR. STERLING

Oh. You knew then.

MRS. STERLING

Yes…I knew. A well intentioned friend.

MR. STERLING

And you never mentioned it?

MRS. STERLING

I couldn't…not then. I was too numbed by the blow. And then the hating took over. I hated her so —

MR. STERLING

It wasn't all Melissa's fault —

MRS. STERLING

Really.

(Withdrawn now)

MR. STERLING

If only you hadn't known.

MRS. STERLING
(Bitterly)

It's just as well. I'd have had to know sooner or later, I suppose. You were married then.

MR. STERLING

Yes.

MRS. STERLING

And she brought up my children? Did they have a happy childhood?

MR. STERLING

Oh, yes.

MRS. STERLING

They didn't get everything they wanted? You left them things to want?

MR. STERLING

It was hard sometimes not to give them everything.

MRS. STERLING

What is it they want most…to be, I mean?

MR. STERLING

Paul wanted to be a flyer always. He had his own plane ever before the war.

MRS. STERLING

Is that what he's doing in the war? Flying? It's what you did in the last war.

MR. STERLING
Yes…but it's a lot different now…much worse this time.

MRS. STERLING
Oh, God!

MR. STERLING
Forgive me. I didn't mean to upset you. I keep forgetting that you've been cut off from everything.
(Suddenly realizing)
Just as I am now. I've only just begun to realize —

MRS. STERLING
(The stronger now)
It's hard at first…and then you get used to it.

MR. STERLING
A strange place…and yet curiously familiar. The manager says there's never any sun here. What's he mean?

MRS. STERLING
Just that…the sun never shines here.

MR. STERLING
Do you mean that in all the time you've been here —

MRS. STERLING
That's right.

MR. STERLING
Then why did you stay on here?

MRS. STERLING
I had to.

MR. STERLING
Oh…yes, of course…you were waiting. Well. We'll leave first thing in the morning.

MRS. STERLING
Oh, Eric…we can't leave here —

MR. STERLING
What d'you mean we can't leave…What's to stop us?

MRS. STERLING
I don't know exactly…something within ourselves.

MR. STERLING
Nonsense. Time you left this place, my girl. I can see now the purpose of my coming here. Couldn't see it at first…before I knew you were here.

MRS. STERLING
Oh, Eric, try to understand. I know it's hard at first. We can't leave this place until we're called.

MR. STERLING
Called? By whom?

MRS. STERLING
I don't know exactly. But Mike comes with a list of names occasionally.

MR. STERLING
Mike?

MRS. STERLING
The driver. He brought you.

MR. STERLING
Oh, yes…who does he work for?

MRS. STERLING
I don't know…not anybody, I don't suppose.

MR. STERLING
He must work for somebody…unless he's in business for himself. But don't you worry. I'll manage to use a little influence and see that we get on the first list going out.

MRS. STERLING
(Slightly amused)
There's no such thing as influence here. Money and position are useless here. They're illusions.

MR. STERLING
Money and position illusions? They're the only tangible —

MRS. STERLING
They don't exist here. They're not needed.

MR. STERLING
Then what is this…a sort of Shangri-La? It couldn't be…not if there isn't any sun. And by the way…if the sun never shines how is it the delphinium do so well here?

MR. DUKELY
(Has come out of the bar and crosses to the news stand)

MRS. STERLING
The delphinium? Here?

MR. STERLING
Haven't you seen them?

MRS. STERLING
No. No…I haven't.

MR. STERLING
But, my dear, how could you have missed them? There're acres and acres of them.

MRS. STERLING
I'm sorry but I haven't seen them.

MR. STERLING
Extraordinary. But then you never were very observing.

MRS. STERLING

Really!
(Remembering Melissa)
I daresay you're right.

MIKE
(Has come in with the tea)
Teapot's hot. Don't burn yourselves.

MRS. STERLING

Thank you, Mike.

MIKE

Don't mention it.

MR. STERLING

Mike? Oh...I'd like to talk to you about —

MRS. STERLING

Eric! I've told you —

MR. DUKELY
(Has been eyeing this)
Want out, h-mm?

MR. STERLING

Right. We'd like to leave here. Can you —

MR. DUKELY
(With a sudden derisive laugh)
We're in this together, Bud.
(He walks away, into the bar. Then over his shoulder, says)
Take it up with your former self.

MR. STERLING
(Staring after him)
What's he mean...former self. Who is he?

MRS. STERLING

One of us.

MR. STERLING

Us?

MRS. STERLING

Yes…he's a member of the human race.

MR. STERLING

Human? Him?……How about a walk?

MRS. STERLING

It's dark out now.

MR. STERLING

Tomorrow, then. I'll show you the delphinium. Would you like that?

MRS. STERLING

Yes. Yes…I would.

MR. STERLING

Good. We'll take a walk in the morning. It's quite a sight.

MRS. STERLING

Why is it that in all this time, I haven't seen them?
(The elevator door opens. The Innkeeper comes out.)

- BLACKOUT -

ACT ONE
Scene 2

Scene: The same on the following evening.

COCO
(Wearing a different costume is performing as intricate pantomime. At its conclusion he bows elaborately but there is no response.)

MR. DUKELY
(Has been wandering about restlessly)
You're not Coco…so you're not funny.

COCO
(Wearing a different costume, is performing an intricate pantomime. At its conclusion he bows elaborately but there is no response)

MR. DUKELY
(Has been wandering about restlessly)
You're not Coco…so you're not funny.

COCO
But…I am Coco

MR. DUKELY
You just think you are.

COCO
But I am. I ca — n prove it!

MR. DUKELY
Yes. How?

COCO

Why…look…I'll prove it with this act.
(He begins to tingle with excitement but this is coupled with deep uncertainty and anxiety)
You claim that you saw me…when I was…at my best.

MR. DUKELY

YOUR best?

COCO

This is an act that I originated. No one was ever able to duplicate it. Not ever. Now watch carefully.
(He does the act)

MR. DUKELY
(Watches stonily)

COCO

Well? Now do you remember?

MR. DUKELY

Oh, yes…very well.

COCO
(Relieved)
So. So now you must admit —

MR. DUKELY

Admit? Yes…I'll admit. I'll admit that it's a good life-less imitation. Almost a caricature. But not quite sharp enough to be a caricature.

COCO
(In deep pain)
Caricature! Imitation!! But it's my own. I created it back in —

MR. DUKELY

You mean you stole it.

COCO

Stole it! I never stole anything in my life? Even when I was hungry as a boy…

MR. DUKELY

To steal…nothing new in that.

COCO

To steal! No! To make something of myself…to become someone…to have something…

MR. DUKELY

Yes. Well you did all right.

COCO

Yes I did! I fought my way to the top…I was known…as the great Coco.

MR. DUKELY

YOU? He was incomparable.

COCO

That's what the critics said. I still have the notices…in my scrap books… Would you like to see them?

MR. DUKELY

So you stole those too!

COCO

Stole my own scrap books…my own reviews? What are you talking about?

MR. DUKELY

Look, my friend —

COCO

I'm NOT your friend. And you're not mine either.

MR. DUKELY

A figure of speech. There's no such thing as friendship.

COCO

No such thing as friendship.

MR. DUKELY

Left the sinking ship?

COCO
(Afraid of looking back)
I traveled a great deal…I was never in any one place long enough…to plant roots…to establish…any lasting —

MR. DUKELY

To establish anything. So you resorted to stealing another man's work.

COCO

Oh, no!

MR. DUKELY

Even his identity.

COCO

His identity? What are you trying to do to me?

MR. DUKELY

I'm trying to set you straight…that's all.

COCO

Set me straight? Like a pin ball…so that you can knock me down again?

MR. DUKELY

Not a bad idea. Now look, old man, stop kidding yourself. What you do here is meaningless.

COCO

You said that once before.

MR. DUKELY

And I'll say it again if I have to. Just to set the record straight. In the interest of justice.

COCO

Justice?

MR. DUKELY

You killed Coco.

COCO

I? I killed…myself?

MR. DUKELY

Who's talking about you? You're an insufferable egotist. Now you're even claiming his death.

COCO

I'm not claiming anything except —

MR. DUKELY

He had nothing left.
(Shrugs complacently)
So…he took to drugs…heroin…became an addict. Finally…suicide.

COCO

Oh, no! That's not true! I didn't commit suicide. And I never took drugs. It was my heart. I died alone…the way I'd lived. Alone. But I had my costumes there. All of them. They were my friends. I'd created them. They remained with me in that small crowded room…right to the end. But my end was not suicide.

MR. DUKELY

Nobody's talking about you.
(He walks away)

COCO

(in his misery looks about at his preoccupied audience as if appealing for support. Crushed and forlorn, he sits at the nearest table.)

INNKEEPER
(To Mr. Dukely)
Why don't you leave him alone? He says he's Coco. And I believe him.

MR. DUKELY

Did you ever see Coco?

INNKEEPER

I see him every day.

MR. DUKELY

How long have you been here?

INNKEEPER

Oh…a very long time.

MR. DUKELY

Exactly! Then how could you have known Coco? The real Coco? And that's not him. I should know. I was a great fan of his.
(And again he walks away)

MIKE
(Rushes up from the pit)

Hey, pop! Just had a call. Gate three again. Gezz! They breeze in here all kindda hours. No schedule. Y'know somethin', pop? I didn't better myself at all comin' here. I'm in the same rut I've always been in.
(He leaves)

INNKEEPER

All right, Mike.

MRS. HOLLOWAY

Maybe my daughter —

INNKEEPER

No, madam.
(He goes to Coco)

COCO

Is that what they say about me? That I look…that I —

INNKEEPER

That's just what he says. It's only one man's malice. Don't let —

COCO

But I did not…believe me I didn't.

INNKEEPER

I do believe you.

COCO

Drugs…suicide. How can he say such things? Invent such lies —

INNKEEPER
(Sadly)

The humanity in man —

COCO

I lived too long…just a few years too long. Those last years of failure destroyed my whole life's work…in people's minds.

INNKEEPER

What des it matter what's in other people's minds?

COCO

Matter?…It matters a lot. I know it shouldn't but it does. It matters a lot to me what he says and thinks. It matters because…the life I led? I lived for my work and that's all.

INNKEEPER

I wish that I could have seen you on earth. He's told me that you were the greatest of them all.

COCO

Yes…but he also claims that I am not Coco. That I am not myself… Well, if I'm not myself then who am I?

INNKEEPER

I like your defiance, my friend. But don't question yourself too much. Maybe that's what's led you into the dark —

COCO

I'm going down stairs…to work.

INNKEEPER
Perhaps you work too hard, Coco.

COCO
(Grateful)

Coco? Thank you.
(He crosses to the elevator and during the ensuing scene, sit on the bellhop's bench)

ANN STRATTON
(Comes out of the elevator and goes to the desk)

INNKEEPER
(Goes to her)

ANN STRATTON
The manager, please.

INNKEEPER
I am the manager.

ANN STRATTON
Oh. Oh, yes. I remember now. Can't seem to wake up. Did I sleep long? What time is it?

INNKEEPER
It's late evening. And you arrived yesterday.

ANN STRATTON
Good Lord! Did I sleep all that time?

INNKEEPER
You must've needed the rest.

ANN STRATTON
Yes…but I can't afford the time. A whole day wasted. I'd like to send a cablegram, please.

INNKEEPER
Yes, but you see, Miss, that's not possible here.

ANN STRATTON

Look…it doesn't matter very much where I am. As long as I can get a message through.

INNKEEPER

But that's the point. You cannot send a message from here. I tried to tell you yesterday.

ANN STRATTON

Oh. Oh, yes. Thought I'd dreamed that. I'm a little confused. Sorry. Well then, I'd like to take the first plane, ship or train out of here? Would you mind seeing to my tickets?

INNKEEPER

Tickets? But where to? You can't leave here.

ANN STRATTON

Oh…a war prisoner…

INNKEEPER

War prisoner…you?

ANN STRATTON
(Looking about her)

No…I guess not…now that I look around me. The enemy would never put us up like this. Doesn't keep us from being fools though.

MR. CHARLES
(has been sitting at a table, staring ahead of him. He's been so still that no one has been aware of his presence. But hearing the 'enemy' mentioned releases his busied torment)

I remember! The children! The furnace! The flames searing! Flesh hissing! The screams…children screaming! Screaming in pain. Screaming in terror. Terror of death. The children. Save the children! Tomorrow's citizens burning. Save them! Save the world! Save the children!…it's impossible —
(He buries his face in his hands)

INNKEEPER
(Is beside him now, and by the laying on his hand, succeeds in calming him)
It's over now. It's behind you. And it won't ever happen to you again.

MR. CHARLES
To me? The children! Are they all right?

INNKEEPER
They're all right now.

MR. CHARLES
Where are they?

INNKEEPER
They're well taken care of. They're resting. Asleep.

MR. CHARLES
Asleep? They are safe?

INNKEEPER
They're safe.

MR. CHARLES
But…I was with them…in the furnace.
(Rubbing his forehead)
I tried so desperately to save them…from being captured. But someone betrayed them…betrayed those poor innocents. So they were captured and I with them. I'm so glad I was with them. How did we escape?

INNKEEPER
Escape? You didn't escape.

MR. CHARLES
But the flames were licking my flesh. You say I did not escape. And yet I am here. How can that be?

INNKEEPER
It will come to you.

BELLHOP
(Has come out of the bar with a tray. He places a cognac on the table for Mr. Charles)

MR. CHARLES
No, I cannot afford it. Thank you. At one time I could. But not now. Thank you.

INNKEEPER
But there's no charge. No charge for anything here.

MR. CHARLES
(Suddenly suspicious)
Oh. You want information. You think I will sell you the list of the children we still have hidden for a glass of cognac and a comfortable room!

INNKEEPER
List of children? I'm afraid I don't understand.

MR. CHARLES
No one will find those children! The ones who have not yet been captured. They are safely hidden! Where no one will ever find them. Put me to the torture. You will learn nothing form me!

INNKEEPER
I am your friend.

MR. CHARLES
You are my friend? Good. Then tell me. Where are those children? The ones that you say are all right. I want to see them. Where are they?

INNKEEPER
I'm sorry…but they're not here.

MR. CHARLES
Then where have you put them?

INNKEEPER
They have returned to God.

MR. CHARLES
(Slowly grasps the truth)
They have returned to God…And me?

INNKEEPER
You, too, are dead.

MR. CHARLES
Me too. I failed in my mission. I failed. May God forgive me.

INNKEEPER
You gave up your life for those children.

MR. CHARLES
I failed —

MR. STERLING
(Seated at a nearby table with Mrs. Sterling)
Poor chap.

MRS. STERLING
Children burned in a furnace! It's not possible.

ANN STRATTON
(Repeating the Innkeeper's remark to herself)
You, too, are dead…dead! Deadbeat. Deadline.
(Her head up and looking out)
Dead. Well. C'est la guerre.
(And she goes out to the bar)

MRS. STERLING
Oh, Eric…it's too awful. It can't be true. He must be ill. Shell shock probably…

MR. STERLING
(Trying to console her)
Probably.

MR. CHARLES
(Staring into space)

The enemy fears the children.

INNKEEPER

A weak opponent then, I should think…a very weak opponent.

MR. CHARLES

Oh, no. Our foe is composed of desperate madmen. Treacherous, unpredictable madmen. Beasts who prey upon children.

INNKEEPER

Children? But why?

MR. CHARLES

They are tomorrow's citizens. And madmen fear the future.

INNKEEPER

In my time war was not pleasant…No. A man went off to fight…with a gun…

MR. CHARLES

Civilization has changed. A great deal.

INNKEEPER

Yes. It must have. From what I can gather great structural changes have taken place on earth. Very puzzling changes. Tell me something, Mr. Charles. What is a cablegram?

MR. CHARLES

A cablegram?

INNKEEPER

That's what she called it…the young lady. Something like a telegraph. Though actually I don't know what a telegraph is either. She wanted to know where the telegraph office is. Can you explain what a cablegram is? I'd like to help her. She's quite disturbed.

MR. CHARLES
You mean you do not know what a cablegram is?

INNKEEPER
I'm not very well informed, I guess.

MR. CHARLES
(In the interest of another, he stops his torment, which is precisely what the Innkeeper hoped for)
Well, now it is a little difficult to explain. It is so simple.

INNKEEPER
Yes…and simple things are sometimes very difficult to understand.

MR. CHARLES
A cablegram is a message that you send by submarine telegraph.

INNKEEPER
Oh…I see. And what is a submarine? No. Believe me. I would like to know what a cablegram is and that's all.

MR. CHARLES
Yes…well…marine. You know what that means?

INNKEEPER
Oh, yes…pertaining to the sea

MR. CHARLES
And sub means under. That's all. It's very simple.

INNKEEPER
Yes…but why do they have such things?

MR. CHARLES
Why? For the sake of speed. A cablegram saves time.

INNKEEPER
Why should people be so intent upon saving time when there's so much —

MR. CHARLES
No! You are wrong. Quite wrong. There is very little time for anything. A little more time and I could have saved those children. I could have saved them from the furnace. Tell me, monsieur, where are the children?

INNKEEPER
The children? They are resting…in God's mercy. I've told you. Why won't you believe me?

MR. CHARLES
Because I do not know you.

INNKEEPER
I understand. When I was on earth, I, too, had to employ caution. But it was a much quieter age I lived in. The ones who've been coming here lately are so confused. Well…they're all confused when they first get here. But these days, they're so lost and so isolated…so burdened by their failures…what they believe to be their failures. It takes some of them so long to realize that failure can be an illusion too. You see, Mr. Charles, you did not fail. No. You saved those children from the madmen…from corruption. They might have been lost forever.

MR. CHARLES
I wish I could believe you.

INNKEEPER
A wish is a good beginning. I wish I could understand this new civilization and its frenzy.

MR. CHARLES
I would like to help you but I do not know the answers.

INNKEEPER
Now, that's mighty fine of you to want to help me. That makes me very happy. Come drink your cognac now.

MR. CHARLES
(Reluctantly picks up the glass. The Innkeeper leaves him and goes back to his desk)

MRS. STERLING

It must be true about the children. Oh, Eric, have men really become such beasts?

MR. STERLING

They're madmen, of course. They started the whole thing…slowly at first. But now they're being conquered.

MRS. STERLING

But will reason be able to survive such bestial —

MR. STERLING

Yes, as long as people believe in reason.

MRS. STERLING

What a world we brought our sons into. What is it that Paul does in this war? He flies you told me.

MR. STERLING

He flies a bomber. He's got over thirty missions to his credit, without even a scratch to himself. He's got unbelievable luck.

MRS. STERLING

What is it he does on these missions?

MR. STERLING

Why…he bombs cities…and the industrial plants of the enemy.

MRS. STERLING

He destroys cities…the cities that men have built. What a destiny.

MR. STERLING

It's only temporary, my dear. After all, the enemy must be defeated.

MRS. STERLING

And after the war?

MR. STERLING

Why he'll do what I did…

MRS. STERLING
It'll be harder for him than it was for you. This is a much more terrible war.

MR. STERLING
You'd have faith in Paul if you could see him.

MRS. STERLING
I've just got this awful concern —

MR. STERLING
Don't have.

MRS. STERLING
Don't have? How can you say that? He's our son. He's flying a bomber. He could be —

MR. STERLING
You should've gone with me on that walk this morning. It would've done you good.

MRS. STERLING
Did you see the delphinium again?

MR. STERLING
The delphinium? No. No…I didn't walk that far.

COCO
(Approaches the Innkeeper who is back at his desk)
Tell me, my friend…

INNKEEPER
Yes, Coco.

COCO
Do you think that there is anything I could do? For the children, I mean. I have a costume that they would like. I know they would like it. There are pictures painted on it. I painted them myself. Very funny pictures. Perhaps if I could make them laugh —

MR. DUKELY
(At the news stand)
You couldn't make a horse laugh. Just you leave those poor children alone. They've been through enough. Just leave them alone.

COCO
(Whirls about and faces Dukely)
Why don't you leave <u>me</u> alone? Why do you torment me like this? I've never done you any harm. Why do you torment me? Why don't you leave me alone? Why do you have to keep following me?

MR. DUKELY
What? I follow YOU?

COCO
You followed me about one earth you said. I didn't know about it then. And now that I do know about it I don't like it. Stop it. Stop following me. Leave me in peace so that I can do my work.

MR. DUKELY
You, my good man, are suffering from delusions of grandeur. I follow you? I did follow Coco. But I do not follow you. You are not Coco. Those are the facts.

COCO
Stop it! Stop telling me that I am not myself. You have no right…You have no right to tell me that I am <u>not</u>. I have the right to believe…I have the right to believe that I <u>am me.</u> And you have no right to take that away from me. You have no right to destroy me…my work.

MR. DUKELY
You are out of your mind!
(And he walks away)

COCO
Out of my mind!

INNKEEPER
D'you know…I think maybe <u>he's</u> crazy.

COCO
Does one of us have to be crazy?

INNKEEPER
Well...one of you has to be wrong.

COCO
But I am Coco. Believe me...I am.

INNKEEPER
I do believe you. That's what makes me think that maybe he's crazy.

COCO
He followed me about until he caught up with me here. I never knew him on earth. Or maybe I did and don't remember. What's he after? What does he want of me?

INNKEEPER
Control...Dominion probably.

COCO
But why?

INNKEEPER
Maybe, because he has no control over himself.

COCO
Why does it have to be me?

INNKEEPER
You were his idol. He made you his idol.

COCO
Why? So that he could have something to destroy?...Where are the children? They would laugh. I know that they would. Their innocence... that's what makes them able to laugh. That's what we lose. And it it's place we take on cruelty...If he would only leave me alone.

INNKEEPER
I think you convinced him that you're not afraid of him.

COCO

Afraid? Of him? Is that what he thinks? Is that why he hounds me so? Because he thinks that I'm afraid of him? Oh…I'd like to show him —

MIKE
(Rushing up from the pit)

Say, pop, wait! Wait'll you see…

INNKEEPER

See what, Mike?

MIKE

Gee, he's gett'n outta the car now. I gotta go an' get his things…help him. I just hadda tell ya. Gee!
(He runs down into the pit)

INNKEEPER

Well, Coco?

MIKE
(Returning from the pit)

This way, Colonel. Don't let the stairs yet you. Watch it now. Some of the steps 're loose. One of the things about this place that could throw ya. The way up. That's it, Colonel. Here we are.
(To the Innkeeper)
Say, pop. Get a load of the ribbons!
(To the soldier, a flyer, taut and impatient)
This, her, is pop. It's what I call him. Reminds me of my grandfather…on my mother's side. Gee!

COCO
(Feeling displaced by the arrival of the soldier has wandered back to his seat near the elevator)

SOLDIER
(Crossing to the Innkeeper)

You've been expecting me, I daresay. Colonel Sterling. Is my room ready?

INNKEEPER
(Startled, glances at the Sterlings seated at their table)
Your room, sir? We have plenty of rooms —

SOLDIER
What're the civilians doing here?

INNKEEPER
Civilians?
(His gaze following the soldier's)
Oh…Oh, those are people.

SOLDIER
Yes…yes. But what're they doing here?

INNKEEPER
Why…they belong here.

SOLDIER
Quite different from Brampton Hall, I must say.

INNKEEPER
Brampton Hall, sir?

SOLDIER
Yes…Yes…The place I'd been ordered to before…a holiday from the show.

MR. STERLING
(Has been watching the arrival of the soldier. He is up and goes to his son)
Paul…

MRS. STERLING
Paul?

SOLDIER
Why, dad! What're you doing here?

####### INNKEEPER
####### *(Concerned for Paul)*
The Colonel seems to be a bit confused by our Inn. He was just saying, sir, that it's not a bit like Brampton —

####### SOLDIER
You remember Brampton Hall, dad…I wrote you from there.

####### MR. STERLING
Oh, yes…Yes, of course. You'd been ordered there for a rest.

####### SOLDIER
Right. Nice of you to meet me here, dad. Be good to have a chat. But how did you know I'd be here? Were you notified? Think I'd like a drink before I clean up. How about it, sir?

####### MR. STERLING
Oh, fine…fine, my boy. Could do with one right now myself.

####### SOLDIER
Where're the girls?

####### INNKEEPER
The girls, Colonel?

####### SOLDIER
The hostesses.
####### *(Sees Coco)*
Oh, a clown. Entertainment tonight, eh? Good. I could do with a laugh.
####### *(Just the word 'laugh' kindles excitement in Coco)*
This is a bit unusual, you know, dad. All these civilian visitors. Must be another change in regulations. I'm for it. It's good to see you.
####### *(To the Innkeeper)*
Where's the bar? How about it, dad?

####### MR. STERLING
There's someone else her to see you. Someone you haven't seen in a very long time, my boy.

SOLDIER

That so? How about that drink first though? I really need it.

MR. STERLING

Yes. Oh, yes. Order me a whiskey and soda, will you. And I'll join you. Right?

SOLDIER

Right, Sir.

(He goes into the bar)

MIKE

Did you see them ribbons, pop? Gee!

MR. STERLING

(Has returned to Mrs. Sterling)

MRS. STERLING

(In her torment, can only look mutely at him)

MR. STERLING

(With a great effort at being casual)

Fine looking boy. We can be mighty proud of him.

MRS. STERLING

Paul…our son…in this place…Oh, Eric, what —

MR. STERLING

He doesn't know yet. We'll have to break it to him very gently. He must've had a crash…been shot down. He thinks he's in one of those rest centers they have in the army for the flyers. Pretty wonderful system they have these days. The army doctors mingle with the boys between flights…looking for symptoms. If they notice that a chap is a bit nervy…they tap him and off he goes for a rest…whether he likes it or not. Some of the chaps don't like stopping —

MRS. STERLING

Go to him, Eric. Stay near him. He knows you…he doesn't know me. He'll need someone when —

MR. STERLING

All right, my dear.

SOLDIER

Oh…there you are, dad.
(Coming from the bar, he crosses to the Sterlings)
Thought we might have our drinks out here. I don't like that room. Reminds me too much of the inside of my ship. Makes me feel hemmed in…and yet in space.
(Shuddering for a moment, then determined to defy the invasion of recollection)
Doesn't make sense. Here. I've brought your drink.

MR. STERLING

Oh. Oh, yes. Thank you, my boy. Oh…by the way this is —

SOLDIER
(Cutting him off, to Mrs. Sterling)
You look like my mother. Exactly like a picture I have of her. Got it right here. I'd like to show it to you. Here it is. Always carry it with me. Gives me a feeling of protection always. Wouldn't think of going on a mission without this picture. Yes…she's brought me luck.
(Showing the picture to Mrs. Sterling)
Beautiful, isn't she? You do look so much like her.

MRS. STERLING

Thank you.
(Looking hungrily at her son)

SOLDIER

May I sit down her with you?

MRS. STERLING

Oh. Oh, yes. Of course. Forgive me. Do please sit down. Would you pull up another chair, Eric?

SOLDIER

You one of the hostesses here?

MRS. STERLING

Hostesses? No...No I'm not.

PAUL

Forgive me. I'm —

MRS. STERLING

Of course.

PAUL

But it is extraordinary how much you look like my mother. Makes me feel as though I'm dreaming somehow. You couldn't be my mother, of course.

(Rubs at his forehead)

I'll snap out of this. Maybe I am a bit flak happy. Maybe the doctors were right in ordering me here. But they're such a waste of time...these holidays. Necessary though...we're told. But a waste of time. I hate stopping. The job's not finished yet. And what's the good of stopping.

MRS. STERLING

But you need the rest.

PAUL

You can't really rest though. Not until you know the job is finished. Done with. So that you can go back to your work. Your own work.

MRS. STERLING

You like flying, don't you? You've always liked it...even before —

PAUL

Why yes...how did you know?

MRS. STERLING

Your father has told me about you.

PAUL

Oh, dad...yes. He didn't approve of my flying when I first started. Did you, dad?

MR. STERLING

Afraid I didn't, my boy.

PAUL

Even though he'd been a flyer himself in the last war.

MRS. STERLING

Perhaps that's why he didn't approve. He knew how hazardous it was.

PAUL

It's no more hazardous now than anything else in the world…Not very long ago I happened to see a farmer plowing his field. He was using a horse plow…a tranquil and safe occupation…wouldn't you say?

MRS. STERLING

Why yes…of course.

PAUL

That's what I thought. So I turned to watch him. I felt peaceful watching him. And then in the next instant he was hurled into the air… his plow and his horse with him. A shell had exploded nearby. And that was the end of his safe occupation.

MRS. STERLING

How awful.

PAUL

Yes. But it made me realize how safe I am in my work. In my plane…I have guns…ammunition…bombs. I can defend myself. <u>I mete out destruction.</u>

MRS. STERLING

You say that with such pride!

PAUL

Certainly. Why not?

MRS. STERLING

…as though you believe in destruction.

PAUL

It's the only thing I believe in.

MRS. STERLING

NO! Oh, no…that's not true. It can't be true.

PAUL

It's the only thing I can afford to believe in.

MRS. STERLING

You're so bitter.

PAUL

Why shouldn't I be bitter? You're all alike…you civilians. You're smug. That's what's wrong with you. Prattling about how bitter we are. It's our bitterness that keeps us going. It's our anger that fives us the energy we need. Right now it's my job to destroy. And in order to be good at my job I've got to believe in destruction.

MRS. STERLING

Yes. Yes, of course. Forgive me for upsetting you. It's hard for me to understand…that's all. We hear about the war occasionally here. But actually we have no conception what it's really like.

PAUL

Haven't you had any bombings here?

MRS. STERLING

Bombings, here? No —

PAUL

Lucky. No wonder you don't understand. No one can know what it's all about unless they've been in the thick of it. You haven't been here very long I take it —

MRS. STERLING

Been here? Oh, yes…quite long —

PAUL

Don't like it, eh?

MRS. STERLING
I don't think anyone likes it here particularly.

PAUL
We chaps do. They treat us very well in these places.

MRS. STERLING
Oh, yes. I keep forgetting.

PAUL
They must've turned this over to us just recently. I've never heard of it before.

MR. STERLING
Nor had I.
(In an effort to cover, though he feels utterly inadequate)

PAUL
I must say I don't relish spending my month's holiday here with —
(Indicating the others)
I don't understand this new arrangement. Another experiment I'll wager. They probably think it's time we were beginning to adjust to civilian life again. Stupid fools! The war is not half over. Won't be for a long time. Not until the world is a shambles probably.
(Looks about him)
How the hell do they expect us to rest among this bunch of —

MR. STERLING
Mind your manners, Paul. You're speaking to your mother.

MRS. STERLING
Oh, Eric

MR. STERLING
I'm sorry, my dear

PAUL
(Strangely calm now)
What was that you said, dad? That I'm talking to —

MRS. STERLING

Your mother.

PAUL

My mother?

MRS. STERLING

Yes, my son.

PAUL
(Turns on his father)
Then why did you tell me she was dead?
(To Mrs. Sterling)
Why? Were you afraid to tell me that you were divorcing mother so that you could marry Melissa? That awful bitch!

MRS. STERLING

Oh, Paul. No.

PAUL

That's all she was. An awful bitch! Still is probably. She led father a merry chase. But I can see now that he had it coming. What a farce. What a dreadful, awful farce we live.

MRS. STERLING

Lived, Paul. Your father did not lie to you.

PAUL

What are you talking about, mother? Mother. Seems odd to suddenly call you mother. What d'you mean he didn't lie? He told me you were dead.

MRS. STERLING

I was. I am.

PAUL
(Hasn't grasped it yet)
What is it you're after? What is it you want of me? I've a bad case of flight nerves. I know that. And I have a bad kind of confusion sometimes. So don't…please…I beg you…don't talk in riddles.

You've come to visit me here. I wish you hadn't. I'm afraid I must ask you to go. If you don't go I'll probably crack up and never be allowed to fly again. And if I have to give that up I might as well be dead. Please leave at once.

MR. STERLING

I'm afraid we can't do that, my boy.

PAUL

You must do it. If you've a shred of feeling you'll leave at once.

MRS. STERLING

Paul, dear. Listen to me.. won't you? I'm not going to say that I know what you've been through. I don't. It's very apparent that you've undergone indescribable torments that no one else can possibly understand. Only someone who was at your side and experienced every pain you felt could know you now and possibly help you. We can't help you. We're not good enough for that. Much as we'd like to be.

PAUL

(Subdued now, and almost like a child)

I've got to get some rest, mother. I've got to get some rest quickly. So that I can get back. Back to my job. Back into action.

MRS. STERLING

Try not to worry about getting back. There's plenty of time —

PAUL

Plenty of TIME? But time is important. More important than —

INNKEEPER

(on the pretext of bringing cigarettes, has come to them)

You may find, Colonel, when you've been here a while, that time can be mighty unimportant. There's so much of it here.

PAUL

Why should there be more time here than anywhere else? Have you cornered the market on time?

(And he laughs at his own feeble joke)

INNKEEPER

It's beginning to seem to me that time has become a kind of reward for death. That when people die they come into the time they've been so anxious about.

ANN STRATTON

(Who has been sitting at a nearby table with her drink)
Maybe, that's why they can go so gallantly to face their deaths. I've seen men and women and children herded like cattle and marched toward death. Death in a gas chamber. But unlike cattle they were blesses with a brain and so they knew they were going to their slaughter. Men less fortunate that cattle! And they walked with their heads up. Unflinching. With all the dignity that man can muster. I was there among them. And I might've met my death with them then. But it happened I didn't. I felt their despair. Marveled at their great dignity…the dignity of man. Those wonderful, valiant people going to their death without a whimper. I wrote about that. And sent the story to my paper. Just as I'd sent all the other stories about all the other horrors. My editor wired back 'great story' and ran it. And the people read it. I'd had a great hope. I'd hoped that I could awaken the people at home to the fast spreading evil in the world. But most of them read with lazy acceptance. I'd hoped that once made aware of the horrors and butcheries, they'd demand and make a better world. Maybe they will some day. They haven't really begun yet. My efforts were worthless. I'd failed and I'd become so tired. So tired of the race with time. And so I was returned to an inactive status…an inactive status. By death.

PAUL

Why do you all keep harping on death? I'm on my holiday. This is a rest center.

ANN STRATTON

This is Limbo, soldier. Try to grasp that and leave the rest behind, where it belongs.

PAUL

Limbo?

ANN STRATTON
You've heard of Limbo?

PAUL
Heard of Limbo! Don't make me laugh. I couldn't take it. If this is Limbo, what's the war area?

ANN STRATTON
The war area is Hell…the Hell you learned about in Sunday school. Man created his own Hell. Hell on earth. You've been promoted, soldier. Promoted into Limbo.

PAUL
(Slowly beginning to realize)
D'you mean I'm dead? That we're all dead?

ANN STRATTON
Right!

PAUL
(A pause. Then he takes up his glass, raises it high)
Well. Cheerio. Here's to the living.

-CURTAIN-

ACT TWO
Scene 1

>Scene: The same. It is almost dawn, the same evening.

PAUL
(Is pacing with the intense restlessness that comes from exhaustion)
I thought I saw the target. Thought? I was sure. My map...my instruments...everything checked. It was the moment...my moment of dominion. What happened?

ANN
(Seated at a table)
You were the target. It was your moment all right...We got ours at sea. Oh, the commencement exercises were very impressive. A shark was the valedictorian. Very appropriate, wouldn't you say?

PAUL
Very...and was the flak flying?

ANN
Oh, yes. Flying high. There we were high in the heavens...hidden by the clouds. I felt so safe. I leaned my head back...that I remember.

PAUL
There isn't any safety. Not any more. Not even in the clouds.

ANN
I learned about that.

PAUL
We were born into the wrong time, you and I.

ANN

Oh, I don't know. Safety is not what I ever wanted to settle for. I just wish that I'd had more time…a chance to even up the score. The place was raided while I was still a heavy loser.

PAUL

And you think you might've won back your losses.

ANN

Could be.

PAUL

What's your system?

ANN

Mine wouldn't do you any good, soldier. I don't think. It won't do me any good either. Not any more.

PAUL

What's the answer?

ANN

To what?

PAUL

To life!

ANN

This place.

PAUL

To death.

ANN

You've got me.

PAUL

To us. To you. To me. To all of us here. What's it all mean?

ANN

I don't know yet. But if there's a story here I'll get it.

PAUL

And if you get it what'll you do with it?

ANN

I'll let you read it, soldier.

PAUL

Words. Words. Words! The dark night filled with words. What good are they?

ANN
(Softly, groping)

In the beginning was the Word, and Word was with —

PAUL

Oh, No! Not that. Not here. Not now.

ANN

Why not here? And why not now? Maybe that's what's wrong. We keep putting Him off. Not now. Not yet.

PAUL

There're those who wouldn't agree with you.

ANN

And there're those I wouldn't agree with.

PAUL

Words! Life is action.

ANN

And action? Destruction. As we've known it.

PAUL

Destruction was my assignment. I had to believe in destruction. Just as well, I suppose, that I didn't live on.

ANN

That kind of thinking and a nickel will get you a ride on the merry-go-round. Circular thinking I call that. It's no good.

PAUL
(His anger mounting)
It's no good, is it?

ANN
No.

PAUL
Is my thinking to be circumscribed too, now?

ANN
Only by yourself.

PAUL
That stolid calm of yours. Born with it, eh?

ANN
No. A gift I acquired.

PAUL
I recommend that you go in for pity and some of the finer arts…more becoming to your sex.

ANN
Oh, I reveled in that kind of luxury once. You wouldn't believe it, but I went in heavily for the gentler things in life…then I traded them all in. Had to the way things were going.

PAUL
Why? Maybe the world'd be a better place if you women didn't mess about doing men's work. It's a man's world.

ANN
Yeah. And just look at the damn place.

PAUL
Women being men.

ANN

And men? You're real angry. With yourself, maybe? What was it you did…or didn't do…that makes you so angry with yourself?

PAUL
(Doesn't answer)

ANN
(Watches him with a certain compassion)
Our angers and our fears. What they do to us. They blunt us. I don't feel with all of me. The way I should. I'm like a piano with toneless keys. It's why I'm here maybe. To find the tune of me in myself. The silent notes that should sing the tune of the complete self.
(Beginning to comprehend)
Too mush head. That's me. Yes. What right did I have to go into a man's world? Look where it got me. Women today…trying to be men. It's what you just said. Maybe you've got something there. Maybe that's why men become…the sons of their wives.

PAUL
I wouldn't know about that.

ANN
No wife?

PAUL
No.

ANN
Me too. No husband.

PAUL
What are we after? What do we want?

ANN
Another chance.

PAUL
Don't make me laugh. What good would that do? It's too late.

ANN

'Who knows if life be not death and death life,' unquote. I remember reading that somewhere.

PAUL

Euripides. Plato quotes him in the Gorgias.

ANN

Erudite, eh? Been to the best schools.

PAUL

Yes, and I had great plans for my dream.

ANN

What was your dream?

PAUL

The fastest plane. My plane would conquer time and space.

ANN

No good.

PAUL

Why not?

ANN

Bombs conquer time and space too. The dreams that end in war.

PAUL

Not if the world becomes a brotherhood of nations.

ANN

That's the dream for me. That one I'll buy.

PAUL

The barrier of distance will yield to speed. When we get to know each other we'll like each other. Mistrust and fear and bias will be overcome and we'll all work together…a dream. What good's a dream now?

ANN

No good. Or NO! Maybe dreams drifting about in space can be harnessed.

PAUL

And used? Like electricity.

ANN

Why not?

PAUL

Dream on.

ANN

'if life be not death and death life.' Maybe we're alive and don't know it. Just like a lot of people I know. Know? Knew. Who're dead and don't know it.

PAUL

Not very funny

ANN

Sorry. The best I could do. Under the circumstances.

PAUL

Dead. Life. Death. Dead.

ANN

I used to know a lot of wise sayings about life and death. Things like —

PAUL

Skip them.

ANN

Okay. D'you know something? I haven't clocked you. But I'll bet you anything you've walked a good ten miles these last hours. Right here in this room. And if you're dead you don't need the exercise. The way I look at it.

PAUL

Look here. I can accept this. Whatever you want to call it. But I cannot accept what went before.

ANN

Why not? It's over and done with now.

PAUL

That's what I cannot accept.

ANN

Oh, Think you could have even up the score too.

PAUL

I know damn well I could have. The things I dreamed of doing. The work I'd mapped out. The plans I'd made. And now it's over.

ANN

Or maybe, just beginning.

PAUL

What kind of talk is —

ANN

Yes. Beginning. Maybe this is another chance. Yes. It must be.

PAUL

Chance? For what? We're dead.

ANN

Maybe we always have been. Maybe this is our chance to become really alive.

PAUL

Alive? How?

ANN

I don't know. Yet. All I know is what I feel now. And I feel there's something missing.

PAUL

Oh. There's life missing. That's all.

ANN

Oh, come off it. Stop harping. Start seeking.

PAUL

For what?

ANN

Okay. You had everything on earth. Money. The works.

PAUL

And yet I had nothing. That's what you were going to say?

ANN

Yeah. Maybe I was. Maybe we're here to do a job with ourselves. A job that we never got around to on earth. Suddenly it hits me. The difference. I remember now…we were grounded…had to stay in this poverty ridden, miserable village. Boy, I was sore. My flight interrupted. There I was with nothing to do. On Sunday, the church bells rang. I shrugged and went. Yes. I went to church. Told myself maybe I could find a story there.

PAUL

And did you?

ANN

Not then.

PAUL

When?

ANN

Now. I'm beginning now to see again and to understand at last the light in the faces of those poor hungry people. The light of love. They were in love. With God.

PAUL

A god of poverty. A god of war…of misery…

ANN

Oh, shut up…And I had nothing but scorn for them then.

PAUL

Oh…and what made you change?

ANN

I don't know. Something new in myself. The missing notes. The missing element. A tiny flame…still too small to see by.

PAUL

The missing element!

ANN

Yes. We were too busy always to think about that. Too busy getting ahead. To what? Okay…this place. So there's a reason. This is the place where we must find —

PAUL

I don't know what you're talking about. You women —

ANN

You know something? For two cents, I could get pretty sore at you. Only where would two cents get me? Your anger's become a disease.

PAUL

That so? And where's the cure?

ANN

In yourself.

PAUL

In myself.

ANN

Right. We've got to dig out the hating that's in us.

PAUL

Oh, you too?

ANN

Me too. I was sore at my readers. Because they didn't get my message. What right did I have to expect them to think and feel the way I did? I was sore at them. No wonder they didn't like me. Me, the self appointed leader…the self-righteous judge of others.

PAUL

You were doing your job.

ANN

What I thought was my job. Maybe it wasn't. It wasn't as important as I wanted it to be. As I wanted to be. That's it. I wanted to be important. Yes. And I never really loved anyone. Just thought I did.

PAUL

Love…

ANN

…is the other person. Love is lots of things. The element that unites… Hate? Is the absence of love. The darkness.

PAUL

I just don't understand a word —

ANN

I'm just talking to myself. I might as well. The delicate…intangible… elusive…missing —That's it! Without it there's chaos. War. We're used to war. And it's hard to give up what you're used to. We're still fighting…you and I.

PAUL

And how do we stop?

ANN
(Shrugs, shaking her head)

I don't know.

PAUL
(Derisive)

Don't tell me —

ANN

I don't know, soldier. I thought I did…thought I was beginning to —
But I don't know. If I knew maybe I wouldn't be here.

PAUL

The name is Paul

ANN

Oh, Mine's Ann.

PAUL
(Tired now from his inner warfare)

Ann. How do we stop?

ANN

By wanting to. I guess.

PAUL

But what else is there…for us?

ANN
(The word surprises her)

Us?
(They look at each other, as though seeing each other for the first time)
Yes, us. The beginning maybe. If we can find the way to each other.
And from there…maybe the way to…all the others.

PAUL

That makes sense.

ANN
(Laughs with delight)

PAUL

I like that.

ANN

What?

PAUL

Hearing you laugh.

ANN
(Surprised)

I did laugh, didn't I? In I don't know how long. I've always been a scowler.

PAUL

You, too?

ANN

Me, too.
(She laughs and he does too)
But what are we laughing at?

PAUL

Does it have to be at something?

ANN

No. No, it doesn't.

PAUL

I was laughing with you.

ANN

With? It's a lovely word.

PAUL

It is, isn't it?

ANN

With. The link.

PAUL

Tell me —

ANN

Tell you? What?

PAUL

Anything.

ANN

But just a minute ago you —

PAUL

That was a minute ago. Now I want to know you.

ANN

Why, thanks. But I don't know myself…so how can I — I spent too many years running away from myself. From myself into action. Life is action. That's what you said. It's the way I lived my life. Trying to hide my fears with action. It didn't work. It wasn't enough.

PAUL

No. It wasn't enough for me either.

ANN

Poor, Paul.

PAUL

That's what we are. Both of us. Poor. Even though my father gave us everything. Everything that money could —
(The memory brings back the anger)
My father! A great fellow, my father.

ANN

Oh, Paul!

PAUL

We can't get away from it, can we?

ANN

We were beginning to.

PAUL

Why did he have to follow me here? What does he want of me?

ANN
But he didn't follow you. He arrived when I did. And you came later.

PAUL
Oh. Then why did I follow him? What is it I want of him? What is it he wants?

ANN
Maybe the same thing. The missing —

PAUL
My father? Money was all eve ever wanted. Money. Success.

ANN
They couldn't have been enough. He's here. Just as we are.

PAUL
Yes.
(Regarding her)
That uniform —

ANN
Don't like it? I'm tired of it, too.

PAUL
That's got to go. It no longer suits you.

ANN
But I haven't anything else. Been wearing it for I don't know how long.

PAUL
We'll find you something. What's your favorite color…Quick?

ANN
And you the erudite *(well read)* one!

PAUL
It's a game. Your favorite color.
(Snaps his fingers)

ANN

White. What's yours? Quick!

PAUL

Blue!

ANN

Then I want a blue dress.
        (And a blue dress floats down)

PAUL
(Sees it first, takes it and offers it to her)

ANN

No! I can't believe it.

PAUL

Put it on.

ANN

Not now. Not here.

PAUL

Right now. Right here.
        (He is unbuttoning her jacket, helping her)

ANN
(Chattering)
I've never seen such a color. Such an exquisite shade of blue. Look. It changes in the light.

PAUL

Now slip it on. Over your head.

ANN

But my —
        (Looking down at her pants)

PAUL

Those will have to go too. You're blushing!

ANN
Lord. We don't seem to leave any of our habits behind.

PAUL
Did you always blush?

ANN
Yeah. Damned inconvenient at times.

PAUL
It's very becoming.

ANN
Thanks.
(Having turned her back she has somehow succeeded in getting into the dress and out of the pants)
It's the loveliest dress I've ever had on. Look. The design at the waste. Flowers. What are they?

PAUL
Delphinium, I think. Off with the boots.

ANN
But I haven't any —

PAUL
Shoes?
(They appear)
Here they are.

ANN
It's magic. And they match perfectly.

PAUL
Mi'lady.
(He ushers her to a chair, then kneels to put the slippers on her feet)

ANN
The magic slippers.

PAUL

They fit?

ANN

Perfectly.

PAUL

Try dancing in them.

ANN

I haven't danced in —

PAUL
(He takes her in his arms and they dance)

ANN

I'm dreaming this. I must be. It's the loveliest dream.

PAUL

This is the beginning.

ANN

I don't want to wake up. Please, God. I don't want to wake up.

INNKEEPER
(Has come in from the dining room, stands watching them)

ANN
(The first to notice him)

Oh! Oh, no. It's over.

PAUL

No. It's not.

ANN

The music's over.

INNKEEPER

It needn't be. Well. You'll be leaving soon, I think.

ANN
Oh, no. But why? We've only just —

PAUL
We haven't made any plans to leave.

INNKEEPER
Planning's not the answer here. You've seen the delphinium. The fields on the way here —

PAUL
I arrived at night.

ANN
But I arrived during — And I'm a reporter!

INNKEEPER
What's that, miss?

ANN
Observing is my trade. Was my trade.

INNKEEPER
Oh, yes. The men and women and children herded like cattle and marched toward — Well, that's all behind you now. You've earned the right to rest and happiness and freedom.

PAUL
Beautiful words. Rest. Happiness. Freedom.

ANN
Where is all that? Where does one find —

INNKEEPER
You have found it.

ANN
Imagine! Imagine not realizing! And you, Paul?

PAUL

I have everything.

INNKEEPER

Hold to it. Hold it close. The precious element.

ANN

Paul. The delphinium.
(Showing the floral design on her dress)
(The elevator door opens with a musical clang)

COCO
(Comes out of its cage. He is in a festive costume)

PAUL
(On seeing Coco)
The circus. Ann. Look. The circus is in town!
(To Coco)
I saw you here last night, sir. But I was tired then. Still I hoped you were going to do your turn for us.

COCO
(Overwhelmed)
You did? You mean you really wanted me —

PAUL

Why, of course.

COCO

But that's extraordinary.
(Trembling with excitement)
I've worked out a new act. I spent the whole night working on it. It's for the children.
(Turning to show his costume)
How do you like it? Do you think the children —

PAUL

Wonderful. Isn't it, Ann?

COCO

The pictures —
    (He points them out)

ANN
(With a child's delight)

Elephants and monkeys —

COCO

Do you think they'll make the children laugh?

PAUL

They make me want to laugh.

COCO

Really? You mean that?

PAUL

A giraffe! Look, Ann.
    (He is examining the pictures closely with the curiosity of a child)

COCO
(Glowing with pride)

I painted them myself. And I've worked out an act to go with the pictures. Would you like me to —

ANN

Now? Would you?

COCO

Of course. I'm ready. All set.

PAUL

Where shall we arrange a stage? Where shall we move the tables and chairs?

COCO
You needn't move anything. Just sit at that table.
(They sit on the edges of their chairs, watching expectantly)
(Taking 'props' out of his voluminous pockets, arranges them on the table at his side)
Now. The curtain is going up.
(Whispers this to Ann and Paul as if letting them in on a delightful secret)

PAUL
This is the most exciting moment.

COCO
(Affecting surprise. The curtain went up before he was ready. He backs up, pulls himself together and makes a formal entrance, looking about at an imaginary audience, finally centers his attention on Paul and Ann. He does a juggling routine)

(Paul and Ann are back in their childhood, awed and expectant)

(Expands in this new climate. Everyone is happy. The Innkeeper is beaming. His friend is finding himself)(The elevator door opens silently and out steps Mr. Dukely. He stands there watching Coco)(Coco is sensing the presence of the enemy, looks in Mr. Dukely's direction. Just seeing him is enough. Coco begins to falter. He drops one of his props. The magic is gone.)

PAUL
(Retrieves the prop from under the table)
Here it is.

COCO
(Stands there, his head bowed in defeat)
It's no good.

ANN
It was very good. It's a wonderful act.

PAUL
Please don't stop.

COCO
(Shaking his head)
I dropped it. Didn't you see? I dropped it. You picked it up.

PAUL
But you meant to do that, didn't you? It seemed to be part of the act.

COCO
(Surprised, and the temptation to lie is great)
Part of the act?
(And in raising his head his eyes meet those of Dukely)
No. It's no good. I'm not…good……it's not good.

INNKEEPER
I think that was good, Coco. Very good. And tonight — tonight we'll…

ANN
A big opening night! That's what we'll have.

PAUL
With banners and posters. I'll see to everything.

INNKEEPER
And I'll have a stage built. A real stage, Coco. It'll be like a musicale… but without music. You won't need music. Your act will be enough.

COCO
Thank you. But —

INNKEEPER
(Anxious to protect the young ones from becoming infected by Coco's despair)
Now, why don't you two go and have a look at the fields of delphinium. The sun is coming up. That's odd. Go. Both of you.

PAUL
We'll come back though.

ANN
Yes. We'll be back early to help.

INNKEEPER
(Is taking them to the door at back right)
Yes. Yes. It might be better if —
(They have gone out into the faint sunlight that did come up but now goes down again)

MR. DUKELY
The sun, eh? Didn't last very long.

INNKEEPER
You have no sense of…of…anything!

MR. DUKELY
(His gaze still on Coco)
I know the truth when I see it.

INNKEEPER
(Appalled)
You?

MR. DUKELY
A musicale! A musicale without music!
(Then a derisive, triumphant laugh)

COCO
(Has covered his ears. Now all of the despair that has been lodging in his soul comes forth in one wail as he whirls about to the back wall. This wall becomes his haven as he rests against it. Then he raises his arms and beats it with his fists, as though fighting back hopelessly, his inevitable doom.)

-BLACKOUT-

ACT TWO
Scene 2

Scene: The same. It is early evening of the same day. There is a large urn filled with delphinium on a table back center. Poster for Coco's show are on the news stand and the desk.

MRS. STERLING
(Is sitting at a table brooding, waiting, oblivious to what is happening)

COCO
(Comes out of the dining room looking for the Innkeeper. Dejected, he stands there, waiting, uncertain.)

BELLHOP
(Comes out of the elevator, sits on the bench)

COCO
Oh, you wouldn't happen to know where he is?

BELLHOP
The boss?

COCO
Is that what YOU call him?
(Looking around, forlorn)
He isn't here.

BELLHOP
No.

COCO

I need him.
(Absently engrossed)
I need someone. I've got an idea…but I need —
(Studies the Bellhop)
Maybe you could — You a member of the profession?

BELLHOP

(Nods ruefully)

COCO

Were you any good?

BELLHOP

I thought I was until —

COCO

Then you know something about audience reaction. Unpredictable. You think you know them because they know you. Then suddenly you're strangers. And it's over. Why?

BELLHOP

I guess maybe I don't know what you're talking about.

COCO

But you were an actor.

BELLHOP

An actor? Me?

COCO

You just said you were a member of the profession.

BELLHOP

Oh, profession. I thought you said depression. I was a member of that all right. Nickel tips!

COCO

Too bad. I might've been able to use you…what size do you wear? No. Never mind.
(To himself again)
I'll have to do it alone. Maybe I'll be able to. Maybe. I used to be able to a long time ago. But now, time has become my enemy…time and being forgotten. That's not it either.

ANN

(Has come out of the dining room, concerned for Coco. The change in her is quite apparent now. She seems younger, softer and more radiant. She is wearing the blue dress.)
I was wondering why you stopped.

COCO

Oh.
(Evasive)
I've got to find something.

ANN

What? Maybe I can help you.

COCO

(Shaking his head)
Something within myself. Buried somewhere.

ANN

The tiny flame —

COCO

Flame? Do you think it's still there?

ANN

Of course it is.

COCO

What makes you so sure?

ANN
I've been watching you rehearse in there. You're great. You're such a tireless worker —

COCO
Maybe I work too hard. It's what he keeps telling me.. my friend.. my one friend. Where is he now?

ANN
The manager?

COCO
(Proudly)
He's my friend. But where is he?

ANN
I don't know.

COCO
I need him. That's the trouble with friends, I guess. When you need them most they're busy.

ANN
And that's the lonely time.

COCO
The terrible time. When you're nowhere.

ANN
I'm your friend. I'd like to be.

COCO
(Quite surprised)
You'd like to by my — but I've never had anyone who wanted to be my friend. Except him here. Before that my costumes were the only friends I had.

ANN
(She laughs as she speaks)
Well, I'm not a costume, but —

COCO
Say, you're laughing. It's the first time I've heard anybody laugh since I've been here. You have a very musical laugh.

ANN
Thank you. That's the nicest compliment. Thank you.

COCO
But you don't need compliments.

ANN
Oh, yes. We all need —

COCO
Acceptance. Yes, without that we're —

ANN
Isolated.

COCO
You know about that? At your age you shouldn't know that much about pain.

ANN
Pain. The diminishing force. It'll pick on anyone who'll let it.

COCO
And I let it? But why? Why? Why?

ANN
I think maybe that' why we're here. To find out.

COCO
Where's the answer?

ANN
In ourselves.

COCO
That's a large place. Too small sometimes and yet too large.

ANN

Of confusion?

COCO

Yes, the confusion.
    (He looks about him as if for the answer, sees the posters, crosses to them)

ANN

Of course

COCO

But will they laugh?

ANN

Of course they'll laugh. They're bound to.

COCO
(Defiant, in pain)

They're bound up in themselves. All these people. But I can free them, if they'd laugh, they'd be —

ANN

They'll laugh.

COCO

Not if he's there. If he weren't there. Always following me about with his — Why does he have to keep following me?

ANN

That man last night?

COCO

He never gives me any peace. Never a moment's peace. He's always there. Who does he think he is anyway, a part of the act? A part of the act —Oh, God —

ANN

Maybe he won't come. We just won't ask him.

COCO

Not come? Him? He's like a flea on a dog. Biting anyway. A part of the act…
(In despair)
It won't do any good. What's the use?

ANN

No. Don't say that.

COCO

I had it. I've had it for a very long time. They laughed. They roared with laughter. It was like being showered with rose petals. So long ago. And then it changed so suddenly. Time stopped for me like a clock in the night. And you wake up to the wrong time.

ANN

It can change again

COCO
(Skeptical)

It can?
(Then grasping at the straw)
Do you really think so?

ANN

I really think so.

COCO

How? How can it change again?

ANN

I believe it can. Changing is living. Yes, it is. We can change if we just let ourselves live.

COCO

'Let ourselves live?' But how can I? He won't let me. He'll be there and I'll tighten up, unsure of myself. There's something about him. If he'd only stay away, just for this one day. That's all I need. If he would only just stay away.

ANN

Maybe I could —

COCO

I'll bet you could. Will you do it? Keep him away?

ANN

I'll do my hardest! I'll put on a show for him myself if I have to.

COCO

But then you wouldn't be at my — and I want you to be there.

ANN

Oh, I'll be there.

COCO

How will you keep him away?

ANN

Leave that to me. You think about your show.

COCO

Yes. I must get back. Back to my work. That's a very nice stage they had built. So quickly too. That should help. Perspective. It's not good trying to entertain in here. Too close to the audience. No perspective. Thank you, my dear.
(He goes back into the dining room)

ANN
(Looks about, worried, sees Mrs. Sterling)
Mrs. Sterling?

MRS. STERLING
(Does not recognize her)
Yes.

ANN

I'm sorry to disturb you. I'm Ann Stratton. Last night —

MRS. STERLING
Oh, yes. I didn't recognize you in that dress.

ANN
It is quite a change, isn't it? Tell me, have you seen the manager anywhere about?

MRS. STERLING
He hasn't been here.

ANN
(Alarmed)
You don't suppose he's gone? Left this place, I mean.

MRS. STERLING
I'm afraid I wouldn't know.

ANN
Oh, dear.

MRS. STERLING
Where is my son? You sat up with him most of the night.

ANN
Yes, we talked things out.

MRS. STERLING
He didn't want me to stay up with him. And I did so want to talk to him. I want to help him. He's so bitter.

ANN
Not any more, I don't think.

MRS. STERLING
(Feeling rejected, futile and alone)
Oh, well, I'm glad. Very glad. I'd never have known him. He was a little boy when —

ANN
Yes. He's told me

MRS. STERLING
(Jealous)
He has? So soon. So quickly? But he's only just met you.

ANN
I know.

MRS. STERLING
What's brought about this great change in you?

ANN
Love…friendship.

MRS. STERLING
And my son?

ANN
He's changed too.

MRS. STERLING
(Envious, barren)
It should make me happy. But I've only just seen him again. And now to lose him so quickly.

ANN
Lose him? Why should you have to lose him. Unless you want to.

MRS. STERLING
(Pangs of buried guilt)
Want to? Really! I never wanted to leave my babies. Never. But I had no choice.

ANN
Maybe we do have a choice.

MRS. STERLING
Are you implying that I wanted to die? I wanted to live.

ANN
You must've wanted something else too. Something else more.

MRS. STERLING
(Fighting back the guilt)
I did want to live. I was expecting to go home. But you're too young to understand. You've never had any children.

ANN
No. But I did have the things I wanted. The things I thought were important. The wrong things. Because I was afraid to want the right thing.

MRS. STERLING
And what is the right thing?

ANN
The ability to love, I think. It wasn't until I got rid of the fear and the anger that I was able to love.

MRS. STERLING
(Thinking inward, searching)
Rid of the fear. Is that what I was? Afraid?

ANN
Of living, maybe?

MRS. STERLING
(A faint gasp of horror now that the truth is coming to the surface)
Yes. I didn't want to go on living. Because —
(sighs, wearied, resigned)
And the fear's been with me all these years. Still is. But I'd never been afraid. Not until that day when —

ANN
Yes! There's always such a day for each of us. The day that changes everything. When we either give in or win out.

MRS. STERLING
And I gave in. Had I lived I might've been able to change —

ANN
You still can.

MRS. STERLING

How?

ANN

You'll find the way if you want to.

MRS. STERLING

If I want to! I'm afraid I don't understand you. You're so odd.

ANN

Odd? I hope not. Unimportant, that's what I am. At last! Helps me to feel that I belong, to myself, to others. Only why did it take me so long to find that out?

MRS. STERLING
(Has lapsed into her brooding again)

I wouldn't know.
(Just by way of being courteous)
I wish that I could help you.

ANN
(Trying to bring her back)

You can!

MRS. STERLING

I can? How?

ANN

Help me with the show that Coco is giving.

MRS. STERLING

The show? But how can I —

ANN

By coming to it. By laughing.

MRS. STERLING

Laugh? I laugh? In the face of...why I couldn't possibly.

ANN

But it's what he needs.

MRS. STERLING

You know, he's really not very funny.

ANN

But he's trying so hard to get through to us. It would make him so happy.

MRS. STERLING

I'm really not terribly interested in his happiness.

ANN

But, why not?

MRS. STERLING

Please. I have my own problems.

ANN

Why not get rid of them? Stop clinging to them. We must let go.

MRS. STERLING

How?

ANN

The quickest way I know is getting interested in someone else's pain. But that's hard to do when you've begun to wallow.

MRS. STERLING

Aren't you being impertinent?

ANN

Sorry. I'm only trying. It's a rough, bumpy road…the way to each other.

MRS. STERLING
(Has lapsed into her withdrawn state)

PAUL
(Comes out of the elevator)

Ann.

ANN

Yes. Rested?

PAUL

Wonderfully.

ANN

Good. Your mother...I've been trying. But I lost the way somehow. She needs you.

PAUL

Right.
(As she goes into the elevator. He is not at ease with his mother)
Quite a girl.

MRS. STERLING

What? Oh, a very odd girl, I'd say. She's so blunt.

PAUL

Yes. She takes short cuts. But that's kindness.

MRS. STERLING

Is it? I don't know. But it doesn't matter. We're such strangers, you and me. You're my son. There shouldn't be this gulf between us.

PAUL

It's all I've ever known. I've never been able to relate to anyone...not until Ann helped me.

MRS. STERLING

But it's what I wanted to do. What I've been waiting for all these years. She's kind, you say? She told me that I —

PAUL

What was it, mother?

MRS. STERLING

I gave up. I gave in to myself. I gave way to grief, I called it. And then there was my pride. Was it my pride I valued most? It must've been. And then the hatred. I hated her so for taking your father —

PAUL

My father!

MRS. STERLING

And I've been so unforgiving. A trivial thing —

PAUL

It wasn't trivial! He betrayed you. He —

MRS. STERLING

No, Paul. Don't blame him. It wasn't all his fault.

PAUL

How can you say that?

MRS. STERLING

Of course.
(Looking about her as if seeing the place for the first time)
What lovely flowers. I've never seen flowers in this place.

PAUL

Ann brought them back.

MRS. STERLING

They're lovely, Ann. And that dress is so right on you. You look lovely in it.

ANN

Thank you. And I'm sorry —

MRS. STERLING

Don't be. It was good what you did. Now run along about your show.

ANN

You're coming?

MRS. STERLING
Oh, yes. And I'm going to laugh too.

ANN
(Impulsively embraces her)
I love you!

(She and Paul leave in the elevator)

MRS. HOLLOWAY
(Coming out of the elevator)
Well, you've got your son and your husband too. I guess you've forgotten what it's like to be alone. Alone like me. How did you do it? Influence. Yes. The rich have the influence. Lucky. That's what you are. Just plain lucky. Your cup must be running over. But that's the way it is, I guess. Some get everything they want and some don't get anything at all, like me.

MRS. STERLING
I'm very sorry. I wish there was something I could do for you.

MRS. HOLLOWAY
That's what they all say. But it doesn't help. I should've taken my life. That's what I should've done.

MRS. STERLING
Oh, no. Don't say that! It's what I —

MRS. HOLLOWAY
What would you know about it? You've got everything. You got what you wanted. Why shouldn't I?

MRS. STERLING
What I wanted? This unhappy place for them? No. No. I didn't want them to come here. I've told you that before. I didn't want that. I couldn't have —

(Mrs. Holloway has wandered off)

MR. STERLING
(Returning from his walk)

MRS. STERLING
(Upon seeing him)
Oh, Eric, the awful thing I did.

MR. STERLING
Come, come, my dear.

MRS. STERLING
I'm like her. I've been just like her.

MR. STERLING
That dreadful old woman? Don't be absurd.

MRS. STERLING
I see myself in her. Something of myself. I've been doing nothing but trying to justify —

MR. STERLING
Justify? What? What are you talking about?

MRS. STERLING
My illness. My attitude. My death —

MR. STERLING
(On edge)
Must we go back to that again?

MRS. STERLING
I'm afraid we must. I must. I've got to get at the complete truth.

MR. STERLING
(Mistaking her meaning, warily)
What truth?

MRS. STERLING
The truth in myself. I'm only just beginning now. Beginning to let myself see that with my dying I thought I could strike back at you. I wanted to punish you. I wanted to hurt you as you had me. Yes. I wanted to kill you.
(They stare at each other)
Yes. That's what I really wanted.

MR. STERLING
Because of Melissa.

MRS. STERLING
Yes. I saw only my pain. Only myself. Only my needs.

MR. STERLING
And me? I only saw what I wanted to see. How blind I was. How comfortably blind. Going after and getting what I wanted always. What I thought I wanted. Until — I was even self righteous when the doctors told me I had cancer. Why me, I wanted to know. I asked that! Me! God, I was smug. So smug in by blindness.

MRS. STERLING
Cancer? You had cancer?

MR. STERLING
The living death in the body. The racing death.

MRS. STERLING
How awful for you.

MR. STERLING
The thing I couldn't conquer. The only thing I could not conquer. The defeat that I had to accept. And then I began to see. First I saw you. As you lay dying. Not until then did I even begin to feel what I should have felt when you were still there…the remorse…the guilt.

MRS. STERLING
But it was I who — I failed you —

MR. STERLING
It was more than Melissa. It went deeper than that, I'm afraid. The truth? I never loved you. I'd never loved anyone. I'm realizing that now.

MRS. STERLING
Then she didn't really take you away from me.

MR. STERLING
She was just another conquest.

MRS. STERLING

Why did you marry me?

MR. STERLING

Why? You had money…position. Your father had great power… tremendous influence —

MRS. STERLING

But you were so attentive…so romantic…

MR. STERLING

I had to be. In order to get what I wanted. It was your father I was courting, He doted on you.

MRS. STERLING

And that's why he turned his business over to you.

MR. STERLING

Yes. And then when he died —

MRS. STERLING

You could afford to be indifferent. Yes. And I kept telling myself it was your work that used up so much of you.

MR. STERLING

And then when you became ill, I was relieved. The truth?

MRS. STERLING

But you saw to it that I had the best of care.

MR. STERLING

That was to cover the truth. I wanted you dead. Yes, I actually hoped you'd die. Why? So that I'd be free. Freedom was to be my biggest conquest. You had become the rebuke, the constant reminder, the price I'd paid. I had to be free of you. It took me a long time to realize that this 'freedom' was the biggest responsibility of all. The lonely road it became. The road that led me into the vacuum of myself. I finally had only myself. It was then that I was faced with the truth. The truth? The doctors had told me about the new drug. The drug that might have saved your life. The decision was up to me. And —

MRS. STERLING

Oh, no —

MR. STERLING

Yes, I told the doctors that the drug might be too experimental. That I could not take the risk. The truth? I was afraid you might recover.

MRS. STERLING

We were quite a match for each other.

MR. STERLING

Why do we have to go back?

MRS. STERLING

I was just a rung on your ladder. Until —
(Suddenly savage)
Why in hell didn't you ask me for a divorce, instead of —

MR. STERLING

I had political ambitions too!

MRS. STERLING

And a divorce would have —

MR. STERLING

Yes.

MRS. STERLING

So, instead, you killed me. Let me die. Well, I'd asked for it! Right from the start. You hadn't a chance. I'd made up my mind the first time we met. You were struggling…ambitious. Hard to reach. Hard to know. Hard to get at. And so I had to have you. I knew I held the winning cards. I was so sure that I could mold you into my way…my dream. The dream that I could manipulate with my advantages.

MR. STERLING

And I had to strike back at you?

MRS. STERLING

With Melissa. I hadn't counted on that. I was too smug. I'd been too protected always. And she wouldn't have happened if my father had lived.

MR. STERLING

No, I don't suppose she would have.

MRS. STERLING

She was only a…symptom? Yes. That's all she was. The right had been there all the time. The truth? I'd had lovers too…many of them. Cowardly affairs that lived vengefully…only in my mind. I guarded my self-righteousness jealously. Finally, my illness became the sublime refuge. My dependence, my clinging, my demands…all so ready to justify. You were right to let me die.

MR. STERLING

Can you ever forgive me.

MRS. STERLING

I forgive you? Can we forgive each other? We fed on each other like wild animals. We lied to each other and to ourselves. The hidden motives behind the pretty masks.

MR. STERLING

My whole life was a lie. The deceptions multiplying like my cancerous cells.

MRS. STERLING

Lying was our way of life. And I waited all these years…for this? Yes. For this. For the truth.

MR. STERLING

The cruel weapon…

MRS. STERLING

No…the purging…that might mean —

MR. STERLING

Freedom? Yes. The freedom that I was really looking for. How simple it might have been.

MRS. STERLING

Yes. And we took the hard way. The short cuts. Thinking they'd be easier. Yes. And the children? I didn't really want them. I was furious when I realized I was pregnant with Paul. I tried not to have him. I went to an abortionist…and then…I didn't go through with it. My great concern all this time? I was covering my guilt.

MR. STERLING
(Sighs, still too troubled about his own pain)
Paul? I must have a talk with him.

MRS. STERLING
Was he always so bitter?

MRS. STERLING
I didn't really see very much of him. Not enough to know…

MR. STERLING
We neither of us really cared. He must've known that.

MRS. STERLING
He hated Melissa. That's when —

PAUL
(Has returned)
She gave you what you had coming, didn't she, father?
(He is changed now, angry, relentless)

MR. STERLING
Yes…I daresay —

PAUL
You daresay! Your wife was sick. Dying. While you were in bed with that whore!

MR. STERLING
I thought I loved —

PAUL

Yes. And the word love justified anything. Ruthlessness went sailing under the banner of love! And when that so-called love is ruthless, there's no decency in anything!

MRS. STERLING

Paul, aren't you being ruthless now? With your father?

PAUL

How can I be otherwise? I'm his son.
(Turns on his father)
You had wealth, power, position. How did you use them?

MR. STERLING

Why, to the best of my ability.

PAUL

To the best of your ability! The Klepac family. Do you remember them?

MR. STERLING

Klepac? No?

PAUL

You're worse than I thought. He'd been an associate of yours. One of your most trusted delegates. He wound up in a concentration camp together with his family. You could have prevented that but you didn't. You couldn't risk getting involved. And then there was Van Dussell. You let him down too.

MR. STERLING

I wasn't aware —

PAUL

Precisely. You weren't aware. Just as you weren't aware of Peter and myself when we were away at school. Where were you when Peter had pneumonia? The headmaster had sent you word that Peter was dying.

MRS. STERLING

Peter dying?

MR. STERLING
(Trapped, on trial)
But I was away at that time. I had heavy responsibilities. Banks were failing. There was a panic. You were young, at school. You didn't know. But there was this terrible depression. It was a good thing I stayed on the job. Instead of losing what I had…most of them did, you know. Well…I managed by astute manipulation to almost double what I —

PAUL
So! While others lost their very shirts you managed to profit!

MR. STERLING
But it was for you. For you two…you and Peter. My sons.

PAUL
And the others? Our bothers? The brotherhood of man was our dream. But it hadn't a chance against you and your kind. We knew that the world was sick. And we saw what it was that had made it sick. The lack of principle. The greed. Evil was on the ascendant and those who rode with evil won. But not for long. You were fortunate that you died when you did. Before you were dethroned. The fates would have caught up with you. That's what you were afraid of. You hoped that your plane would crash even before you took off. To the devil with the other passengers. You wanted to die. You thought you could escape —

MR. STERLING
It was the cancer that killed me.

PAUL
The cancer. Yes. The alien thought, which feeds on the healthy mind and eventually, destroys it.

MR. STERLING
But death hasn't brought me peace.

PAUL
Had you earned it?

MR. STERLING

I don't know. No…I don't suppose…but I'd hoped…I'd tried. We all tried. Brilliant thinkers are working hard to —

PAUL

Brilliant thinker! Peace is in the minds of men. Yes. But is it in their hearts?

MR. STERLING

In their hearts? Why…I had taken that for granted.

PAUL

Just as you took everything else for granted. You and your generation with its wishful thinking. When the world was sick you thought it was just hypochondria. It would get well if you let it alone. That was the alien thought. The cancer that feeds on the world.

MR. STERLING

But we tried. They're still trying. There's Lord Inner-Shalom. I'd always thought his plan the best of all. But now I remember an incident. Seemed unimportant at the time. We were walking down the street, he and I, late one night. He stopped to buy the morning paper…threw a silver coin at the newsboy…a sickly looking youngster. Then rather harshly…I noted…he demanded his change.

"Change, mister?" the youngster asked, his huge eyes so black, his face so pale. "Yes, my change, damn it, and don't look so innocent about it. I've got three pennies change coming." The youngster, without saying a word, handed back the silver coin. My friend, in a rage, threw the newspaper at the boy…with such force that the child staggered —
   (Realizing now what he has inadvertently revealed, he covers his face with his hands)
— and nearly fell. I'm appalled now that I look back.

PAUL

What did you do about the child?

MR. STERLING

Nothing. That's what's so appalling. I did nothing.

PAUL

And your friend?

MR. STERLING

He walked away.

PAUL

And you?

MR. STERLING

I followed him.

PAUL

You followed a great leader.

MR. STERLING

I'd thought him brutal at the time. But only for a moment. Only for a moment…because he was who he was.

MRS. STERLING
(Almost to herself)

'in their hearts'…love. There was no love. No love in any of us.

ANN
(Has returned)

Paul? Have you found him?
(She gets no response)
Paul! You said that you'd find pop! Paul! Coco's show!

PAUL

This isn't the time for it.

ANN

Not the time? But — what's the matter with you? What's happened?

PAUL

Something more important.

ANN

More important? But Coco is expecting us. Our being there means everything to him.

MRS. STERLING

Love…
(To Ann)
You've found it. If only you could show us the way.

ANN

But I am. I'm trying to.

MRS. STERLING

It's so hard. It's such a big change. How can we possibly —

ANN

By being willing. Willing to see the past for what it was…willing to let go of it.

MRS. STERLING

But your past I'm sure is less hideous than ours.

ANN

Who knows?

MRS. STERLING

We always took. From the world. From each other. We never gave.

ANN

Well, we can begin now.

MRS. STERLING

How? With what?

ANN

Ourselves. With our hearts.

MRS. STERLING

Our cold hearts?

ANN
We can warm them by giving them to each other.

MRS. STERLING
Yes. I'm beginning to see–

ANN
Good. Good for you. Now let's go. Coco is waiting.

PAUL
Sorry. I'm not up to it.

ANN
You're not up to it? Your old self again. Ready to let another man down.

PAUL
(Startled, looks to his father)

MR. STERLING
(Still guilt ridden)
Yes. It's what I did.

PAUL
Is that why I had to face you here? To see myself. In you? That's what I hated most. Being your son. Being known as your son.

ANN
Oh, Paul! That's over and done with.

MR. STERLING
(His gaze has wandered to the delphinium)
To repent. To resolve to amend. To hope for another chance. The way to peace. To brotherhood. Forgive me, my son.

PAUL
(Humbled by this humility, he gropes)
Forgive you? I forgive you? Who am I to forgive you? I condemned you. I! What right had I? Who am I to judge? I spent my life hating. Telling myself always that I had this dream. This dream of brotherhood. The dream that concealed the hating. War was the welcomed outlet. Father —
(He extends his hand)
I'm grateful for this meeting. To this place. For what it's given me.
(Mr. Sterling has taken his son's hand)
Forgive me, Father.

MR. STERLING
We must try to forgive ourselves, my son. And make whatever amends we can.

PAUL
I feel now as though I'm at the bottom of an abyss. As though I'd been afraid all my life. Of failing. To the bottom. As though I'd always grabbed at anything. To break the fall. To keep from hitting bottom. And now the fear is gone. Completely. And I'm glad I'm at the bottom.

ANN
Right. So let's go…Up!

PAUL
Will we be able to make it?

ANN
We can't miss. We have each other. All of us.

INNKEEPER
(Has returned)

ANN
(The first to see him)
Oh, pop. We've been looking for you.

INNKEEPER
I've been in Mr. Dukely's room.

ANN

The only place we didn't look.

INNKEEPER

I've been talking to him. Trying to persuade him to stay away from Coco's show.

ANN

And?

INNKEEPER

He was putting on his tie when I left him.

ANN

Then I must —

(She starts toward the elevator)

INNKEEPER
(Restrains her)

No. You must stay together now. You four. Get the show started. I'll try to delay him. I'll keep him out here as long as I can.

COCO
(Has come in from the dining room)

ANN

Coco! What're you doing out here? It's time for your curtain to go up.

COCO

Yes. But —

ANN

We're all looking forward to your performance, Coco.

MRS. STERLING
(Rallies)

Yes, indeed we are.

COCO

Thank you. I hope you'll find it amusing. I hope you'll —

ANN

Of course, we'll laugh.

PAUL

A good laugh is just what we need.

COCO
(Kindling)

Laughter frees people. That is the philosophy upon which I based my work.

ANN

No wonder you were so great. Everything you did had meaning.

COCO

It did?
(Suddenly not able to believe her yet wanting to)
You were too young —

ANN

Oh, no. I went to the circus every year of my life. Ever since I was knee high. And I saw you. I'll swear I saw you.
(She nudges Paul in a way that is not apparent to Coco. Paul rallies)

PAUL

I remember seeing you perform, sir. We talked about nothing else for months. Isn't that so, mother?

MRS. STERLING

Oh, yes. You remember, Eric.

MR. STERLING

Yes. Yes. Of course.

ANN
(Trying to get Coco to go)
Come on. You mustn't keep your audience waiting.

COCO

No, but I must speak to —
> *(He indicates his friend the Innkeeper)*

INNKEEPER
> *(Quickly, imperatively)*

You'd better take your seats. All of you.

ANN
> *(Worried)*

Yes, let's go.
> *(As they leave to Coco)*

I really did see you. And I always roared with laughter.

INNKEEPER

What can I do for you, my friend.

COCO

They lied very well, didn't they?

INNKEEPER

What do you mean? Lied?

COCO

Of course they did. But I appreciate it. How good of them to lie like that. Now I've forgotten what it was that I wanted to talk to you about. But —It really was good. Good of them to lie to me. I know they were lying and yet I believe them. Because I want to, I guess.

INNKEEPER

They must've seen you at some time or other. You haven't been here that long.

COCO

They might've at that.

INNKEEPER

So there you are.

COCO

Yes. I wonder what it was that I wanted to talk to you about.

INNKEEPER

Was it something important?

COCO

It must've been. I certainly wouldn't have left my work if it weren't important.

INNKEEPER

I wish I could help you to recall —

MR. DUKELY
(Comes out of the elevator)

COCO
(Sees him)

That's it. That's what was on my mind.

INNKEEPER
(Seeing Dukely)

Oh. Him.

COCO

He's right on time too. Just as if he were part of —Why couldn't he have lived?

INNKEEPER

I don't know. Sometimes I wish he had.

COCO

He's coming to the show, I suppose? Yes, of course he's coming. What could keep him away? So. It'll be just another failure. No. No. I can't face it. Not again. Not that hollow silence where there should be laughter. No. No. Call the performance off. Tell them I'm sick. Tell them anything. But call it off. Just call it off. I can't. That's all.

INNKEEPER

Who is he after all? Why should —

COCO

He's the public. Don't you see? The public is my collaborator. A part of myself. My work. Without the public I do not exist. My work lives only when they react. When they laugh.

INNKEEPER

Yes. But they're the public too. In there. They're ready. Waiting. And you let him do this to you.

COCO

But he's become — With him always there I can't —

INNKEEPER

You've let him become too important.

MR. DUKELY
(During this has walked to his haven, the news stand)
Well? What's holding up the works? I thought we were going to have a musicale. A musicale without music.
(His laughter is harsh)

COCO
(His last shred of hope gone)
You are coming then?

MR. DUKELY

But, of course.

COCO

You couldn't be induced to stay away? Just this once?

MR. DUKELY

Stay away? From a performance given by the great Coco?

COCO

Oh. You admit then that I am Coco-

MR. DUKELY

Certainly not.

COCO

Then I don't understand —

MR. DUKELY

You don't?

COCO

No. First you say that I am not Coco. Then you say that you could not be induced to stay away from a performance given by Coco.

MR. DUKELY

Right.

COCO

But, I am giving the performance!

MR. DUKELY

Right.

COCO

And still you say that I am not Coco! Say what're you trying to do? Drive me crazy? If I'm not Coco who am I?

MR. DUKELY
(Shrugs)

Just anybody.

COCO

Just anybody? Well, if I'm just anybody why in hell do you want to come to my show?

MR. DUKELY

You really want me to stay away, don't you?

COCO

I sure do.

MR. DUKELY

Well, I'll tell you what I'll do with you, my friend.

COCO

Friend? That again!

INNKEEPER
(Anxious to calm Coco)

Now, if —

COCO

What? What will you do with me?

MR. DUKELY

I'll make a pact with you.

COCO

A pact?

MR. DUKELY

Yes, it's this. I'll stay away from your performance if you'll admit the truth.

COCO

The truth? What truth?

MR. DUKELY

That you're not Coco. You admit the truth and I'll stay away from your performance. And we'll have no further discussions. Those are the facts.

COCO

Facts! Truth! Say, listen. What seems a fact to you is not necessarily the truth. I am —

MR. DUKELY

No. You're not. Well. My offer still stands.

COCO

I admit that I am not myself. Otherwise —No! I won't admit. It's not the truth!

MR. DUKELY

Very well then.
(*He strides past Coco. Then in the doorway of the dining room, over his shoulder*)
Well, good luck. I hope you make it.
(*He goes*)

COCO
(*Enraged*)
Make it! He hopes I'll drop —
(*Startled*)
Where I am!

INNKEEPER

Dismiss him, Coco. Dismiss him from your mind.

COCO

Maybe he's right. Maybe I'm not —Maybe I just think I'm Coco. It's what he keeps saying over and over. Until it's become like a swarm of bees in my head. Maybe he's right. Facts! Truth? What in hell is he talking about?

INNKEEPER

Dialectics. Isn't that what they call it?

COCO

Dia —What? Look. If I'm not Coco…Who am I?

INNKEEPER

You think you're Coco, don't you?

COCO

I did. But now…with him always yacking that I'm not —how can I be sure? How will I ever be sure?

INNKEEPER

They're waiting in there. They're ready. Go in. Give your performance. If they laugh you can be sure you're Coco. Isn't that so?

COCO

If they laugh. But he's in there too. My identity hangs on —

INNKEEPER

Forget about him.

COCO

Forget? How can I? When he's always there. Always telling me that I'm not — that I couldn't make a horse laugh. Who wants to make a horse laugh? I only want to make those people laugh.

INNKEEPER

Then go in and make them laugh.

COCO

You don't understand. As long as he's there it's just hopeless.

INNKEEPER

Is he God?

COCO
(Suddenly indignant)

God? Him?

INNKEEPER

Then why believe in him? You said you'd like to show him. This is your chance.

COCO

I had a chance last night with those eager young ones. And I muffed it.

INNKEEPER

Forget about last night. Forget all the yesterdays. Do you know that sometimes I wonder. If it really matters so much who we are. Maybe all that we have to believe is that we are. Doubt is death, I think. Belief is life, my friend.

COCO
(Beginning to comprehend)
Belief is life. Maybe I never really believed. Just thought I did. Just wanted to. That's not enough.

INNKEEPER
Not quite.

COCO
Yes. "It can change again," she said. Yes.
(Distracted by the reflection of a pink glow that has been coming from the dining room)
That lighting is very good. Very good. I put some pink gelatins on some of the spots.

INNKEEPER
Pink gelatins?

COCO
Always carry them with me. And that stage. Wonderful. Perspective. Well. It's time for the curtain to go up.

INNKEEPER
Good luck, Coco. You'll make it.

COCO
He hopes!
(Then he smiles at his friend and eases off)

MIKE
(Enters. He has a sheet of paper in his hand)
Gee. Hey, pop! Whadda ya know? Kelly had a flat! It would happen to him. Noth'n ever happens to me. An' does he appreciate it? No. You'd remember that when I was on earth, I wouldna appreciated it neither. I had too many there. That's all life was. Flats. Blowouts. Lights. Fenders. And cops. Them cops. With them tickets. All I ever wished for was that some day I should go to a heaven where there wasn't no traffic. And no lights. No flats. An' no cops. So I come here. And that's just what I got. No noth'n. Noth'n ever happens. It gets on my nerves. That's what. I

aint got enough relaxation. A state of mind. That's what it is. A state of mind.

(From the dining room we hear a sudden burst of laughter, one laugh particularly shrill)

INNKEEPER

Well. There's his answer.

MIKE

Say! What's go'n on?

MRS. HOLLOWAY
(Has wondered in)
(There is another outburst of laughter)

MIKE

Gee! Somebody musta busted a cop on the nose.

MRS. HOLLOWAY

What're they laughing at? I don't see anything to laugh at.

— BLACKOUT —

ACT TWO
Scene 3

>Scene: The same. Immediately after Coco's performance.

COCO
(Accompanied by applause, comes out of the dining room)
They laughed! Did you hear them? They laughed!

INNKEEPER
I heard them. You were very funny, Coco.

COCO
I was?
(With some surprise)
D'you know something? I suddenly feel very young. Actually I'm an old man. But right now I feel young again.
(Seeing Mike)
Hello. How are you?

MIKE
(Surprised)
Me? I'm fine. Yeah. Great. Say. You never said hello to me before.

COCO
Is that so? I guess you're right. I never saw you before.

MIKE
But I saw you all right. I saw you.

COCO
And I didn't see you.

MIKE

I don't get it.

COCO
(Looking about him)

This is a fine place. I never took much notice of this room before. I think I'm going to like it here. Yes. Well, they're free. In there, they laughed and now they're free.

INNKEEPER

There you are, Coco. You did it. You made them laugh.

COCO

You helped me. And she did too. "It can change again"…and it did. D'you know something? I don't feel so alone anymore. All those lonely years. We're not alone. We don't have to be.

INNKEEPER

We never are. Except in our thinking.

COCO

That's it. I didn't stop to think when I went on. That was it. That's why I wasn't afraid. It's no good. This thinking.

INNKEEPER
(To himself)

"In the moment that ye think not."

COCO

That's when I started to get in trouble. When I started thinking. About how I could surpass…myself! Why…I made a rival out of myself! The egotist at war with his talent. That's what I'd become. No wonder I lost my audience. I'd stopped working for them. Stopped caring about them. That's what it was. I blamed everyone and everything but myself. So I found myself alone. Thinking about myself always. Saying I had to work when I was trying to escape. D'you know it was really myself I was working at. Battling. Destroying myself.

INNKEEPER
(Very gently)

Leave yourself alone.

COCO

Yes. What does it matter who we are. That's what you said. It doesn't make a damn bit of difference. D'you know we should have these musicales often. Everyday. It would do people good. Why we could —

MIKE

Say, pop, don't he know?

INNKEEPER

Know?

MIKE

Oh, I forgot. I got the list here.
(He hands it over)

INNKEEPER

Mike, how often have I told you that you're not to look at the names on these lists?

MIKE

Aw, gee, pop, I gotta do something to break up the monotony. You don't know what it's like. The monotony I got. Driv'n weary from nowheres to no place. As far as I can see. Once in a blue moon I get a hack like this here lieutenant. But he don't give me a tumble. Gee.

COCO
(Has been happily creating)

Say! I've got an idea for a new act.

INNKEEPER

Your name is on this list, Coco.

COCO

My name? That so? What list is that?

INNKEEPER
It's the list of those who've been called to leave.

COCO
Oh, Is that so? Another booking, eh? Well, what's the next place like?

INNKEEPER
Nobody knows.

COCO
Nobody knows? Well, don't you have an advance man who sends you a report?

INNKEEPER
No. We don't get any reports.

COCO
And you have no idea what it's like?

INNKEEPER
Oh. We all have ideas. Ideas of our own. But no one actually knows. It could be —I don't know. I feel that it's a step forward. Into tomorrow. Like waking from a —

COCO
Does everyone have to take that step?

INNKEEPER
No. You have a choice.

COCO
Of what?

INNKEEPER
You can either go on or stay here.

COCO
Has anyone ever —

INNKEEPER

I chose to stay.

COCO

You did?

INNKEEPER

It was a long time ago. You're thinking of staying, aren't you?

COCO

I could be useful here.

INNKEEPER

You want to hold on to what you've found here today. Yes. And you think that by staying —That's what I thought. I wanted my moment to be eternal. But we, none of us, can stay in the present. So because I was unwilling to go into the future, I drifted back into the memory of my failures and my debts. It's hard to give up the pattern of the past. Because it has form.

(Shaking his head)

The thing that I'm beginning to see is that the pattern becomes the trap. The cage. *Our todays produce the tomorrows.* And we should be willing to go on. There's freedom in the future. Maybe I was too afraid of freedom, so I kept going back into the cage. I'm only just beginning to see.

COCO

The cage?

(He shudders)

You think I should go on then?

INNKEEPER

You must decide for yourself.

COCO

Yes.

(Thinks about it)

Well, I've got a lot of packing to do. I'd better take my costumes with me. I'll be needing them. Unless, of course, there's a restriction of some sort.

INNKEEPER

There aren't any restrictions.

COCO

Well, that sounds very promising. No restrictions. I wish you were going.

INNKEEPER

I missed my chance.

ANN

(Comes from the dining room, followed by the Sterlings. They all talk at once)
Coco, you were wonderful!

MRS. STERLING

Congratulations, Coco. And I want to thank you. For helping me to laugh at myself.

PAUL

You surpassed yourself, Coco.

COCO

Surpassed myself? No. I got rid of myself. That's what I think happened. Rid of that part of me — Well, never mind. You laughed. The music came back. It turned out to be a musicale after all. For me anyway.

ANN

For us especially. Free! That's what I feel.

PAUL

All of the confusion's gone. Gone completely, mother. It's like waking from a terrible dream. What was it I dreamed? There're only tiny, passing fragments. Flames. Smoke. I can't remember.

ANN

Why try? It's over. Over and done with at last! Say, did you ever play "London Bridge?"

PAUL

London Bridge?

ANN

No. You were good at Greek. London Bridge. Why do I think of that now? Oh, I get it. We crossed it!

COCO
(Mystified)

If you'll excuse me. I think I'd better get on with my packing. I've got quite a number of costumes.

ANN

Packing? Are you leaving us, Coco?

COCO

I'm hoping that we'll all be leaving together.

MRS. STERLING

Oh, has Mike brought a list?

INNKEEPER

Yes, madam.

COCO

I'll be right back.

(He leaves)

ANN

Any of us on the list?

INNKEEPER

You four and Coco.

MRS. STERLING

Thank God!

ANN

Where do we go?

INNKEEPER

Into the unknown.

MRS. STERLING

The unknown?

PAUL

That sounds great! That's what was so exciting about flying. That sense of being in the heavens. Nowhere and everywhere. You must've felt the same thing, dad. The unknown.

MR. STERLING

Yes. Yes, I did.

INNKEEPER

But I must tell you. You don't have to go. You have a choice.

MRS. STERLING
(Quickly)

A choice?

MR. STERLING

My dear, you're not thinking of staying here? In this dismal —

MRS. STERLING

But I'm used to it here. And it's Peter I'm thinking of. He'll need me if he should come here. I can't abandon him again.

PAUL

He won't need anything, mother.

MRS. STERLING

But everyone who comes here —

MR. STERLING

He won't be coming here, my dear.

MRS. STERLING

How do you know?

MR. STERLING

He must've gone to another area.

MRS. STERLING

You mean?

MR. STERLING

Yes.

MRS. STERLING

Then why didn't you tell me?

MR. STERLING

I was still too confused when I first arrived. Later, I became too engrossed in my own —

ANN

Just like the rest of us.
(To Mrs. Sterling)
I'm sure he must've gone to a much happier place. So be glad for him.

MRS. STERLING

Yes. Thank you.

MR. STERLING
(To the Innkeeper)

How soon are we leaving?

INNKEEPER

There's a cab waiting, sir.

MRS. STERLING
(Troubled)

But —

MR. STERLING

My dear, if you stay I shall stay too!

MRS. STERLING

You'd stay here? But you hate this place…and you'd stay because of me? Then that means —

MR. STERLING

Yes.

MRS. STERLING

Then I've got to go on.

PAUL

We must all go on, mother.

MRS. HOLLOWAY
(Has come back)

So, you're leaving are you? All of you together. A happy family.
(To Mrs. Sterling)
And you're satisfied to go and not care at all about ever seeing your other son again. Yes, but you always were a strange one. Didn't want this one to come here in the first place…and yet he came…and your husband, too. You've got everything…you have. While I — they wouldn't even let me have my own daughter's baby. That husband of hers. She never should've married him. I hate him. And I'll go on hating him. Where is it you're going? I'd like to go too. Maybe I'll find my daughter there.

INNKEEPER

No, ma'am. You cannot leave here yet.

MRS. HOLLOWAY

But I might find her where they're going. I've got to find her.

INNKEEPER

But you cannot leave here, ma'am.

MRS. HOLLOWAY

I will if I want to. If these people will take me with them. You will, won't you, ma'am?

MRS. STERLING

We'd gladly take you. But I don't think it's up to us.

INNKEEPER

That's right, madam.

MRS. HOLLOWAY
Then I can't go. I won't ever find her. I know that now. And I'll have to spend the rest of my days in this place. Alone. Without her. Without my daughter. Alone.

INNKEEPER
You'd better come with me, ma'am. I'll get you a cup of tea.

MRS. HOLLOWAY
(Broken and weeping, goes with him into the dining room)
Alone. For the rest of my days. She was everything to me. Yes. Everything. I just lived for my daughter from the moment she was born. Her father was no good. So I just lived for her. Alone.
(They've gone)

MRS. STERLING
If we could only help her.

ANN
Yes, but she's not willing —

MR. STERLING
Well, we'd better get packed. Eva?

MRS. STERLING
It won't take me long. How about you two?

PAUL
I haven't anything to pack. I don't think I'll be needing my maps.

ANN
I'm going as I am.

MRS. STERLING
We'll be down directly.
(They leave)

ANN
The unknown!

PAUL

Intrigues you, does it?

ANN

What a story!
(Laughs at herself)
Here I go again. But I'm done with that. Done with playing a man's part. That inactive status. Why did I take it so hard?

PAUL

It's the big change that frightens us all.

ANN

The big change become the big chance.

INNKEEPER
(Returning)
She'll be all right now. Well, it makes me a little sad to see you go. You're quite extraordinary. You young ones. You're not afraid.

ANN

Oh, yes. We have been. But not anymore.

COCO
(Emerges from the elevator, plus numerous and enormous bags)
My costumes.
(As he hauls them out of the lift)
And my props. You haven't seen them all. Wait 'till we get to where we're going.
(Counting the bags)
Four. Five. Six. Seven. Yes. That's right. Seven.

MR. DUKELY
(Comes out of the dining room, crosses to Coco. They face each other)
Well!

COCO

Hello.
(Bewildered)
Do I know you?

MR. DUKELY

Oh, yes. Very well.

COCO

Too well?

MR. DUKELY

Intimately.

COCO

Is that so? Funny —

MR. DUKELY

Not very. I did not laugh.

COCO

You didn't, eh? Blind? That's too bad. My comedy's all pantomime. No cracks. No gags. No jokes. Just pantomime.

MR. DUKELY

Facts are facts. And the fact remains that you are —

COCO

Oh, yes. Facts. You with your facts. Now I remember. I've known you for a long time. Yes. Too long. Almost. Why, I got to believing that you were a part of the act. A part of me. In a way, the part I believed in. YOU! And now? You're just a stranger. I didn't even recognize you. Funny.
(He laughs a long laugh)
Now I can laugh. At last I can laugh. At myself AND at YOU!

MR. DUKELY

Not very funny.

COCO

Not to you. But you don't matter. Not to me. Not any more.

MR. DUKELY
(Strides to the news stand)

THE STERLINGS
(Coming out of the elevator)

INNKEEPER
Mike. Come along now. Take these bags out to the car.

MIKE
Okay, pop.

MRS. STERLING
(To the Innkeeper)
I'm so very grateful to you. I shall miss you and your great kindness.

INNKEEPER
Thank you, madam.
   (To Mr. Sterling who has been helping Mike)
Good Bye, sir. I know you'll all be happy. Good Bye, children.
   (They all say Good bye and leave)

COCO
(The last to go, takes the Innkeeper's hand, glances at Dukely, indicating him with his head)
Who does he think he is? Everybody!
   (He leaves)

MIKE
(Rushing in)
Say, pop, whadda ya think?

INNKEEPER
Yes, Mike, what is it?

MIKE
Kelly just come with a new one. Cutt'n in on my territory!

INNKEEPER
But you were busy here, Mike. And the newly passed should never be kept waiting for transportation. You know that.

MIKE
Yeah, but — Here he is. Name is Cameron.

MR. CAMERON
(Has come in. He is middle-aged)
Good evening.

INNKEEPER
Good evening, sir.

MR. CAMERON
I'm from the earth. The earth world.

INNKEEPER
Yes, I know.

MR. CAMERON
Oh, you know that. I didn't live long enough. Do you know that too?

INNKEEPER
(Nods)

MR. CAMERON
Remarkable. You're a research worker too?

INNKEEPER
I don't think so.

MR. CAMERON
Amazing. The world's too busy to be cured of its illnesses. Too busy making war machines. Intercontinental ballistic missiles. Bomb shelters. Stuff like that.

INNKEEPER
Too bad.

MR. CAMERON

Yes. Too bad. I spent my life working on a cure for cancer. Found it too. Tried it on my mother. The growth is gone. She's still alive. They were very much impressed. Those doctors. Yes, very much impressed. Until the haggling began. The haggling over the distribution rights.

(His bitterness is more apparent now)

So then they started claiming that it couldn't have been cancer to begin with. That it must've been a misdiagnosis. I fought back. But I got no place. You can't buck the machinery of politics. So in a bitter rage, I burned up my lab and everything in it. Can I work here?

INNKEEPER

Work here? Oh, yes.

MR. CAMERON

Have to begin all over again. But I can do it. Got the formulas in my head. The cure is there. Everything is there. In the world. Ready to be used. Everything but acceptance. Rejection is what I got for my whole life's work. Cancer can be cured. I've proved it. But it'll take them a long time to believe it. Well. I'd like to get to work. I can do it. I can find it again. If course I can.

INNKEEPER

I'll take you to your room, sir.

MR. DUKELY
(Has been listening carefully)

A cure for cancer! Hah!

MR. CAMERON
(Turns, stares at Mr. Dukely)

Do I know you?

MR. DUKELY

Why, I think you do!

-CURTAIN-

AFTERWORD BY LIESL EHARDT

It was a typical sunny day, with temperatures in the low seventies, on the afternoon of November 15, 2005, in Burbank, CA, where I had been living for about two years. I had just returned to my apartment from an audition, for my favorite soap opera, "The Young and the Restless." Upon returning home, I checked my e-mail. There was a message from Rick Atkins and I was instantly intrigued.

By way of background, a couple years prior to this, while living in New York City, after my graduation with a Bachelor of Fine Arts degree in Acting, I learned that I was related to a successful 1920s and 30s actor by the name of Zita Johann. My father, John Ehardt, had related family stories about her, and Dad's sister, Jane Moore, my aunt, had been doing genealogy research to develop a family history, which included Zita Johann. It turns out that Zita's mother and my great grandmother were first cousins on my father's side, making Zita my second cousin twice removed. In addition, her birth name was Elisabeth, which also happens to be what my name, Liesl, derives from in German.

Unfortunately, the family had lost track of Zita in the 1950s, and only the stories and my aunt's research were left. I included this information along with photos of Zita on my website. And that is where Mr. Atkins found me.

So, why was I so intrigued by Mr. Atkins message? In it he mentioned that he not only knew Zita, but that they were "dear friends" for "eleven years prior to her passing." He was interested in finding out more of what I knew about her and sharing what he knew. Needless to say, I was interested!

Upon my first learning of Zita, I realized that I knew very little about her, aside from the family stories and what I had been able to find in mini biographies printed in various places online, some of which contained inaccurate information. I knew of no one who actually knew her personally before that first note from Rick. However, while trying to educate myself, I was struck by Zita and my unique resemblance. It seemed that she was almost a brunette version of myself, and her eyes, my family remembered, were a carbon copy of my own. In fact, in his note of November 2005, Mr. Atkins wrote, "you and she do favor" each other. This was most touching, coming from someone who had actually known her and who had looked into her enchanting eyes, face to face, something that I, to this day, wish I had had the opportunity to do.

Although I never got the chance to meet Zita, I feel as though Rick had entered my life for a reason. Through him, I was given the chance to know my cousin. He brought her into my life and has helped, through this book and beyond, to keep the essence of her brightly alive, for which I know she would be proud. I feel so honored and touched that I turned out to be the reason *Guest Parking: Zita Johann* has been brought to print. I am so excited knowing that others will now get the chance to be introduced to Zita Johann and learn more about who she was, via Rick's touching account of events and memories.

Through this book and all the letters, clippings, articles, cards, pictures, e-mails, recordings and more, which Rick has so openly shared with me over the years, my knowledge of Zita has fully emerged. I realize now how alike she and I are, not only physically, but also through our goals, values, views of Hollywood, belief in patience and the power of listening to young ones, and our strong desire to help children with disabilities.

You see, from a very young age, and long before any knowledge of Zita, I have had a profound understanding of and love for children. I have great interested in the arts, choir, teaching and performing. This interest has always been with me while living overseas, in London and the Middle East, as well as in the States. My first performance was a role in the play, *The Wizard of Oz*, while in 8th grade at the age of 13. My passion for acting grew during high school, where, luckily for me, the arts were strongly supported, and I was exposed to a wider variety of one-act plays, comedy, drama and musical theater.

However, before entering college, I struggled with the conflict between my desire to teach and work with children and my love for acting. My hope is that this platform might someday allow me to open my own children's charity foundation. Without knowing about Zita, I began acting on stage, just as she had done. About the time I began to find out about Zita, I was pulled towards Hollywood and film acting, just as she also had. Now, just as she, I am hopeful that someday I will be able to move into charity work with children.

Since that sunny afternoon in mid November of 2005, Rick and I have stayed in close contact. We have become friends. During his yearly visits out to Los Angeles, we meet for lunch each October, during which I feel as though Zita is there with us, smiling, as we catch up and reminisce about how she unconventionally brought us together.

Unlike Zita, who strongly believed in an afterlife, I'm not sure what my feelings are on life after death. However, her memory is present for me on an almost daily basis, and has given me a newfound reason for why

Liesl Ehardt in a playful shot for the author. Liesl "couldn't resist" this pose at the Egyptian Theatre in Los Angeles, October 20, 2009. PHOTO BY THE AUTHOR

I do what I do, and why I believe I was born to act, entertain, as well as to help and work with children, hopefully through a charity of my own.

Before Zita's death, she took on a different role, this time as writer of a mystical play titled, *And Then It Was Morning*. The plot ironically, centers around Ann Stratton, in a house where people are unknowingly ushered in as they die, and only Ann is aware of this. After reading it, I honestly

At home in 1986. PHOTO COURTESY OF ZITA JOHANN

feel that Ann's character is supposed to be Zita and that she placed herself in the role of the lead character so she could live on, only in another form, mirroring her belief in life after death.

In the end, despite the role one plays or how people enter and exit one's life, the road through life is filled with incredible highs and pesky lows, especially for an actor. I'm sure Zita also encountered all of this, in some form or other on her journey through life. When I find myself among those pesky lows, questioning not only myself, but also my occupation, Rick's book about Zita's story helps me push forward. Ultimately, I hope that my journey through life, both as an actor and with my future charity work, makes my cousin Zita proud.

SELECTED BIBLIOGRAPHY

Abramson, Abraham (Project manager), *The New York Times Film Reviews* (Volumes 1 & 2: 1913-1938, of) Six volumes; 1913-1968 (*The New York Times*, 1971).

Atkins, Rick, *Let's Scare 'Em!* (Grand Interviews and a Filmography of Horrific Proportions, 1930-1960) (Jefferson, North Carolina and London; McFarland and Company, Inc., 1997).

Brook-Shepherd, Gordon, *The Last Empress: The Life and Times of Zita of Austria-Hungary 1893-1989* (New York, London; Harper-Collins Publishers Ltd., 1991).

Clarens, Carlos, *An Illustrated History of the Horror Film* (New York; G.P. Putnam's Sons, 1967).

Edwards. Anne, *The DeMilles: An American Family* (New York; Harry N. Abrams, Inc., Publishers, 1988).

Falk, Byron A., *The New York Times Theatre Reviews* (10 Volumes: 1920-1970) (New York City; Arno Press, 1971).

Grobel, Lawrence, *The Hustons* (New York; Charles Scribner's Sons, Collier Macmillan, Inc., Canada, 1989).

Hanson, Patricia King (executive editor) and Gevinson Alan (associate editor), *The American Film Institute Catalog of Motion Pictures Produced in the United States* (Feature Films 1931-1940); (Berkeley and Los Angeles, California; University of California Press, 1993).

Houseman, John, *Unfinished Business: Memoirs (1902-1988)* (New York; Applause Theatre BookPublishers, 1989).

Johnston, Julia Michael, *Mary Baker Eddy: Her Mission and Triumph* (Boston, Massachusetts; The Christian Science Publishing Society, 1946).

Koszarski, Richard, *Hollywood Directors 1914-1940* (London, Oxford, New York: Oxford University Press, 1976).

Lamparski, Richard, *Whatever Became Of...? (Fourth Series)* (New York; Crown Publishers, Inc., 1973).

Meredith, Burgess, *So Far, So Good (A Memoir)* (Boston, New York, Toronto, London; LittleBrown and Company, 1994).

Riley, Philip J. (Editor), *The Mummy:(Volume 7) Original 1932 Shooting Script* (Absecon, New Jersey; MagicImage Filmbooks, 1989).

Smith, Cecil A. and Litton, Glenn, *Musical Comedy in America: From Black Crook to SouthPacific, From The King and I to Sweeney Todd* (New York; Routledge/Theatre Art Books; member of the Taylor & Francis Group; Subsequent Edition, January 7, 1987).

Tornabene, Lyn *Long Live the King: A Biography of Clark Gable* (New York; G.P. Putnam's Sons,1976).

Wolff, Geoffrey, *The Art of Burning Bridges: A Life of John O'Hara* (New York; Alfred A. Knopf,2003).

Yurka, Blanche, *Bohemian Girl: Blanche Yurka's Theatrical Life* (Athens; Ohio University Press,1970).

Zita at home in the early 1960s. PHOTO COURTESY OF ZITA JOHANN

APPENDIX

Stage

He Who Gets Slapped (1922)
Written by Leonid Andreyev.
Produced by Robert Milton.
Garrick Theatre (NY): January 9. 1922-June 1922*
The New York Times review — January 10, 1922 (page 15: column 1).
Zita Johann was understudy to actress Margalo Gillmore as Consuelo in summer tour production. David Manners a.k.a. Rauff Acklom and/or Michael Dawn for a short time, was understudy to Basil Sydney's Alfred Bezano during summer tour production only. John Rutherford played Alfred Bezano otherwise.
CAST: Philip Leigh *(Tilly)*, Edgar Stehli *(Polly)*, Ernest Cossart *(Briquet)*, Frank Reicher *(Mancini)*, Helen Westley *(Zinida)*, Martha-Bryan Allen *(Angelica)*, Helen Sheridan *(Estelle)*, Edwin R. Wolfe *(Francois /Conductor)*, Richard Bennett *(He)*, Henry Travers *(Jackson)*, Margalo Gillmore *(Consuelo)*, John Rutherford *(Alfred Bezano)*, Louis Calvert *(Baron Regnard)*, John Blair *(A Gentleman)*, Kathryn Wilson *(Wardrobe lady)*, Charles Cheltenham *(Usher)*, Philip Loeb *(Pierre)*, Renee Wilde *(A Sword Dancer)* Oliver Grymes *(Ballet Master)*, Dante Voltaire *(Thomas)*, Joan Clement *(A Snake Charmer)*, Richard Coolidge *(A Contortionist)*, Kenneth Lawton *(A Riding Master)* and Francis G. Sadtler *(A Juggler)*.

* Source: Internet Broadway Database. *Used with permission. (Applies to production dates only.)*

Peer Gynt (1923)
Written by Henrik Ibsen
Produced by Theodore Komisarjevsky
Garrick Theatre (NY): February 5, 1923-September 1923*
Translated by William Archer and Charles Archer
Music by Edvard Grieg
The New York Times review — February 6, 1923 (page 14: column 1).
Zita Johann was understudy to actress Selena Royle as Solveig during summer tour production. David Manners was understudy to William W. Griffith as Solveig's father in summer tour production.
CAST: Joseph Schildkraut *(Peer Gynt/His Son)*, Louise Closser Hale *(Aase, a peasant widow)*, Bertha Broad *(Ingrid)*, William Franklin *(Mads Moen/The Troll Chamberlain/and Fellah)*, Ellen Larned *(Bridegroom's Mother)*, Philip Leigh *(Bridegroom's Father/Troll Courtier/Trumpeterstrale / Peer's Son)*, Stanley G. Wood *(Asiak and a Smith/Troll Courtier/Mr. Cotton)*, Stanley Howlett *(Bride's father/Hussein/The Lean One)*, William M. Griffith *(Solveig's father/Troll Courtier)*, Elizabeth Zachary *(Solveig's Mother)*, Selena Royale *(Solveig)*, Francene Wouters *(Helga/and The Ugly Brat)*, C. Porter Hall *(Old Man of Hegstad)*, J. Andrew Johnson *(Another Old Man)*, Helen Westley *(The Troll King's Daughter)*, Dudley Digges *(The Troll King)*, William Franklin *(The Troll Chamberlain)*, Armina Marshall *(Kari)*, Albert Carroll *(Dancer)*, Edward G. Robinson *(Von Eberkopf)*, Romney Brent *(Thief)*, Alfred Alexandre *(Receiver)*, Charles Tagewell *(Officer)*, Lillebel Ibsen *(Anitra)* and Charles Halton *(Begriffenfeldt)*.

The Devil's Disciple (1923)
Written by George Bernard Shaw
Produced by The Theatre Guild (Philip Moeller)
Garrick Theatre (NY): April 23, 1923-October 1923*
The New York Times review — April 24, 1923 (page 24: column 1).
Zita Johann was understudy to actress Martha-Bryan-Allen as Essie. David Manners was again understudy to Basil Sydney as Richard Dudgeon during summer tour production.
CAST: Beverly Sitgreaves *(Mrs. Annie Primrose Dudgeon)*, Martha-Bryan Allen *(Essie)*, Gerald Hamer *(Christie)*, Moffat Johnston *(Anthony Anderson)*, Lotus Robb *(Judith Anderson)*, Alan MacAteer *(Lawyer Hawkins)*, Byron Russell *(William Dudgeon / Mr. Brudenell)*, Kathryn Wilson *(Mrs. William Dudgeon)*, Lawrence Cecil *(Titus Dudgeon)*, Maud

Ainslie (Mrs. Titus Dudgeon), *(Basil Sydney, (Richard Dudgeon)*, Roland Young *(General Burgoyne)* and Reginald Goode *(Major Swindon)*.

Shakespeare's As You Like It (1923)
Written by William Shakespeare
Produced by Robert Milton
48th Street Theatre (NY): April 23, 1923* (8 performances)
The New York Times review — April 24, 1923 (page 24: column 1).
Zita was understudy to Marjorie Rambeau as Rosalind. Rollo Peters was understudy to Ian Keith as Orlando and opened his own short-lived production of the play.
CAST: Albert Powers *(A Shepherd)*, Ian Keith *(Orlando)*, Arnold Lucy *(Adam)*, Jerome Lawler *(Oliver)*, Hal Higley *(Denis)*, Stanley Kalkhurst *(Charles)*, Marjorie Rambeau *(Rosalind)*, Margalo Gillmore *(Celia)*, Edgar Norton *(Le Beau)*, John Craig *(Frederick)*, Frank Arundel *(Amiens)*, A.E. Anson *(Jacques)*, J. Malcolm Dunn *(The Duke)*, William Williams *(Silvius)*, Hortense Alden *(Audrey)*, Gwynedd Vernon *(Phoebe)*, Percival Vivien *(William)* Ernest Lawford *(Touchstone)*, G. Anderson *(First Page)*, Norton Myers *(Second Page)*, Walter Abel (A Lord/Jacques De Bois) and Mercedes De Cordoba *(Hyman)*.

Man and the Masses (1924)
Written by Ernst Toller
Translated by Louis H. Untermeyer
Produced by The Theatre Guild
Garrick Theatre (NY): April-June 1924*
The New York Times review — April 15, 1924 (page 25: column 2).
Zita Johann as First Woman Prisoner.
CAST: Blanche Yurka *(The Woman)*, Ullrich Haupt *(The Man)*, Jacob Ben-Ami (The Nameless One/The Spirit of the Masses), Arthur Hughes *(The Companion)*, A.P. Kaye *(First Banker)*, William Franklin *(Second Banker)*, Erskine Sanford *(Third Banker/A Priest)*, Leonard Lean *(Fourth Banker)*, Barry Jones *(Fifth Banker/An Officer)*, Charles Tazewell *(Sixth Banker)*, John McGovern *(The Condemned One)*, Maurice McRae *(First Working Man)*, Allyn Joslyn (Second Working Man), Marling Chilton *(Third Working Man)*, Samuel Rosen *(Fourth Working Man)*, Pauline Moore *(A Working Woman)*, Mariette Hyde *(Second Woman Prisoner)* and Sidney Dexter *(Messenger Boy)*.

Dawn (1924)
Written by Tom Barry
Produced by Walter Vincent and Sidney Wilmer
Sam H. Harris Theatre (NY): November 1924 — January 1925*
The New York Times review — November 25, 1924 (page 27: column 1).
Zita Johann as Judith Slayton.
CAST: Howard Lang *(Matthew Slayton)*, Emma Dunn *(Mary Slayton)*, Helen Strickland (Margaret Slayton), Hartley Power *(Robert Carter)*, Richard Carlyle *(David)*, Perce R. Benton *(Mr. Marvin)*, William Williams *(Billy Randolph)*, Day Manson *("Speed" Farnum)*, William Morgan (Ely Robbins), Raymond Van Sickle *("Rabbitt" Trundell)*, Florence Peterson *(Jane Marvin)*, Camella Campbell *(Lula Maynard)*, Robert Montgomery *(Louis Rhodes)*, Elizabeth Allen *(Ann Perkins)*, Lee Smith *("Squeak" Maynard)* and Dorothy Tierney *(Cora Adams)*.

Aloma of the South Seas (1925)
Written by John B. Hymer and LeRoy Clemens
Lyric Theatre (NY): April-June 1925*
Produced by Carl Reed
Staged by A. H. Van Buren
The New York Times review — April 21, 1925 (page 18: column 1).
Zita Johann as Aloma. Vivienne Osborne replaced Zita Johann, due to poor health after several performances.
CAST: Marion Barney *(Mrs. Ridgely)*, Denis Gurney *(Reginald Ridgely)*, Penelope Hubbard *(Taula)*, Priscilla Knowles *(Hina)*, Vivienne Osborne *(Aloma)*, Arthur Barry *(Sumner Ridgely)*, Ben Johnson *(Andy Taylor)*, Walter Glass *(Shorty)*, Arthur R. Vinton *(Red Malloy)*. George Gaul *(Nuitane)*, William Gargan *(Boano)*, Al. Roberts *(Hongi)*, Frank Thomas *(Bob Holden)*, Anne Morrison *(Sylvia Templeton)*, Richard Gordon *(Van Templeton)*, Andrea McKinnon *(Luana)*, Lola De Rome *(Moana)*, Dorotha Denise *(Unola)* and Korola Alleneve *(Nahoma)*.

Grand Street Follies (1925)
(A Revue in two acts and ten scenes.)
Book and Lyrics by Agnes Morgan
Featured songs and lyrics by Marc Loebell and Dan Walker
Choreography by Albert Carroll
The Neighborhood Playhouse (NY): June 18, 1925-November 1925*

The New York Times review — June 19, 1925 (page 24: column1).
CAST: Edgar Kent, Albert Carroll, Whitford Kane, Irene Lewisohn, Helen Arthur, Esther Mitchell, Marc Lobell, Dorothy Sands, Paula Trueman, Junius Matthews, Vera Allen, Ian Maclaren, Otto Hulicus, Lily Lubell, Michel Barroy, and Thomas Tilton. Featuring: William Beyer, George Bratt, Edla Frankau, George Heller, George Hoag, Zita Johann, Helen Mack, Philip Mann, Lewis McMichael, Harold Minjer, Mae Noble, Madeline Ross, Ann Schmidt, J. Blake Scott, Lois Shore, Sadie Sussman, Blanche Talmud, Allen Vincent, Dan Walker and Polaire Weissmann.

Drift (1925) (An off-Broadway production)
Written by Maurice V. Samuels
Produced and Directed by Hyman Adler
Cherry Lane Playhouse: November 24, 1925 (two week run)
The New York Times review — November 25, 1925 (page 15: column 3).
Zita Johann as Zita Karolyi.
CAST: Edward Eliscu *(Roberts)*, Camilla Dalberg *(Marya)*, Wilbur DeRouge *(Bones)*, Harold Goulden *(Jose)*, Hyman Adler *(Rigo Karolyi)*, Chancellor Warden *(Seaton)*, Adelaide M. Chase *(Vivienne Ranger)*, Wall Spence *(Ralph Clark)*, Cecile Cummings *(Mrs. Ranger)*, F, Karl Stall *(Henry Clark)*, Katherine Cavalli *(Mrs. Marston)* and Charles Seel *(Mr. Marston)*.

Merchants of Glory (1925)
Written by Marcel Pagnol and Paul Nivoix
Produced by The Theatre Guild
Guild Theatre (NY): December 14, 1925-January 1926*
The New York Times review — December 15, 1925 (page 28: column 3).
Zita Johann was used briefly as an understudy to Armina Marshall.
CAST: Helen Westley *(Madame Blanchet)* Betty Linley *(Yvonne)*, Armina Marshall (Germaine Blanchet), Lee Baker *(Grandel)*, Augustin Duncan *(Bachelet)*, George Nash *(Pigal)*, Philip Loeb *(A Man /The Usher)*, Stanley G. Wood *(Secretary to the Prefect / Secretary to Deputy Bachelet)*, Lowden Adams *(Lieutenant Colonel Blancard)*, Charles Halton *(Richebon)*, Jose Ruben *(Monsieur Denis)*, Edward Fielding and *(Comte de Leauville)*.

The Goat Song (1926)
Written by Franz Werfel
Translated by Ruth Langner
Produced by The Theatre Guild
Guild Theatre (The August Wilson Theatre, NY):
January 25, 1926-March 1926*
The New York Times review — January 26, 1926 (page 18: column 1).
Zita Johann as Kruna.
CAST: George Gaul *(Gospodar Stevan Milie)*, William Ingersoll (Gospodar Jevrem Veslie / Scavenger), Blanche Yurka *(Mirko's Mother)*, Judith Lowry *(Stanja's Mother)*, Lynn Fontanne *(Stanja)*, Dwight Frye *(Mirko)*, Helen Westley *(Babka)*, Lorna McLean *(A Maid)*, Philip Loeb *(Young Serving Man)*, Albert Bruning *(Physician)*, Bela Blau *(Messenger)*, Erskine Sanford *(Starsina / Priest)*, Harold Clurman *(Clerk)*, Edward Fielding *(The American)*, Herbert Yost *(Teiterlik)* Edward G. Robinson *(Reb Feiwel)*, Frank Reicher *(Bogoboj)*, Alfred Lunt *(Juvan)*, Anthony Andre *(An Old Man)*, Martin Wolfson *(Innkeeper)*, House Baker Jameson (Bashi Bazook), and William Ingersoll *(The Hangman)*.

The Cradle Song (1927)
Written by Gregorio Martinez Sierra and Maria Martinez Sierra
Translated by John Garrett Underhill
Costume and Set Design by G. E. Calthrop
Directed by Eva Le Gallienne
Civic Repertory Theatre (NY): January 24-March 1927*
The New York Times review (of the Civic Repertory Theatre first run) — January 25, 1927 (page 18: column 2).
A national road tour began in Hartford, Connecticut — September 5, 1927, lasting twenty-three weeks, ending in California in July 1928 with Zita Johann as Teresa.
The national road tour cast included: Mary Shaw, Alexander Kirkland, Harry Davenport, Phyllis Rankin, Mary Hone, Fanny Davenport. Virginia Gregori, and Elizabeth Chester.

Machinal (1928)
Written by Sophie Treadwell
Produced and Directed by Arthur Hopkins
Plymouth Theatre (NY): September 7, 1928-November 24, 1928*

The New York Times review — September 8, 1928 (page 10: column 3).
Zita Johann as The Young Woman (in her New York Stage triumph in 91 performances).
CAST: Millicent Green *(A Telephone Girl)*, Grace Atwell *(A Stenographer)*, Leopold Badia (A Filing Clerk), Conway Washburn *(An Adding Clerk)*, Jean Adair *(A Mother)*, George Stillwell (A Husband), Otto Frederick *(A Bellboy)*, Nancy Allan *(A Nurse)*, Monroe Childs *(A Doctor)*, Hal K. Dawson *(A Young Man)* Zenaide Ziegfeld *(A Girl)*, Jess Sidney *(A Man)*, Clyde Stork (A Boy), Clark Gable *(A Man)*, Hugh M. Hite *(Another Man)*, John Hanley *(A Waiter)*, John Waters *(A Judge)*, John Connery *(A Lawyer for Defense)*, James MacDonald (A Lawyer for the Prosecution), Otto Frederick *(A Court Reporter)*, John Hanley *(A Bailiff)*, Conway Washburn (A Reporter), Hugh M. Hite *(Second Reporter)*, Hal K. Dawson *(Third Reporter)*, John Hanley (A Jailer), Mrs. Charles Willard *(A Matron)*, and Charles Kennedy *(A Priest)*.

Troyka (1930)
Written by Lula Vollmer
Adapted by Hungarian Imre Fazekas
Produced by Laura D. Wilck
Hudson Theatre (NY): April 1930 (15 performances)
The New York Times review — April 2, 1930 (page 32: column 6).
Zita Johann as Natascha.
CAST: Weldon Heyburn *(The Captain)*, Albert Van Dekker [later Albert Dekker] *(Ivan)*, William Parke *(First Soldier)*, Jack Roseleigh *(Semion)*, Philip Leigh *(Avinov)*, George Casselberry *(Izeff)*, Ray Earles *(Selivenoff)*, Martin Noble *(Bogulieff)*, Lewis Milne *(Koska)*, George Bratt *(Bolotoff)*, Frank Dae *(Vassely)*, Eugene Brominski *(Pushkin)*, William G. Edwards *(Gustoff)*, William House *(Sienko)*, Tony Mack *(Second Soldier)*, Edward Hartford *(Kuroff)*, Walter Dreher *(Dymov)*, Mel Tyler *(A Man)*.

The Lake (1930)
Written by John Houseman and Joan Wolfe *(a.k.a. Zita Johann)*.
Produced by Stockbridge Players
Berkshire Theatre *(Pittsfield, Massachusetts)*: August 11-16, 1930
STARRING: Zita Johann, Alexander Kirkland, Molly Pearson, Hugh Buckler, Leo Carroll, George Couloris, Evelyn Beresford, Margaret Love, Francesca Bruning, George Graham, and Frederick Voight.

Uncle Vanya (1930)
Written by Anton Chekov
Translated by Rose Caylor
Produced and Staged by Jed Harris
Costumes by Fania Mindell and Herman Patrick Tappe
Scenic Design by Jo Mielziner
Booth Theatre (NY): September 22, 1930-October 6, 1930*
The New York Times article — September 23, 1930 (page 30: column 3).
Zita Johann as Solya Alenandrovna/Sonya. Zita replaced Joanna Roos, as Sonia, in this two week run and road tour in Boston, Chicago, Pittsburgh and Newark.
CAST: Lillian Gish *(Yelena Andreyevna)*, Osgood Perkins *(Mikhail Ivovich Astrov)*, Walter Connelly *(Ivan Petrovich Voinitsky—Vanya)*, Eugene Powers (Alexander Vladimirovich Serebryakov), Isabel Irving *(Maria Vasilyevna Voinitskaya)*, Kate Mayhew *(Maryina / Nanny)*, Eduardo Ciannelli *(Ilya Ilyich Telegin / Waffles)* and Harold Johnsrud *(Servant)*.

Tomorrow and Tomorrow (1931)
Written by Philip Barry
Produced and Staged by Gilbert Miller
Henry Miller's Theatre (NY): January 13, 1931-July 1931*
(The play later toured in the fall of 1931 in Baltimore, Chicago, Boston, Cleveland, Pittsburgh, Kansas City and Minneapolis.)
The New York Times review — January 14, 1931 (page 26: column 3).
Zita Johann as Eve Redman.
CAST: Harvey Stephens *(Gail Redman)*, Marie Bruce *(Ella)*, Herbert Marshall *(Nicholas Hay)*, Osgood Perkins *(Samuel Gillespie)*, Adele Schuyler *(Jane)*, John T. Doyle *(Walter Burke)*, Drew Price *(Christian Redman)*, Eileen Byron *(Mary)*, Mary Elizabeth Forbes *(Miss Frazer)* and Alice MacIntosh *(Miss Blake)*.

Waltz in Fire (1934)
Written by David Hertz and Dorothy Joseph
Producers — Sidney Harmon and James R. Ullman
Masque Theatre scheduled opening, October 29, 1934 (known today as The John Golden Theatre).
The three-act play was withdrawn before presentation.
The cast was to include Zita Johann, Tom Powers, Howard Phillips and Eduardo Cianelli.

Panic (1935)
Written by Archibald MacLiesh (Librarian of Congress 1939-1944)
Choral movement designed by Martha Graham
Produced by Phoenix Theatre Inc. (Nathan Zatkin and John Houseman)
Imperial Theatre (NY): March 14, 1935-March 15, 1935*
(Three performances)
The New York Times review — March 16, 1935 (page 18: column 4).
Zita Johann as Ione.
CAST: Rose McClendon *(An Old Woman)*, Russell Collins *(A Man)*, Harold McGee *(A Man)*, Joanna Roos *(A Girl)*, Gerrit Kraber *(A Man)*, Bernard Zanville *(A Young Man)*, Eva Langbord *(A Young Girl)*, Paula Trueman *(A Woman)*, Karl Swenson *(A Young Man)*, Orson Welles *(McGafferty)*, George Glass *(Immelman)*, Clifford Heckinger *(Banker)*, Gordon Nelson *(Banker)*, Walter Coy *(Banker)*, Joseph Eggenton *(Banker)*, Edward Mann *(Guard)*, Abner Biberman *(Unemployed)*, William Challee *(Unemployed)*, Albert Lewis *(Unemployed)*, Paul Genge *(Unemployed)*, Wesley Addy *(Unemployed)*, Robin Batcheller *(Unemployed)*, Harold Johnsrud *(Blind Man)* and Richard Whorf *(Griggs)*. CHORUS MALE: Edward Mann, Paul Genge, Wesley Addy, Albert Lewis, Arthur Singer, Yisrol Libman, John O'Shaughnessy and Jerome Thor. CHORUS FEMALE: Elizabeth Morison, Dierdre Hurst, La Verne Pine, Virginia Welles, Amelia Barleon, Elizabeth Timberman, Osceola Archer, Beatrice Pons, Lucille Strudwick, Mary Tarcai, Margaret Craven, Margot Loines and Elaine Basil.

Seven Keys to Baldpate (1935)
Adapted by George M. Cohan from the novel by Earl Derr Biggers
Produced by The Players Club
Staged by Sam Forrest
National Theatre (today known as the Nederlander Theatre, NY):
May 27, 1935-June 1, 1935
The New York Times review — May 28, 1935 (page 30: column 2).
Zita Johann as Mary Norton.
CAST: *(Foreword written by A.E. Thomas told by actor Otis Skinner)* WITH: Francis Conlan (Elijah Quinby), Josephine Hull *(Mrs. Quinby)*, George M. Cohan *(William Hallowell McGee)*, Ernest Glendinning *(John Bland)*, Irene Rich *(Mrs. Rhodes)*, James T. Powers *(Peters)*, Ruth Weston *(Myra Thornhill)*, Ben Lackland *(Lou Max)*, Edward J. MacNamara *(Jim Cargan)*, George Christie *(Thomas Hayden)*, James Kirkwood *(Jiggs Kennedy)*, Percy Moore *(First Policeman)*, Allen Delano *(Second Policeman)* and Walter Hampton *(Hal Bentley)*.

Flight Into China (1939) (An-off-Broadway production)
Written by Pearl S. Buck (her first play).
Sets by Peggy Clark
Directed by Lee Strasberg
Paper Mill Playhouse (Milburn, New Jersey): September 11, 1939 (two week run).
The New York Times review — September 12, 1939 (page 28: column 1).
Zita Johann [in her return to the stage after four years] as Leah, a Jewess.
CAST: Tonio Selwart *(Reinhardt)*, Uta Hagen *(Mollie Chang)*, Jose Ferrer *(Curio Vendor)*, Thelma Schnee *(Peony)*, Wesley Addy *(David)*, Albert Bergh *(Ezra)*, Grace Coppin *(Madame Ezra)*, and Ruth Tobin *(Kwei Lan)*.

The Burning Deck (1940)
Written by Andrew Rosenthal
Produced by Jack Small
Staged by Robert Milton
Maxine Elliott's Theatre (NY): March 1, 1940-March 2, 1940*
(Three performances)
The New York Times review — March 2, 1940 (page 9: column 2).
Zita Johann as Nina Brandt.
CAST: Dennis Hoey *(Captain Applegate)*, Ivan Triesault *(Nicholas)*, Alfred A. Hesse *(Don Juan)*, Russell Hardie *(Jeffrey Brandt)*, Marion Mill *(Baroness Maude De Rossi)*, Gregory Gaye (Niki De Vobourg), Onslow Stevens *(Rex Wolfson)*, Edith King *(Margaret Eaves)*, Vera Allen *(Cornelia Lauren)*, George Lloyd *(Roby Lauren)*, Frank Dowling *(Raphael)*, Mary Howes (Ava Andrus) and George Calvert *(A Native Boy)*.

Broken Journey (1942)
Written by Andrew Rosenthal
Produced by Martin Burton
Staged by Arthur Hopkins
Henry Miller's Theatre (NY): June 23, 1942-July 11, 1942*
The New York Times review — June 24, 1942 (page 22: column 2).
Zita Johann as Rachel Thatcher Arlen.
CAST: Tom Powers *(Hale Thatcher)*, Helen Carew *(Essie)*, Phyllis Povah *(Belle Newell)* Warner Anderson *(Dan Hardeen)*, Edith Atwater *(Christina Landers)*, Joan McSweeney *(Trina)*, and Gordon Nelson *(Howard Newell)*.

Special Stage Performances

Ellery Queen Radio Mystery (March 27, 1940)
Benefit party for the Red Cross at the Rockland Theatre (location: 36 North Broadway, Nyack, NY).
CAST: Zita Johann. Helen Hayes, Will Geer, and Harry Bellaver. (The Rockland Theatre opened in 1928 and closed in 1967. It was razed in 1978.)

Salute Tomorrow (1940, An Off Broadway play)
Written by Marjorie Leonard
County Theatre in Suffern, New York opening: July 25, 1940.
STARRING: Zita Johann, McKay Morris, Hugh Marlowe and Richard Taber.

Rockland Riot (August 22, 1942, One night only.)
Written by Maxwell Anderson.
Directed and Produced by Larry Adler & Bernard Shedd at Clarkstown Country Club in South Nyack, NY; Outdoor Theatre.
A twelve-act celebrity-variety benefit for the Russian War Relief. In one act, Zita Johann played Queen Elizabeth to Helen Hayes' Mary of Scotland. Other cast members included, Ed Wynn, Mary MacArthur *(12 year-old daughter of Helen Hayes and Charles MacArthur)*, Hesper Anderson *(8 year-old daughter of Gertrude Anderson)*, John Hoystradt, Jane Froman, Will Geer, Lotte Lenya, Kurt Weill, John Wray, Kerry Stuart, Harry Bellaver, Alfred Dixon and Tily Losch.

One Woman Show...
Zita Johann as: *Lady Macbeth, Queen Gertrude, Juliet, Katherine ("Taming of the Shrew")* and *Medea*, which were performed at the Rockland Theatre soon after "Rockland Riot."

Battle for Heaven (1969)
Written by Michael O'Shaughnessy and Randolf Carter
Directed and designed by Brad Gromelski
Technical director — Jonathan Lawson
Produced by the Seton Players
Elizabeth Seton College (October 8-11, Yonkers, New York)

The Dobbs Ferry Sentinel review — October 9, 1969 *("News of the Muses" by Doris Krauss).*
CAST (in order of appearance): Dwight Marfield *(Calvin Frye)*, MaryAnn Barrett (Molly Peterson), DeNola Pyrch *(Mary Tomlinson)*, Cathy Fediw *(Laura Leonard)*, Zita Johann (Mary Baker Eddy), Pamela Rivers *(Mrs. Augusta Stetson)*; Melanie O'Neill *(First Practitioner)*, Meg Baker *(Second Practitioner)*, Bill Newell *(First Reporter)*, Ann Marie Bendetto (Second Reporter), Robert Rohan *(Third Reporter)*, Edward J. Sliva *(George Glover)*, Alan Brock (Mr. Frank Streeter), William Young *(Senator Chandler)*, Cecil Kersten *(Judge Aldrich)*, Anthony Di Caprio *(Dr. Jelly)*, Lon Waterford *(Mr. Strickler)*, Katherine Cantillon *(Mrs. Babcock)*, and Angela De Marzo *(Lucy Pierce)*.

Motion Pictures

The Struggle (1931)
DIRECTOR: D.W. Griffith.
D.W. Griffith, Incorporated (Copyright November 25, 1931). Distributed by United Artists Corporation: February 6, 1932; New York opening, December 10, 1931.
ASSISTANT DIRECTOR: Richard A. Blaydon.
STORY AND SCREENPLAY: Anita Loos and John Emerson.
PHOTOGRAPHY: Joseph Ruttenberg.
FILM EDITOR: Barney Rogan.
MUSIC EFFECTS: Philip Scheib.
MAKEUP: Edward Scanlon.
PRODUCTION MANAGER: Raymond A. Clune.
PRODUCTION ADVISOR: A. Griffith Grey.
STILL PHOTOGRAPHY: Frank Kirby.
PRODUCTION DATES: July 6-August 14, 1931 at Audio Cinema Studios, Bronx, New York. *(Original running time: 87 minutes.)*
The New York Times review — December 11, 1931, page 35: column 1. *Zita Johann as Florrie Wilson.*
CAST: Hal Skelly *(Jimmie Wilson)*, Charlotte Winters *(Nina)*, Evelyn Baldwin *(Nan Wilson)*, Jackson Halliday *(Johnny Marshall)* and Edna Hagen *(Mary Wilson)*, Claude Cooper *(Sam)*, Arthur Lipson *(Cohen)*, Charles Richman *(Mr. Craig)*, Helen Mack *(A catty girl)*, Scott Moore *(Al, a gigolo)*, Dave Manley *(Tony, a mill worker)*.

Tiger Shark (1932)
DIRECTOR: Howard Hawks.
First National Pictures, Inc., controlled by Warner Bros. Pictures, Inc. (Copyright September 3, 1932); Distributed by First National Pictures, Inc., The Vitaphone Corporation, September 24, 1932.
ASSISTANT DIRECTOR: Richard Rosson.
Based on the original story "Tuna" by Houston Branch.
SCREENPLAY: Wells Root (and an uncredited John Lee Mahin and Howard Hawks).
PHOTOGRAPHY: Tony Gaudio (Sequences filmed on location at Catalina Island).
ART DIRECTION: Jack Okey.
MARINE SUPERVISION BY Captain Guy Silva.
FILM EDITOR: Thomas Pratt.
GOWNS BY Orry-Kelly.
VITAPHONE ORCHESTRA CONDUCTOR: Leo F. Forbstein.
SOUND: C.A. Riggs and A.D. Mair.
STILL PHOTOGRAPHER: Mac Julian.
Production dates: April 28, 1932-June 24, 1932. *(Original running time: 80 minutes.)*
The New York Times review — September 23, 1932, page 22: column 2 *Zita Johann as Quita Silva.*
CAST: Edward G. Robinson *(Mike Mascarenhas)*, Richard Arlen *(Pipes Boley)*, Leila Bennett *(Muggsey, the barber)*, J. Carroll Naish *(Tony)*, Vince Barnett *(Fishbone)*, William Ricciardi *(Manuel Silva)*.

The Mummy (1932)
DIRECTOR: Karl Freund.
Universal Pictures Corporation; Carl Laemmle President (Copyright December 14, 1932; title credit on the film itself bears a COPYRIGHT MCMXXXIII by Universal Pictures Corp.). Distributed by Universal Pictures Corporation, December 22, 1932.
SCREENPLAY: John L. Balderston.
STORY: Richard Schayer and Nina Wilcox Putnam.
PHOTOGRAPHY: Charles Stumar (and Jerry Ash).
CAMERA OPERATOR: James Drought.
ASSISTANT CAMERAMAN: Art Glouner.
MUSIC: James Dietrich (Western Electric Noiseless Recording).
SPECIAL EFFECTS: John P. Fulton.

FILM EDITOR: Milton Carruth.
STILL PHOTOGRAPHER: Fred Archer.
PRODUCTION DATES: mid-September to October, 1932. *(Original running time, excluding other cuts made: 78 minutes).*
The New York Times review — January 7, 1933, page 11: column 2
Zita Johann as Helen Grosvenor a.k.a. Princess Anck-es-en-Amon.
CAST: Boris Karloff (*Ardath Bey a.k.a. Imhotep*), David Manners *(Frank Whemple)*, Arthur Byron *(Sir Joseph Whemple)*, Edward Van Sloan *(Doctor Muller)*, Bramwell Fletcher *(Ralph Norton)*, Noble Johnson *(The Nubian)*, Kathryn Byron *(Frau Muller)*, Leonard Mudie *(Professor Pearson)*, James Crane *(The Pharaoh)* Henry Victor *(The Saxon Warrior a.k.a. Marion)* Arnold Gray *(Knight)*, Tony Marlow *(Inspector)*, Eddie Kane *(Doctor)*.

Luxury Liner (1933)
DIRECTOR: Lothar Mendes.
Paramount Productions, Incorporated. A B.P. Schulberg Production (Copyright February 3, 1933). Distributed by Paramount Produuctions, Inc., February 3, 1933.
Based on the novel *Die Überfahrt* by Gina Kaus, translated by Otto Frederick Theis (New York, 1932).
SCREENPLAY: Gene Markey and Kathryn Scola.
PHOTOGRAPHY: Victor Milner.
ASSISTANT CAMERAMAN: Guy Roe.
CAMERA OPERATOR: William Mellor.
SOUND: Western Electric Noiseless Recording.
FILM EDITOR: Eda Warren.
STILL PHOTOGRAPHER: William E. Thomas
PRODUCTION DATES: not available. *(Original running time: 70 minutes.)*
The New York Times review: February 3, 1933, page 21: column 3.
Zita Johann as Miss Morgan.
CAST: George Brent *(Dr. Karl Bernhard)*, Vivienne Osborne (*Sybil Bernhard*), Alice White *(Milli Lensch)*, Verree Teasdale *(Luise Marheim)*, Frank Morgan (*Alex Stevanson*), C. Aubrey Smith *(Edward Thorndyke)*. Henry Wadsworth *(Fritz)*, Wallis Clark (*Dr. Veith*), Billy Bevan *(Schultz)*, Theodor von Eltz *(Exl)*, Barry Norton *(Prince Vladimir Gleboff)*, Henry Victor *(Baron von Luden)*, Edith Yorke *(Mrs. Webber)*, Christian Rub *(Peasant Father)*, William Mahlon *(Baby)*.

The Man Who Dared: An Imaginative Biography (1933)
DIRECTOR: Hamilton MacFadden.
Fox Film Corporation (Copyright June 30, 1933). Distributed by Fox Film Corp., July 14, 1933.
ORIGINAL SCREENPLAY: Dudley Nichols and Lamarr Trotti.
PHOTOGRAPHY: Arthur Miller.
ASSISTANT CAMERAMAN: Bill Abbott and Milton Gold.
SECOND CAMERAMAN: Joe La Shelle.
SETS: Duncan Cramer.
FILM EDITOR: Al DeGaetano.
COSTUMES BY Royer.
MUSICAL DIRECTOR: Samuel Kaylin.
SOUND: E.F. Grossman (Western Electric Noiseless Recording).
PRODUCTION DATE: mid-May 1933. *(Original running time: 75 minutes.)*
The New York Times review: September 9, 1933, page 9: column 3.
Zita Johann as Teena Pavelic.
CAST: Preston Foster *(Jan Novak)*, Joan Marsh *(Joan Novak)*, Irene Biller *(Tereza Novak)*, Clifford Jones *(Dick)*, June Vlasek *(Barbara Novak)*, Leon Wykoff [later Leon Ames] *(Yosef Novak)*, Douglas Cosgrove *(Dan Foley)*, Douglass Dumbrille *(Judge Collier)*, Frank Sheridan *(Senator John McGuinness)*, Leonid Snegoff *(Victor Posilipo)*, Elsie Larson *(Ruzena Novak)*, Lita Chevret *(Miss Rainey)*, Vivien Reid *(Ronda)*, Matt McHigh *(Karel)*, Jay Ward *(Jan Novak, the boy)*.

The Sin of Nora Moran (1933)
DIRECTOR: Phil Goldstone.
Majestic Pictures Corporation. Distributed by Majestic Pictures Corp., December 13, 1933.
CO-DIRECTOR: Howard Christy.
ASSISTANT DIRECTOR: J. McClosky.
Based on a play by Willis Maxwell Goodhue.
SCREENPLAY: Francis Hyland.
PHOTOGRAPHY: Ira Morgan.
ART DIRECTION: Ralph Oberg.
FILM EDITOR: Otis Garrett.
MUSICAL SUPERVISOR: Abe Meyer.
ORCHESTRA DIRECTION: S.K. Wineland.
SOUND ENGINEER: Earl Crain (RCA Victor "High Fidelity" Sound System).

PRODUCTION DATE: June 1933 at the Mack Sennett Studio. *(Original running time: 65 minutes.)*
The New York Times review: December 13, 1933, page 29: column 3.
Zita Johann as Nora Moran.
CAST: Cora Sue Collins *(Nora Moran as a child)*, Alan Dinehart *(the District Attorney John Grant)*, Paul Cavanaugh *(Governor Dick Crawford)*, Claire DuBrey *(the Governor's wife Edith Crawford)*, John Milijan *(Paulino)*, Henry B. Walthall *(Father Ryan)*, Sarah Padden *(Mrs. Watts)*, Aggie Herring *(Mrs. Moran)*, Otis Harlan *(Mr. Moran)*, With: Ann Brody, Harvey Clark, and Sid Saylor.

Grand Canary (1934)
DIRECTOR: Irving Cummings.
Fox Film Corporation (Copyright July 17, 1934). Distributed by Fox Film Corp., July 27, 1934.
Based on the novel Grand Canary by A.J. Cronin.
SCREENPLAY: Ernest Pascal.
CONTRIBUTING WRITERS: David Hertz, Dudley Nichols, Keene Thompson, Clementine Galloway, Gladys Unger and Humphrey Pearson.
PHOTOGRAPHY: Bert Glennon.
CAMERA OPERATOR: Don Anderson.
ASSISTANT CAMERAMEN: Lou Kunkel and Roger Sherman.
SETS: Max Parker.
FILM EDITOR: Jack Murray.
GOWNS: Rita Kaufman.
MUSICAL DIRECTOR: Louis De Francesco.
SOUND: S.C. Chapman (Western Electric Noiseless Recording)
UNIT MANAGER: Earl Rettig.
STILL PHOTOGRAPHER: Emmett Schoenbaum.
SONG: "El amor es una flor," music by Cyril J. Mockridge, English lyrics by Monte Howard, Spanish lyrics by José López Rubio.
Production dates: mid-April to early May, 1934. *(Original running time: 78 minutes.)*
The New York Times review: July 20, 1934, page 11: column 1.
Zita Johann as Suzan Tranter.
CAST: Warner Baxter *(Dr. Harvey Leith)*, Madge Evans (*Lady Mary Fielding*), Marjorie Rambeau *(Daisy Hemingway)*, Roger Imhof *(Jimmie Corcoran)*, H.B. Warner *(Dr. Ismay)*, Barry Norton *(Robert Tranter)*, Juliette Compton *(Elissa Baynham)*, Gilbert Emery *(Captain Renton)*,

John Rogers *(Trout)*, Gerald Rogers *(Steward)*, Desmond Roberts *(Purser)*, Carrie Daumery *(Marquesa)*, Rosa Rey *(Manuella)*, Harrington Reynolds *(First quartermaster)*, Rodolfo Hoyos *(Singer)*, Alan Sanford *(Flower vendor)*, George Regas *(El Dazo)*, Pedro Regas and Chris Pin Martin *(Henchmen)*, Sam Appel *(Bartender)*, Charles Stevens *(Cab driver)*, Douglas Gordon *(Postman)*, Keith Kenneth *(Michael Fielding)*. With: Alphonse DuBois, Chito Alonzo, and B. Fuente.

Raiders of the Living Dead (1986)
DIRECTOR Samuel M. Sherman.
Independent-International Pictures. Distributed by Independent-International Pictures (Copyright 1986).
EXECUTIVE PRODUCER: Charles Baldwin.
PRODUCED BY Dan Q. Kennis.
SCREENPLAY: Sherman Piper.
PHOTOGRAPHY (Duart color): Douglas Meltzer.
FILM EDITOR: John Donaldson.
MUSIC COORDINATOR: Tim Ferrante.
PRODUCTION DESIGN: Ruth Seidman.
ASSOCIATE PRODUCER-ASSISTANT DIRECTOR: David Weisman.
PRODUCTION MANAGER: Timothy Speidel.
MAKEUP EFFECTS: Scott Suger.
"INCEPTIVE EFFECTS AND DIRECTION:" Brett Piper (who originally began making the movie in 1983).
(Original running time: 83 minutes.)
Presentation of a Cineronde-Canada production. US premiere on New York television, November 3, 1989.
Variety review November 29, 1989, p. 32.
Zita Johann as the Librarian.
CAST: Robert Deveau *(Morgan Randall)*, Donna Asali *(Shelly)*, Scott Schwartz *(Jonathan)*, Bob Allen *(Dr. Carstairs)* Bob Sacchetti *(Man in Black)*, Corri Burt *(Michelle)*. With: Leonard Corman, Christine Farish, Nino Rigali and Barbara Patterson.

Radio

Captain Applejack (October 18, 1936)
Lux Radio Theatre on the Air (CBS Radio).
Zita Johann as Anna Valeska. Directed by Frank Woodruff.

The Winged Victory (March 6, 1939)
CBS Radio Workshop.
Zita Johann as Joan. Directed by Brewster Morgan.

The Trojan Women (December 18, 1940)
CBS Radio Workshop.
Zita Johann as Andromache. Produced by John Houseman.

John's Other Wife (1936-1942)
NBC Radio.
The show aired from September 1936, until March 1942. Zita Johann played intermittent characters between 1939 and 1941. Produced by Frank and Anne Hummert (pioneers in creating radio soap operas during the 1930s and 40s).

We Are Always Young (January 1941 until November 22, 1941)
NBC Radio.
Another in a run of first radio soap operas. It was produced out of WOR in New York City. Zita Johann was in the supporting cast. Produced and directed by Robert Lewis Shayon.

Machinal (June 7, 1944)
Arthur Hopkins Presents (NBC Radio).
Zita Johann reprised her role as The Young Woman. Directed by Wynn Wright.

Bill of Divorcement (September 13, 1944)
Arthur Hopkins Presents (NBC Radio).
Zita Johann as Sydney Fairfield. Directed by Wynn Wright.

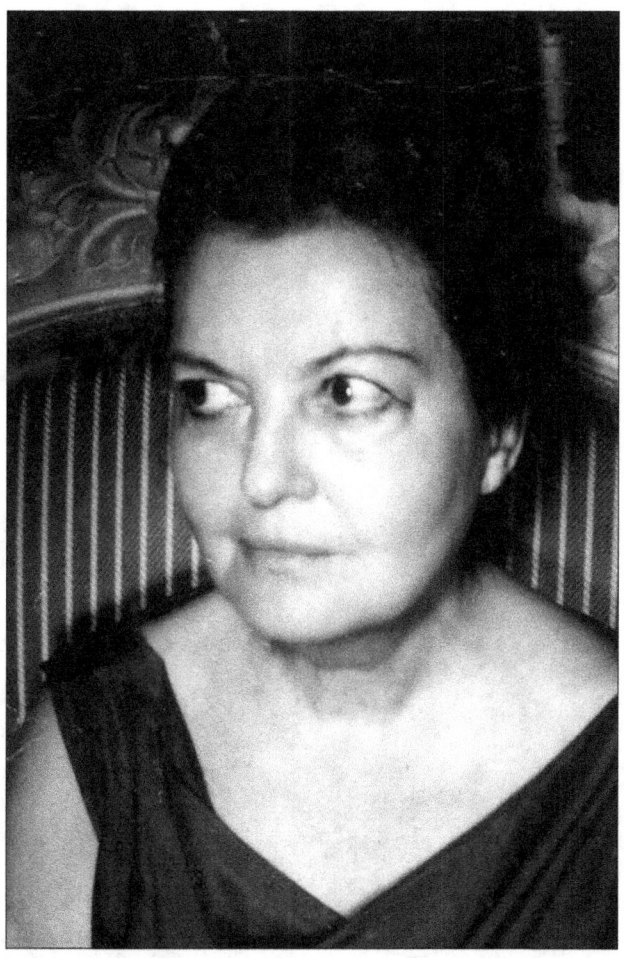

Zita sent this photo to the author in 1989 suggesting to place in his wallet. An inscription reads, "To Rick, with love, Zita."

NOTES

Chapter 1: *Epiphany*

1. The book entitled, *Whatever Became Of...?* was the fourth in a long series of biographical compilations consisting of then and now photographs of celebrated persons. Written by Richard Lamparski, Zita Johann is featured on pages 182 and 183.

2. Rockland County is located in the U.S. state of New York, 12 miles north-northwest of New York City. The name comes from "rocky land," an early description of the area given by settlers. Rockland is New York's southernmost county west of the Hudson River. It is suburban in nature, with a considerable amount of designated scenic parkland. Rockland County is divided into five towns: Clarkstown, Haverstraw, Orangetown, Ramapo, and Stony Point. There are nineteen incorporated villages in Rockland County, twelve of which are located at least partially in the town of Ramapo. There are no villages in the town of Stony Point. West Nyack is one of 25 unincorporated hamlets in Rockland County. West Nyack is in the Town of Clarkstown Rockland County, New York, located north of Central Nyack, east of Nanuet, with is south of Valley Cottage and west of Upper Nyack.

3. Astara is an esoteric non-profit religious institution and publishing organization based on the western mystery tradition. Earlyne and Robert Chaney founded Astara in 1951. Administration has since been passed to their daughter, Sita. Its headquarters are located in Rancho Cucamonga, California. Astara's teachings are primarily drawn on sources from Spiritualism, Theosophy, and Ancient Egypt *(Reference.com)*

4. Zita Johann particularly wanted to share her interests regarding two women in European history sharing her first name…"First, there was Saint Zita, the patron saint of maids, domestic servants, and of lost keys. You'll read about her. She was not complicated in the least. You'll understand dear. She considered that God assigned her employment to her. She always rose hours before the rest of the Fatinelli family whom she was employed for forty-eight years. The story was related one morning in church about Saint Zita. She was giving her own food to the poor. In leaving her chore of baking bread and having prayed as she did each morning, claimed to have found angels in the Fatinelli kitchen baking bread for her. Her feast day in the Church is April 27 [1272], the day Zita peacefully passed away in the Fatinelli house. She was sixty. To this day, families bake a loaf of bread in celebration of Saint Zita's feast day. It's been said that a star appeared above the attic where she slept the moment she passed. This showed that she gained eternal rest." [She was canonized in 1696. Her mummified body rests in the Basilica di San Frediano in Lucca.] "Then there *is* Zita of Bourbon-Parma. She was named after Saint Zita. I am fascinated by her. Some years after we arrived in the United States, Zita was coronated the Queen of Hungary, well Empress of Austria she was. She became a public figure. Franz Joseph had passed away. My father was one of his Hussar officers, you see. There was blood between Franz Joseph and the Empress' husband, King Charles IV of Hungary, so Charles had married Zita. I think that my father really named me after her, to tell you the truth. Between her families, Zita had a tremendous amount of siblings, some of whom were mentally impaired. She was later educated in a convent along with her sister. She traveled a great

deal. I think that she leads a fascinating life. She was brought up a devout Catholic. Later, I decided to become a Catholic by choice. My mother was against it. If I had it all to do over again…I would rather *be a nun!*" [Empress Zita was born May 9, 1892, at Villa Pianore, Tuscany. She passed away March 14, 1989. She was ninety-seven and Austria's last Empress.]

Chapter 2: *The Meeting*

1. Henry Varnum Poor was born in Chapman, Kansas in 1887. He majored in art at Stanford, where he graduated Phi Beta Kappa, in 1910. He traveled to London where he studied with the distinguished British painter, Walter Sickert, at the Slade School. When Poor returned to California, he taught at Stanford and became one of the leading modernist painters on the West Coast. However, in 1919, he settled in New City, located in Rockland County, New York. There he designed his own home and began designing homes for other local residents. He was one of the founders of the Skowhegan School of Painting and Sculpture in Maine where he devoted much of his time and effort. Henry Varnum Poor also played an important role in establishing the American Designers Gallery as well as introducing the possibility of including contemporary exhibitions at the Metropolitan Museum. He passed away in Rockland County, New York in 1970 (Courtesy of Zita Johann and a press release from James Graham & Sons, Art Gallery, New York).

2. *"Adagio for Strings"* from the String Quartet in B minor. It is a 1936 composition by Samuel Barber (1910-1981). The recording was from a portion of a rehearsal at the Los Angeles Philharmonic in April 1982 that Zita acquired from a friend. The actual performance took place in San Francisco at Davies Symphony Hall with Leonard Bernstein, conducting, July 24, 1982 (Courtesy of Zita Johann).

3. In tracing Zita's ancestry, Jane E. Moore, friend to the author, discovered Zita's mothers name. Knowing this told her just how they were related…and that she is indeed related as family legend had it. Jane began her research, however, already knowing from her father that Zita was from the same village as Jane's grandmother: Deutschbentschek. Jane E. Moore is village coordinator of the online website DVHH/Village of Deutschbentschek in Banat.

4. Courtesy of The Newberry Library of Chicago, Zita Johann and Jane E. Moore.

5. Stefan Johann was born December 18, 1876 in Deutschbentschek, Hungary/ Romania. The Stefan Johann family became American citizens July 13, 1916. Not much is known about Stefan Johann since he divorced Magdalena (Zimmermann) Johann. Stefan's second wife Pauline, along with her stepson, Erick Ameis, lived together for an unknown period of time. Stefan Johann's death remains a mystery. Zita suggested to this writer that her father might have passed away in Europe (Courtesy of Zita Johann and Jane E. Moore).

6. Richard Kiley passed away at the age of 76, in Middleton, New York, March 5, 1999 (*The New York Times*, Saturday March 6, 1999).

Chapter 3: *The Intermission*

1. Rollo Peters was born Charles Rollo Peters III, the son of the well-known painter, Charles Rollo Peters Jr., and Mary Murphy Peters, in Paris, France, September 25, 1892. He was reared in California and later studied art in Paris. Upon Rollo Peters' return to America, in 1917, he designed sets and acted on stage as a member of the Washington Square Players at The Bandbox Theatre in New York City.

This enthusiasm led Rollo Peters to venture away from his own canvases and brushes. He joined The Theatre Guild, designed costumes for many theatre productions, and acted in numerous plays. Zita

Johann met Rollo Peters after seeing him in the 1923 stage play *Romeo and Juliet*. "Rollo as Romeo was the first actor that I had a crush on." The two became friends. They appeared together in Rollo's 1923 stage production of William Shakespeare's, *As You Like It*. In 1931, together with producer/playwright, Lawrence Langner, Rollo Peters helped establish the Westport Theatre in Westport, Connecticut. In 1935, Rollo went to Hollywood to work as an assistant director to George Cukor for the filming of the M-G-M motion picture *Romeo and Juliet* that was released in 1936. Rollo Peters was involved in building and renovation of homes in Rockland County. In fact, Rollo did most of the early renovations to Zita Johann's pre-revolutionary Dutch farmhouse in West Nyack. Rollo Peters relocated to California in 1952. He passed away January 21, 1967 in Monterey, California (Courtesy of Zita Johann).

2. Two online articles suggested for reading include: *Franz Joseph I* (Wikipedia, the free encyclopedia) and *History of German Settlements in Southern Hungary* by Sue Clarkson.

3. Zita Johann's sister, Magda Johann was first married in 1929 to Lloyd Eduard Mayer (known as a writer and humorist in Robert L. Johnson Magazines using the name of Lloyd E.M. Mayer). The date of their annulment is unknown (Courtesy of Jane E. Moore).

4. Mother, Magdalena and daughter, Agatha, were then residing at 475 West 159th Street, New York (Courtesy of Jane E. Moore).

5. Zita Johann's mother, Magdalena (Zimmermann Johann) Fernandez, passed away in May 1974 at the age of 87 (Courtesy of Zita Johann and Jane E. Moore).

Chapter 4: *Broadway and Hollywood*

1. Lydia Adele Carll Banghart passed away February 22, 1936 at the age of fifty-three. (*The New York Times* : Deaths, February 24, 1936; L. Adele Banghart).

2. Lawrence Langner founded The Theatre Guild in 1919. The board was organized by former Washington Square Players (producers), Philip Moeller, Lee Simonson, Helen Westley and later Dudley Digges. Armina Marshall, an actress (later Mrs. Lawrence Langner), was a co-administrator of the Theatre Guild with Theresa Helburn (*The New York Times* — Armina Marshall (Obituary), Monday, July 22, 1991, by Glenn Fowler).

3. In reading Zita's articles, she told me that she and David Manners were part of Basil Sydney's touring company in 1922, ten year before she and David Manners appeared in Universal Pictures' *The Mummy*.

4. The Theatre Guild's newly constructed home opened in as the Guild Theatre in 1925. Today, it is known as the August Wilson Theatre. It is located at 245 West 52nd Street in New York City. The Garrick Theatre was later razed in 1932.

5. The final editions of "Grand Street Follies" in 1928 and 1929, were the tenants of the Booth Theatre. The effects after the New York stock market crash closed the *Follies* indefinitely. The *Grand Street Follies* debuted in 1922 and ran annually until 1929. Philanthropic sisters Alice (1883-1972) and Irene Lewisohn (1886-1944), originally founded the Neighborhood Playhouse in 1915. In its beginning, Alice was in charge of dramatic arts while her sister, Irene, was in charge of dance training and costumes for dancers. Martha Graham and Agnes deMille were among the alumni then. After the theatre closed in 1927, it re-opened the following year as an actor training school. It is known today as the *Neighborhood Playhouse School of the Theatre*. Those who later studied under Sanford ("Sandy") Meisner, developed an acting methodology known as the Meisner technique include, James Caan, Steve McQueen, Robert Duvall, Gregory Peck, Bob Fosse, Diane Keaton, Peter Falk, Jon Voight, Grace Kelly, Tony Randall and Sydney Pollack

6. Theater producer, director, playwright and screenwriter, Winthrop Ames, in 1912, had the Little Theatre built. The following year Winthrop Ames had the Booth Theatre built and managed both theatres until 1930. In 1982, the Little Theatre, which was also known as New York Times Hall, was renamed the Helen Hayes Theatre after the actress' namesake theatre. The Fulton (originally named after the actress in 1955) was razed in 1982.

7. *The New York Times* — SUES FOR PRIZE HE WON — E.G. Riley Wants $1,000 and Production of His Play; March 15, 1928.

8. *Long Live the King* by Lyn Tornabene, (G.P. Putnam's Sons, New York/1974) Pp: 114 and 115.

9. The couple had originally set up residence at 320 5th Street in New York City. Eventually, they relocated to New City, in Rockland County. After their separation and ultimate divorce, John Houseman had relocated on his own before Zita Johann settled into her West Nyack home. They never lived together in West Nyack (Courtesy of Zita Johann).

10. Zita Johann was born the day before the famed Russian playwright, Anton Chekov (1860-1904) passed away from tuberculosis July 15, 1904.

11. D.W. Griffith's long movie career began in 1908 as a writer, actor and later a director with the *American Mutoscope and Biograph Company*. In 1909 the business was renamed the *Biograph Company*. Biograph also produced movies in Hollywood, California and opened branches in foreign countries as well. Mr. Griffith launched the careers of such notables as Blanche Sweet, Mary Pickford, Lillian Gish, Dorothy Gish, Lionel Barrymore, Donald Crisp, Bessie Love, Harry Carey, Mae Marsh, Mack Sennett and Richard Barthelmess. Griffith was one of the four leading figures with Mary Pickford, Douglas Fairbanks, and Charlie Chaplin who formed United Artists Film Corporation, February 5, 1919, in Hollywood, California. *The Struggle* was shot between July 6, and August 14, 1931 at the Audio Cinema Studio, at 198th and Decatur Avenue in the Bronx (that was originally the Edison Studio) and other exteriors, such as 175th Street and Stamford Rolling Mills, Connecticut. By 1930, Mr. Griffith had sold off much of his interest in United Artists. *The Struggle* opened to New York audiences December 10, 1931. However, after public criticism that Griffith received for *The Struggle*, it became his last movie production (although Griffith is credited as one of three directors who include Hal Roach and Hal Roach Jr., in the 1940 United Artists release, *One Million B.C.*). United Artists released and distributed *The Struggle* to national audiences February 6, 1932. It was cancelled and withdrawn from circulation August 29, 1935. The copyright was renewed in 1959. In 1996, Kino on Video (VHS) released *The Struggle*. In 2008, Kino International released, *D.W. Griffith: Father of Film* (UK 1993 — Color/B&W), on DVD. The three-part documentary was written, produced and directed by Kevin Brownlow and David Gill. It was first shown over Thames television in the UK and through US Public Broadcasting in March 1993. The documentary features filmed interviews with Zita Johann, Lillian Gish, Blanche Sweet, and Frank Capra, and others. This is a highly recommended and noteworthy documentary of a pioneer and revolutionary in movie making. D.W. Griffith is best remembered for two monumental directing achievements, *The Birth of a Nation* (1915) and *Intolerance: Love's Struggle Throughout the Ages* (1916). David Llewelyn Wark Griffith passed away at the age of seventy-three, July 23, 1948, in Hollywood, California (Courtesy of Zita Johann and David Marowitz).

12. Howard (Winchester) Hawks (1896-1977) was an influential American film director, producer and screenwriter in Hollywood. While working at Warner Bros. on *Tiger Shark,* Zita Johann was making fifteen hundred dollars a week. In January 2010, Turner Classic Movies (TCM) made *Tiger Shark* available on DVD through Movies Unlimited. Howard Hawks passed away at the age of eighty-one, in Palm Springs, California, December 26, 1977.

13. Oliver La Farge (1901-1963), the author of the novel, Laughing Boy, published in 1929. In 1930, La Farge won the Pulitzer Prize. Zita and La Farge met in Hollywood in 1932.

14. *Laughing Boy* producer Carl Laemmle, Jr., and director William Wyler, cancelled the movie project at Universal Pictures. The story was later purchased and released by M-G-M in 1934, starring Ramon Navarro and Lupe Velez. W.S. Van Dyke directed it. It opened to less than successful reviews.

15. In the summer of 2008, Universal Home Entertainment released a 2-Disc (DVD) Special edition of *The Mummy* (1932), with a variety of special features and commentaries (*The New York Times*, Tuesday July 22, 2008; p. E3).

16. Movie offers turned down by Zita Johann include *Show Boat* (Universal, 1929), directed by Harry A. Pollard (Laura La Plante played Magnolia). *The Thirteenth Chair* (M-G-M, 1929); directed by Tod Browning with Bela Lugosi before his fame in *Dracula* at Universal in 1931. After Zita refused the part for *This Mad World* (M-G-M, 1930), with Basil Rathbone, director William DeMille (older brother of Cecil B. DeMille), replaced Zita with Cecil's newest discovery, actress Kay Johnson (mother of actor James Cromwell); For *East Lynne* (M-G-M, 1931), directed by Frank Lloyd, Zita said, "The story was not my cup of tea;" *Thirteen Women* (RKO, 1932), directed by George Archainbaud; Myrna Loy played Ursula Georgi, Zita said, "I refused anything involving the number thirteen. I wasn't kidding you that I am superstitious. I'm not proud of it." *Deportation Train* (RKO, 1932), Zita said, "That melodrama on a train. They tried to get me to act in. I thought it was a terrible part." *Deported* was released by Paramount that same year; It was directed by Paul L. Stein. Zita Johann and Clark Gable were to star but both passed on it. Zita was slated to appear in the World War I spy movie, *Rendezvous*, released by M-G-M in 1935. Production on *Rendezvous* was suspended due to first actress chosen Binnie Barnes was briefly ill. When filming resumed with Barnes, Zita was no longer considered for the role of Olivia Karloff. *Rendezvous* starred Rosalind Russell and William Powell. When auditions were underway at Warner Bros. for *A Midsummer Night's Dream* (released in 1935), Zita suggested to director Max Reinhardt that Olivia DeHavilland would be a better choice to play Hermia. Zita told this writer, " I did not want to create problems between anyone, so I passed on that picture too. Look. I wasn't the only actress turning down parts in pictures. By that time, I was intent on returning to New York and to be back in the theater." (From scrapbooks of Zita Johann and conversations with her by the author, May 2, 1982; West Nyack, New York.)

17. In addition to being a Hollywood director Karl Freund (1890-1969) was an Academy Award winning Cinematographer known by many in the industry as "Papa" Freund. From 1951-1956, he was best known for his cinematography work having filmed 149 episodes of the *I Love Lucy* television program at Desilu Productions in Hollywood California.

18. Excerpted quote of Zita Johann from Page 192 of *Long Live the King* by Lyn Tornabene (G.P. Putnam's Sons, New York/1974).

19. Adolph Zukor (from Hungary) was among the notable people who resided in Rockland County, New York. His 760-acre estate, the Dells was located north of New City, New York. He moved there in 1926 with his wife, Lottie Kaufman. They had two children, Eugene James, and Mildred. In 1956, after his wife passed away, he relocated, maintaining apartments in both New York City, and Los Angeles, California. He passed away in his Century City apartment, Los Angeles, June 10, 1976, at the age of 103 (Courtesy of Zita Johann, *Chicago Sun-Times* Obituary, Friday June 11, 1976; page 92: columns 1 and 2; *also The New York Times* Obituary, Adolph Zukor Is Dead at 103, Built Paramount Empire).

20. Movie director, Lothar Mendes, was born in Berlin, Germany in 1894. He began working in Europe as an actor in silent motion pictures. He began screenwriting and directing in the early 1920s, under the watchful eye of Max Reinhardt. Mendes moved to Hollywood in 1924, and in 1926 he married actress, Dorothy Mackaill. The marriage lasted nearly two years before they were divorced. After the divorce, Paramount hired Mendes. There he worked until directing *Luxury Liner*. In 1933, he moved to London, England continuing to direct movies. After directing the movie, *Moonlight Sonata*, in England, World War II soon began. Mendes returned to America and directed his last four Hollywood movies for Warner Bros., RKO, 20th Century-Fox, and Columbia, respectively. One of his more notable movies as director was the H.G. Wells story *The Man Who Could Work Miracles* starring Roland Young. It was made in London and released in 1937. Lothar Mendes passed away in London, England, at the age of eighty, February 25, 1974, which coincidentally was the day this writer first contacted Zita Johann.

21. *Luxury Liner* was one of over 700 Paramount motion pictures that sold in 1958 to MCA/Universal for television distribution. These movies have since been owned and controlled by Universal (Courtesy of David Marowitz).

22. Hamilton MacFadden (1901-1977) attended Harvard Law School before he began acting in New York theater in the early 1920s. He began directing Broadway plays and remained doing so until the late 1920s. In the early 1930s, MacFadden went to Hollywood, and was hired by Fox Films as a writer, director and actor. Prior to directing, *The Man Who Dared: An Imaginative Biography*, MacFadden was the director who launched the popular Charlie Chan series first starring Warner Oland. When Twentieth Century Pictures and Fox Films merged as 20th Century-Fox, MacFadden continued working there and other studios until the mid-1940s.

23. The movie director of whom Zita Johann was referring was Phil Goldstone (1893-1963). Mr. Goldstone, a Polish immigrant began working as a movie director in Hollywood westerns in 1920. He was the founder of the Motion Picture Relief Fund and former studio head at Tiffany Pictures. He later worked as a film producer at Nat Levine's Mascot Pictures, who bought the old Mack Sennett Studio, where Phil Gladstone directed *The Sin of Nora Moran*. At the time, Goldstone was working for Lawrence J. Darmour's Majestic Pictures, the company that released *The Sin of Nora Moran*, in 1933. By 1935, all of the above mentioned independent production companies and Monogram Pictures merged to become Republic Pictures. Republic was best known for its specialization in quality B pictures, westerns and movie serials. Phil Goldstone produced more movies than he directed. He passed away in West Los Angeles, California, at the age of seventy, June 19, 1963. In the summer of 2000, the UCLA Film Archive announced *The Sin of Nora Moran* as one of their preserved films. That same year, Nostalgia Family Video released *The Sin of Nora Moran* on VHS. Image Entertainment as a double feature has recently produced *The Sin of Nora Moran* with the non-Zita Johann feature *Prison Train* on DVD. (Online: B MOTION PICTURE PRODUCTION COMPANIES; Saturday, July 29, 2000, UCLA: Tenth Festival of Preservation; also: *Variety*, June 26, 1963).

24. *The New York Times (Zita Johann Plans Suit)*, July 10, 1933, p. 11:8 & (*Zita Johann Wins Divorce*), September 13, 1933, p. 22:5. 25. John Huston became a successful movie director. He was an Academy Award winning actor and director who achieved "legendary" celebrity status. He passed away at the age of eighty-six, August 28, 1987 in Middleton, Rhode Island,

26. Irving Cummings (1888-1959) began his acting career in his late teens on Broadway with the legendary Lillian Russell. He was also an American movie actor, and later a movie director, producer and writer. Zita Johann became acquainted with Mr. Cummings through director, Hamilton MacFadden. Irving Cummings later became known for his Technicolor musicals that

featured Shirley Temple, Alice Faye, and Betty Grable that he directed at 20th Century Fox. He passed away at the age of seventy, April 18, 1959, in Los Angeles, California (*Variety*, April 22, 1959).

27. The Production Code (popularly known as the Hays Code or the Breen Office) was the set of industry censorship guidelines. Beginning in 1930, it was the chief administer of enforcement of censorship which became an amendment to the Code in order to obtain a certificate of approval before each release. Thus, was established the (PCA) Production Code Administration in the United States. The first major instance of censorship under the Production Code involved the 1934 movie *Tarzan and His Mate*, in which brief nudity required a body-double for actress Maureen O'Sullivan. In 1968, the Production Code was abandoned entirely. The MPAA (Motion Picture Association of America) film ratings proceeded thereafter. They went into effect November 1, 1968, despite changes made to the rating system since 1984.

Chapter 5: *Transitions*

1. The Adirondack mountain range is located in the northeastern part of New York that runs through Clinton, Essex, Franklin, Fulton, Hamilton, Herkimer, Lewis, St. Lawrence, Saratoga, Warren, and Washington counties. The mountains are often included by geographers in the Appalachian Mountains, but they are geologically similar to the Laurentian Mountains of Canada. They are bordered on the east by Lake Champlain and Lake George, which separate them from the Greek Mountains in Vermont. The Mohawk Valley borders them south and to the west by the Tug Hill Plateau, separated by the Black River. The region is south of the St. Lawrence River.

2. Stories and essays by John O'Hara were published in *The New Yorker* and *The Saturday Evening Post* magazines. In his column entitled, *Appointment with O'Hara*, the author made mention of Zita Johann regarding Hollywood in 1934, which appeared in an unspecified 1955 edition of the Saturday Evening Post that Zita sent to this writer (Courtesy of Zita Johann).

3. *The New York Times* ('WALTZ IN FIRE' SUIT WON BY PRODUCERS) December 8, 1934.

4. On the morning of May 5, 1948, David Hertz' private passenger plane crashed into the Pacific Ocean. His body was never found. The only evidence found some time later was a portion of the planes propeller. His divorced wife, Margaret, and their ten-year-old daughter survived him. During his 14-year career, Hertz worked for RKO, International Pictures, and Metro-Goldwyn-Mayer. He is credited as a writer in various movies: *Beloved Enemy*, *History Is Made at Night*, *Blackmail*, *Love Crazy*, *Journey for Margaret*, and *Daisy Kenyon*. David Hertz was forty-three years of age (*Long Beach Independent* Vol. 10 / No.251–May 6, through June 11, 1948).

5. George M. Cohan wrote the comedy-mystery play "Seven Keys to Baldpate." It was based on the Earl Derr Bigger novel. The play originally opened September 22, 1913 at the Astor Theatre, located at Broadway and 45th Street in New York City,. It had a successful run with over 300 performances, starring Wallace Eddinger as William Hallowell McGee. George M. Cohan appeared as William Hallowell McGee with Zita Johann in the 1935 revival. Several motion picture versions of *Seven Keys to Baldpate* have been made. (Courtesy of Zita Johann and David Marowitz).

6. By 1936, Warner Bros. and First National Pictures merged becoming Warner Bros..

7. Zita Johann and John McCormick returned to New York in August 1936. Zita would made a few more trips to California before she terminated business there (Courtesy of Zita Johann).

8. Portions of information regarding the *Lux Radio Theatre* were provided with permission by Terry Salomonson from Audio Classics Archive, *Radio Broadcast Log Of: Lux Radio Theatre*, online.

9. The Columbia Workshop broadcast, *The Winged Victory*, may be heard currently over *Dum.com* (Old Time Radio Shows — Columbia Workshop — 390306:online).

10. Zita claimed that her first husband, John Houseman owed her $17,000. She told this writer that the money was never paid back to her. This remained a conflict between both parties. Zita said. "I still have the note." After the radio broadcast of *The Trojan Women*, Zita Johann said that she never saw John Houseman again (Courtesy of Zita Johann).

11. *The New York Times* — (Obituary*) Robert Lewis Shayon, 95, Is Dead, Elevated Radio.* (June 28, 2008) Published July 18, 2008.

12. Singer, Lotte Lenya, and her composer husband, Kurt Weill (best known for his productions that include *The Threepenny Opera* and *Knickerbocker Holiday*) met Zita Johann in 1939. This was before the couple made permanent residence in nearby New City in Rockland County. Kurt Weill passed away at the age of fifty, April 3, 1950. Lotte Lenya passed away November 27, 1981, at the age of eighty-three in Manhattan.

13. *Arthur Hopkins Presents* ran 36 episodes between April 19, 1944 and January 3, 1945 over the NBC Radio Network (Audio Classics Archive: Arthur Hopkins Presents: online).

14. Bernard Edward Shedd was born July 27, 1906 in Chicago, Illinois. He passed away at the age of eighty-one in Europe in November of 1987. John Houseman passed away at the age of eighty-six, at his Malibu, California home, October 31, 1988 (*The Los Angeles Times, Actor John Houseman, Dies at 86,* Tuesday, November 1. 1988; Pp.1, 26, 27; and Jane E. Moore).

15. Alan Brock was of Hungarian descent. His given name was Steve Zebrock. He and Zita together attended the Alviene School of Theatre Arts during the early 1920s. Brock left for Hollywood in 1929. He returned to New York at the height of the Depression. It was in New York, where theatrical producer Theodore Hammerstein, suggested that Brock take a position as a theatrical agent. Alan Brock specialized in securing work for Broadway and silent movie stars. Alan Brock passed away at the age of eighty-five, March 19, 1995, in his hometown of Hastings-On-Hudson, New York (Courtesy of David Marowitz).

16. *The Dobbs Ferry Sentinel,* Thursday, October 9, 1969 *News of the Muses* by Doris Krauss; "Battle for Heaven" (Courtesy of David Marowitz).

Chapter 6: *An Awakening*

1. *School Transportation News at STN Media:* Train-Bus Crashes (online) –Page 5 of 11 pages (Train-School Bus Collision: Congers, New York: March 24, 1972).

Chapter 7: *Crescendo*

1. Samuel M. Sherman is a movie writer, producer, director, author and actor. He was born in 1940, in New York City. As of this writing, he continues as the owner of his distribution company Independent-International Pictures. *Raiders of the Living Dead* debuted as a Friday night cablecast on the USA Network, November 3, 1989. In 2002, a two disc DVD set of *Raiders of the Living Dead* and two other versions were made available as added features

Chapter 8: *The Reawakening*

1.*Let's Scare 'Em!* was published in 1997 by McFarland and Company, North Carolina/London *(Chapter 10, Beginning After the End: Zita Johann,* pages 139-148).

2. Rosemary Franck moved with her family to Rockland County in 1964. (MUSEUM HONORS 1.3 MILLION TROOPS/*LoHud.com/The Journal News, May 25, 2008 by Bob Baird.*)

Chapter 9: *And Then It Was Morning*

1. Jean-Paul Charles Aymard Sartre (1905-1980) was a French existentialist philosopher, playwright, novelist, screenwriter, political activist, biographer, and literary critic. Zita was an avid reader of Sartre's books. His 1944 play *No Exit*, was adapted to the cinema, most notably in 1954 by Jacqueline Audry (1908-1977), a French film director.

Charcoal drawing of Zita by Madolin Colby (1951). PHOTO COURTESY OF DAVID MAROWITZ

INDEX

20th Century Fox Pictures 105, 328, 329
Actors Studio 115
Adagio for Strings (musical composition by Samuel Barber) 19, 324
Adirondack Mountains 107, 329
Adler, Larry 118, 313
Aloma of the South Seas 36, 40, 102, 306
Alviene School of Theatre Arts 31, 330
And Then It was Morning (an unpublished play by Zita Johann) 14, 130, 143, 145-294, 300, 331
Anderson, Maxwell 116, 117, 123, 313
Arthur Hopkins Presents (radio series) 320, 330
Appointment in Samarra (book) 107
Appointment with O'Hara (news column) 329
As You Like It (1923 Shakespearian play) 305, 325
Astara 13, 323
Atkinson, Brooks 115
Atwater, Edith 117, 312
Bain, Donald 113
Banat (Hungary/Romania) 20, 324
Barry, Philip 52. 53, 57, 310
Barry, Tom 36, 306
Battle for Heaven (play) 121, 313, 330
Baxter, Warner 101, 103, 318
Beck, Jason 116
Bigger, Earl Derr 108, 311, 329
Bill of Divorcement, A (1939 radio broadcast) 120, 320
Blackmer, Sidney 120
Bogart, Humphrey 62, 64
Brent, George 85, 91, 92, 316
Brock, Alan 36, 121, 314, 330
Broken Journey (play) 116, 117, 312
Bromley, Sheila 116
Browning, Tod 327

Bryant High School 31
Buck, Pearl S. 115, 312
Burning Deck, The (play) 115, 312
Byron, Arthur 64, 66, 67, 316
Captain Applejack (1936 Lux Radio Theatre Broadcast) 111, 112, 320
Carll (Banghart), Lydia Adele (aka Miss Carll) 31, 33, 36, 325
Cayce, Edgar 14
CBS (Columbia Broadcasting System) 111, 113, 115, 320
Cermak, Anton 95
Chekhov, Anton 51, 310, 326
Cherry Lane Playhouse (New York) 41, 307
Chamberlain, George Agnew 43
Children's World, The (unsold TV show) 126
Christie, George 108, 311
Cianelli, Eduardo 108, 310
Civic Repertory Company (Theatre) 43, 308
Claim, The (play) 42
Clemens, LeRoy 36, 306
Cohan, George M. 108, 110, 311, 329
Cohn, Harry 104, 105
Columbia Workshop (Radio) 113, 330
Coney Island 25
Conlan, Francis 311
Cort Theatre (New York) 51
Coward, Noel 57
Cradle Song, The (play) 43, 44 308
Cronin, A.J. 101, 318
Cummins, Irving 101, 318, 328, 329
Dawn (play) 36, 306
Dawson, Hal K. 120, 309
DeHavilland, Olivia 327
DeMille, Cecil B. 111, 112, 327
Deportation Train (RKO, 1932) 327
Deported (Paramount 1932) 83, 327

333

Deutschbentschek 20, 21, 324
Devil's Disciple, The (play) 33, 35, 304
Dillon, Josephine 85
Draper, Stephen 118
Drift (play) 41, 307
East Lynne (play) 327
Eddinger, Wallace 329
Eddy, Mary Baker 121, 301, 314
Ehardt, Liesl 7, 15, 135-137, 297-300
Elizabeth Seton College 121, 313
Emperor Franz Joseph I (of Austria-Hungary) 25, 325
Famous Players-Lasky (later Paramount Pictures) 94
Fazekas, Imre 51, 309
Fenton, Mildred 116
Fernandez, Antonio 21, 26
Fernandez, Magdalena (Zimmermann) 20, 21, 324, 325
Fernandez, Remedios Maria 21
Ferrer, Jose 115, 312
Fletcher, Bramwell 64, 316
Flight Into China (play) 115, 312
Fontanne, Lynn 42, 308
Foster, Preston 95, 97, 98, 317
Fox Films 95, 96, 101, 105, 328
Freund, Karl 64-66, 68-70, 315, 327
Froman, Jane 313
Gable, Clark 43, 46, 83, 302, 309, 327
Garbo, Greta 83
Gabriel, Gilbert W. 43
Garrick Theatre 36, 37, 303-305, 325
Geer, Will 313
Getting to Know You (song by Rodgers and Hammerstein) 125
Gillmore, Margalo 303, 305
Gish, Lillian 51, 310, 326
Goat Song, The (play) 42, 308
Goetz, William 105
Good Earth, The (movie and novel) 115
Grand Canary 101-105, 318
Grand Street Follies (and play of 1925) 38, 39, 41, 306, 325
Gray, Judd 43
Griffith, D.W. (David Llewelyn Wark) 53, 55-57, 314, 326

Griffith, Raymond 105
Hackett, Walter 111
Hagen, Uta 115, 312
Hampden, Walter 108, 311
Harrigan, William 116
Harris, Jed 51, 310
Haussmann, Jacques (also: Houseman, John) 13, 20, 48, 49, 57, 59, 61, 64, 79, 97, 100, 104, 108
    115, 121, 301, 309, 311, 320, 326, 330
Hawks, Howard 59, 60, 315, 326
Hayes, Helen 117, 118, 123, 313, 326
Hayward, Leland 28, 83, 91, 118
He Who Gets Slapped (play) 33, 34, 67, 120, 303
Henry Miller's Theatre 57, 116, 310, 312
Hertz, David 26, 27, 101, 104, 105, 108, 111, 310, 318, 329
Higger, Gertrude (Mrs. Maxwell Anderson, also "Mab" Anderson) 116, 123
Hiroshima 123
Holloway, Ruby 64, 67, 68
Hopkins, Arthur 36, 43, 45, 57, 116, 117, 120, 308, 312, 320, 330
Houseman, John (see also: Haussmann, Jacques or John)
Hull, Josephine 108, 311
Huston, John 53, 62-64, 79, 93, 100, 328
Huston, Walter 53, 111
Hutchinson, Josephine 43
Hymer, John B. 36, 306
Janney, William 116
Johann, Agatha (sister of Zita Johann) (also: Agatha Whitney or Aggie) 21, 26-28
Johann, Magdalena (sister of Zita Johann) (also: Magda J. Tarleton or Maggie) 21, 25, 26, 116
Johann, Magdalena (Zimmermann) (mother of Zita Johann) 25, 26, 28, 49, 92
Johann, Stefan (father of Zita Johann) 20, 21, 324
John's Other Wife (radio soap opera) 115, 320
Johnson, Noble 64, 83, 316
Karloff, Boris 65, 67, 69, 79, 80, 316
Kaus, Gina 85, 316
Kiley, Richard 21, 22, 324
King and I, The (play) 125, 301

Kirkland, Alexander 48, 49, 116, 308, 309
Kline, Adelaide 113
La Farge, Oliver 327
Laemmle, Carl, Jr., 63, 67, 68, 71, 327
Laemmle, Carl, Sr., 43
Lake, The 48, 49, 309
Lamparski, Richard 323
Landis, Jessie Royce 116
Langner, Lawrence 325
Laughing Boy 62, 63, 79, 327
Lasky, Jesse 91
Laurie, Joe, Jr., 116
Lawrence County, Pennsylvania 21
Le Gallienne, Eva 43, 44
Lee, Gypsy Rose 116
Lenya, Lotte (Mrs. Kurt Weill) 117, 123, 124, 313, 330
Loeb, Philip 32, 303, 307, 308
Lorenz, Elizabeth (Mrs. Pare Lorenz) 116
Lorenz, Pare 116
Losch, Tily 313
Lost (play) 43
Lovejoy, Frank 113
Loy, Myrna 327
Lugosi, Bela 327
Lunt, Alfred 42, 308
Lux Radio Theatre of the Air 111
Luxury Liner (Paramount, 1933) 85, 91-93, 316, 328
MacArthur, Charles 313
Macfadden, Hamilton 95, 97, 317, 328
McCormick, John 13, 77, 110, 329
Machinal (play) 43, 45, 46, 48, 51, 85, 99, 120 308, 309, 320
Mad World, This 327
Man and the Masses [Masse Mensch] (play) 36, 38, 305
Man of La Mancha, The 21
Man Who Dared, An Imaginative Biography, The (Fox, 1933) 95-97, 317
Manners, David 7, 64, 66, 67, 84, 133, 303, 304, 316, 325
Mary of Scotland (benefit play) 117, 313
Marshall, Armina 304, 307, 325
Marshall, Herbert 52, 57, 310
Markham, Carl 24

Masque Theatre 108, 310
Metro-Goldwyn-Mayer (M-G-M) 48, 49, 62, 91, 115, 325, 327, 329
Maxine Elliott's Theatre 115, 312
Mayer, Lloyd Eduard (also: Lloyd E.M. Mayer) 325
Merchants of Glory (play) 41, 307
Meredith, Burgess 64, 123, 301
Mendes, Lothar 91, 316, 328
Midsummer Night's Dream, A (Warner Bros. Pictures, 1935) 327
Milton, Robert 115, 303, 305, 312
"Monday's Child" (poem) 29
Montgomery, Douglass 108
Mooney, Ria 43
Moore, Colleen 110
Moray, Mona 116
Morgan, Brewster 113, 320
Morgan, Frank 91, 94, 111, 316
Mummy, The (Universal, 1932) 9, 10, 12, 28, 64-85, 301, 315, 325, 327
Music Box Theatre (Hollywood) 111
National Broadcasting Company (NBC) 111, 320, 330
Nichols, Dudley 317, 318
Nivoix, Paul 41, 307
Nostradamus (also: Michel Nostradamus) 14
Nyack Hospital (Rockland County) 132, 137
O'Hara, John 107, 302, 329
One Woman Show (starring Zita Johann) 313
O'Sullivan, Maureen 111, 329
Osborne, Vivienne 91, 102, 103, 306, 316
Pagnol, Marcel 41, 307
Panic (play) 108, 311
Paramount Pictures 60, 83, 86, 91, 94, 316, 327, 328
Paper Mill Playhouse (Milburn, New Jersey) 115, 312
Pearl Harbor 116
Peer Gynt (play) 33, 36, 304
Perkins, Osgood 51, 57, 108, 310
Peters, Rollo (Charles Rollo Peters III) 23, 24, 102, 116, 305, 324, 325
Players Club 108, 311
Plymouth Theatre (New York) 43, 46, 308
Poor, Henry Varnum 18, 116, 123, 324

Potter, H.C. (Henry Codham) 105
Powers, James T. 311
Putnam, Nina Wilcox 64, 315
RKO (Radio-Keith-Orpheum) Pictures 27, 57, 59, 94, 105, 327-329
Raiders of the Living Dead 129, 131, 319, 330
Rambeau, Marjorie 101, 102, 104, 305, 318
Rathbone, Basil 327
Redstone, David 113
Rich, Irene 108, 311
Riley, Edward Goldsmith 42, 326
Robinson, Edward G. 42, 59, 60, 62, 304, 308, 315
Rockland County (New York) 11, 18, 23, 113, 116-118, 120, 121, 123, 125, 323-327, 330, 331
Rockland Riot (12-act benefit play) 117, 118, 313
Rodulescu, Elie 20
Romeo and Juliet (1923 play) 325
Roos, Joanna 51, 53, 310, 311
Rosenthal, Andrew 115, 117, 312
R.U.R. (*Rossum's Universal Robots*, 1923 play) 31
Russian War Relief 313
St. Agatha's Home for Children 125
St. Dominic's Convent at Blauvelt 125
St. Margaret's of Pearl River 125
Samuels, Maurice V. 41, 307
Sartre, Jean Paul 14, 143, 331
Schayer, Richard 64, 315
Schenck, Joseph 95, 103-105
Schulberg, B.P. (Benjamin Percival) 91, 316
September 11, 2001 (also: 9/11) 29
Seven Keys to Baldpate (1935 play) 108, 110, 311, 329
Shakespeare, William 127, 305
Shayon, Robert Lewis 116, 320, 330
Shedd, Bernard E. (Edward) 13, 116-118, 120, 121, 320
Showboat (Universal, 1929) 327
Shumlin, Herman 24Sierra, Gregorio Martinez 308
Sierra, Maria Martinez 308
Sin of Nora Moran, The (Majestic, 1933) (also: *The Voice From the Grave*) 98-101, 317, 328

Skelly, Hal 54, 56, 314
Skinner, Otis 108, 311
Small, Jack 115, 312
Smith. C. Aubrey (Sir Charles Aubrey Smith) 91, 94, 316
Snyder, Ruth 43
Southampton, Long Island, New York 21
Stehli, Edgar 120, 303
Stock Market Crash of 1929 50, 325
Strasberg, Lee 115, 312
Struggle, The (United Artists, 1931) 53-58, 314, 326
Sydney, Basil 31-34, 67, 303, 305, 325
Szegedi, Maria 21
Szegedi, Mihay 20
Tamiroff, Akim 111
Tarleton, John V. 21, 26
Teasdale, Verree 91, 316
Temesvar, Hungary 20
Thalberg, Irving 49
Theatre Guild, The 32, 36, 37, 41, 42, 67, 304, 305, 307, 308, 324, 325
Thirteenth Chair, The (M-G-M, 1929) 327
Thirteen Women 327
Tiger Shark (Warner Bros. Pictures, 1932) 26, 59-62, 110, 315, 326
Tomorrow and Tomorrow (play) 52, 53, 57, 59, 310
Treadwell, Sophie 43, 46, 308
Trojan Women, (Euripides') The (1940 radio broadcast) 115, 320
Trotti, Lamarr 95, 317
Troyka (play) 50, 51, 309
Twentieth Century Pictures 105, 328, 329
Uncle Vanya (1930 play) 51, 53, 310
United Artists Corporation 54, 58, 105, 314, 326
U.S.S. George Washington 20
Universal Pictures 28, 43, 62-65, 68, 71, 72, 74, 76, 77, 79, 80, 82-84, 315, 325, 327
Van Sloan, Edward 64, 67, 316
Vollmer, Lula 51, 309
Wallace, David 43
Waltz in Fire (play) 108, 310
Warner Bros. Pictures 59-62, 105, 110, 315, 326-329

War of the Worlds (1939 radio broadcast) 108
We Are Always Young (radio soap opera) 116, 320
Weill, Kurt (husband of Lotte Lenya) 117, 313, 330
Welles, Orson 108, 115, 311
Werfel, Franz 42, 308
West Nyack, New York 11, 113, 124, 130, 137, 327
Weston, Ruth 108, 311
Whatever Became Of? (1973 book) 301, 323
Whitney, Agatha Johann 21
Whitney, Elwood 21, 28

Winged Victory, The (1939 radio broadcast) 113, 320, 330
Winter Quarters (and former home of Zita Johann) 113, 116, 138
Wolfe, Joan 48, 49, 309
Wray, John 313
Wurtzel, Sol 95
Wynn, Ed 118, 313
Zanuck, Darryl F. 105
Zita and Friends 126
Zukor, Adolph 91, 327

Bear Manor Media

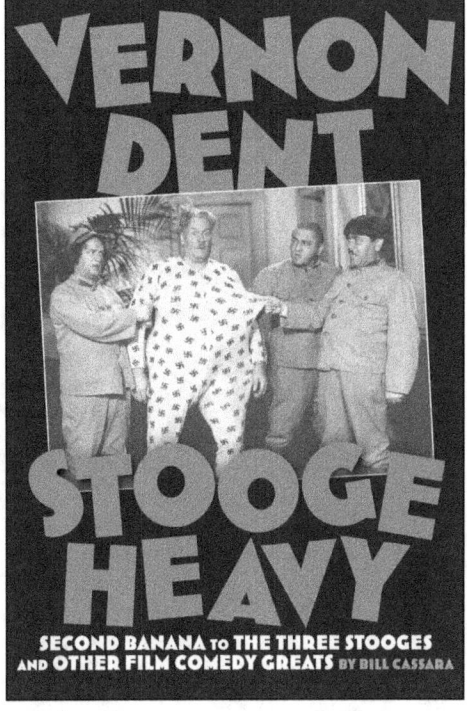

Classic Cinema.
Timeless TV.
Retro Radio.

WWW.BEARMANORMEDIA.COM

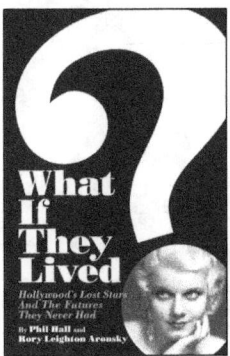

www.ingramcontent.com/pod-product-compliance
Lightning Source LLC
Chambersburg PA
CBHW070230230426
43664CB00014B/2257